Shifting Alliances

Europe, America and the future of Britain's global strategy

Shifting Alliances

Europe, America and the future of Britain's global strategy

Patrick Diamond

Senior Visiting Fellow at the London School of Economics
Transatlantic Fellow of the German Marshall Fund of the United States

POLITICO'S

First published in Great Britain 2008 by
Politico's Publishing, an imprint of
Methuen Publishing Ltd
8 Artillery Row
London
SW1P 1RZ

10 9 8 7 6 5 4 3 2 1

Copyright © Patrick Diamond 2008

Patrick Diamond has asserted his right under the Copyright, Designs and Patents Act 1988 to be identified as the author of this work.

A CIP catalogue record for this book is available from the British Library.

ISBN 978-1-84275-224-1

Set in Bembo by SX Composing DTP, Rayleigh, Essex
Printed and bound in Great Britain by Butler and Tanner, Frome

This book is sold subject to the condition that it shall not by way of trade or otherwise be lent, resold, hired out, or otherwise circulated without the publishers' prior consent in writing in any form of binding or cover other than that in which it is published and without a similar condition being imposed on the subsequent purchaser.

Contents

	About Policy Network	vii
	Preface and acknowledgements	ix
	Introduction	xxi
1.	Bridging the divide?: Europe, America and the future of Britain's global strategy	1
2.	The Anglo-American alliance and British global strategy since 1945	12
3.	British global strategy in the Blair era: managing the forces of globalisation	34
4.	Is Britain back?: beyond decline	47
5.	Tumultuous Britain: the Iraq crisis unfolds	54
6.	Towards a new geo-strategic landscape	86
7.	American perceptions of Britain and the world: facing reality?	96
8.	Europe as a strategic actor in the world: international demands confront domestic restraints	105
9.	The future of Britain and Europe: the awkward partner no longer?	127
	Conclusion: changing perspectives on Europe and America	150
	Notes	169
	Bibliography	185
	Index	197

About Policy Network

What we do

Policy Network is an international think tank dedicated to promoting progressive policies and the renewal of social democracy. Launched in December 2000, Policy Network facilitates the sharing of ideas and experiences among politicians, policy makers and experts on the centre left.

Our common challenge

Progressive governments and parties in the developed world are facing similar challenges. Perceived threats to economic, political and social security linked to globalisation, alongside the limitations of traditional policy prescriptions in the light of rapid social and technological change, mean that progressives must work across national boundaries to find solutions. The insecurities associated with greater immigration flows, terrorism, shifts in economic power and environmental change are increasingly driving the political agenda. Responses to these challenges must be located within an international framework of progressive thinking, rooted in social democratic values.

Our mission

Policy Network's objective is to develop and promote a progressive agenda based upon the ideas and experiences of social democrat modernisers. By working with politicians and thinkers across Europe and the world, Policy Network seeks to share the experiences of policy makers and experts in different national contexts, find innovative solutions to common problems and provide quality research over a wide range of policy areas. Through its programme of regular publications and events, Policy Network's focus is to inject new ideas into progressive politics and provide social democrats with the intellectual framework necessary to meet the policy and political challenges of the twenty-first century.

Recent publications

Patrick Diamond (ed.), *Public Matters: the Renewal of the Public Realm* (London: Politico's, 2007).

Anthony Giddens, Patrick Diamond and Roger Liddle (eds), *Global Europe, Social Europe* (Cambridge: Polity, 2006).

The Hampton Court Agenda: a Social Model for Europe (London: Policy Network, 2006).

Contact

Policy Network
Third floor
11 Tufton Street
London
SW1P 3QB
United Kingdom
Telephone: +44 (0)20 7340 2200
Fax: +44 (0)20 7340 2211
Email: info@policy-network.net

For more information about Policy Network and its activities visit www.policy-network.net.

Preface and Acknowledgements

> There is nothing more difficult to plan, more doubtful of success, nor more dangerous to manage than the creation of a new order of things . . . Whenever his enemies have occasion to attack the innovator they do so with the passion of partisans, while the others defend him sluggishly so that the innovator and his party alike are vulnerable.
>
> Niccolò Machiavelli[1]

This book confronts the central dilemma of Britain's global strategy – the unresolved choice between Europe and America and the impact of that dilemma on the future of British politics.[2] Long-established features of the domestic political landscape are being uprooted or refashioned after Blair, and these changes are far from complete. Abroad, as Professor Andrew Gamble has often reflected, the stark choice between Europe and America has constantly given rise to new defining issues such as whether or not to join the euro, and whether Britain should support the Iraq War. These choices call into question the very nature of the British state and its prospects for survival as a sovereign political community.

The object of this book is to encourage a nuanced discussion of the future of British foreign policy and Britain's role in the world in the twenty-first century. I intend it as a contribution to the debate now going on in many countries about the essential nature of the international order – and Britain's place within it. The book's argument presumes that lasting political change depends on altering the balance of opinion within not only the governing class but the country as a whole. The focus is not the immediate controversies of the special relationship, Iraq or the war on terror, but the historical and institutional forces that have animated Britain's national strategy since the Second World War. These complex issues have too often been shrouded in a fog of sound bites and slogans.

The focus is Britain but the debate is also relevant to the future of American foreign policy. The real danger for the United States is that its natural allies in Europe do not accept its view of the world, even if they live under the benign protection of American military force. As Ivo Daalder and James Lindsay have argued, at some point other countries may decide that they are no longer prepared to merely follow America's lead or that they will actively oppose America's chosen course. 'At that point, America will stand all alone – a powerful pariah state that, in many instances, will prove unable to achieve its most important goals.'[3]

In the aftermath of Iraq, profound questions have emerged at the fore of the debate about the future of British foreign policy. First is the continuing importance and relevance of liberal interventionism, and the use of military force to accomplish humanitarian goals. The international community was badly divided after September 11 2001 and there is now little agreement about how to fashion an interventionist doctrine that will protect the vulnerable and oppressed. The danger is that grave breaches of international law and human rights – such as the genocide and ethnic cleansing recently witnessed in Darfur – go unheeded given the impediments to multilateral authorisation through the United Nations.

The second question relates to the strategic conception of Britain's national interest, and Britain's relationship with Europe and the United States. The Blair administration, like every postwar British government, accepted the primacy of the special relationship. All British premiers for the last sixty years – including even the pro-European Edward Heath – have sought to be an inside player in Washington's power games. This is what the commentator Peter Riddell describes as the 'hug them close' approach.[4] Its weakness is that over Iraq the close alliance with the United States became increasingly high risk, inflaming British public opinion while endangering Britain's capacity to remain fluently engaged in Europe. The claim of the pro-Europeans that Britain traded influence in the EU for closeness to Washington, thereby damaging British interests, has to be confronted.

The debate about liberal interventionism and the strategic conception of the national interest are set to be defining issues for the future. On the one hand, conflict between Europe and America and a divided West have little to offer. Both sides need to co-operate in tackling the multiple threats inherent in the current geo-strategic environment. There are common interests on almost all global issues, from the fight against international terrorism to dealing with climate change. On the other hand, Britain still faces an acute dilemma as the mid-Atlantic point between Europe and America. It is being drawn closer to the European Union by dint of deepening economic integration and the Europeanisation of the British polity since the mid-1970s. Yet a significant section of the British political class prefers the special relationship with the United States, which it views as amenable to the British character and Britain's Anglo-Saxon roots. Globalisation also rekindles memories of Britain as an independent power with a world role.

It is not surprising that Tony Blair found the great balancing act of Europe and the United States difficult to sustain. There are now major divisions within the political class between pro-Europeans, who seek to put Britain at the heart of Europe, Anglo-Americans, who affirm the primacy of the special relationship with the United States, and British multilateralists, who prefer an independent foreign policy based on British identity and 'British' values. The divisions themselves cut across the traditional ideological and party boundaries of right and left.

To suggest that Britain can easily reconcile the contradictions of Europe and America is of course an illusion. There is no easy choice that can be made. This study seeks to confront the dilemmas and delusions that result as they continue to define British politics long into the future. It argues that there is no fundamental choice of alignment between Europe and America, but there is a question of priority for Britain to resolve.

The broader analysis also reflects the author's experience as a special adviser to Prime Minister Tony Blair in his second government (2001–5). It was written during the immediate period before the Blair/Brown handover, in the belief that British politics will benefit from serious debate about the future of global strategy and Britain's role in the world. Britain's foreign policy is in flux as never before and Iraq dominates all discussion of Blair's record in office. But jibes that Prime Minister Blair was merely 'Bush's poodle' are as glib and superficial as accusations that France and Germany did not have serious reasons for opposing the invasion of Iraq.

Shifting Alliances is a blend of historical analysis combined with detailed reflections and insights drawn from the heart of British government. I have avoided the temptation to reveal the details of private conversations and discussions in which I participated. Instead, the approach is deliberately sober and analytical, capturing a wide array of concepts, tools and empirical evidence drawn from the social sciences, political theory, historical monographs, theoretical accounts of international relations and new models of globalisation. It does not pretend to be an original work of scholarship, and draws heavily on theoretical frameworks enunciated by other writers, notably Andrew Gamble, Peter Clarke and Philip Stevens.

The purpose of this book is to understand the substance of Britain's global strategy and the conception of its world role after empire. That has to mean forging an ethically progressive foreign policy doctrine which recognises that basic security is the first priority, yet relies on clear principles of justice: a moral but muscular approach, as Amitai Etzioni describes it.[5] This doctrine must intelligently integrate domestic and foreign concerns, bridging the gap between the perpetual demands for humanitarian intervention and our finite capacity to intervene around the world with real effect. It advocates a new British model of liberal internationalism rooted in a commitment to Europe.

Shifting Alliances: the argument

The conventional wisdom of our age is that Iraq was a seismic event in British foreign policy, as tumultuous as the British failure at Suez fifty years earlier. The conclusion is that no British Prime Minister will ever again support unilateral action by the United States. Numerous commentators argue that the notion of the transatlantic bridge – where there is no conflict between the commitment to Europe and the American alliance – has been fatally undermined by Iraq. The choice for Britain now lies between fuller engagement in Europe and isolationism. The strength of Euroscepticism in the UK may push Britain towards the latter course. But the structural alignment of values between Britain and its European partners combined with the inexorable logic of integration will eventually result in a stronger commitment to Europe and the loosening of ties with America.[6]

That is the new orthodoxy of conventional British pro-Europeanism. This book seeks to provide a subtle critique of those determined to indulge in wishful thinking. It aims to trace the long historical roots of Britain's ambiguous attitude to the EU, examing a number of important contributions to the historiography of decline. Foreign policy is complicated since inevitably it involves balancing objectives rather than subordinating all to a single aim. The Atlantic alliance has deep roots in the British state, British institutions and British identity. It is embedded in the myth of what Andrew Gamble terms 'Anglo-America', an imagined community reaching from the Golden Gate Bridge to the White Cliffs of Dover.

After the Second World War, the US was the essential pillar of collective security, guaranteeing Britain's survival as a democratic society. That defence was grounded in the 'Anglosphere' and the cultural affinity of the English-speaking peoples. America was an important ideological inspiration both for the moderate post-war Labour government and the neo-liberal policies of the Thatcher governments after 1979. The US was crucial to Britain remaining a great power with an independent nuclear capability. Numerous British interests in the armed forces, intelligence and the defence industries were tied up with the United States.

Though the relationship was always unequal, the alliance with America became the new linchpin of British policy. That is unlikely to change in the foreseeable future, as the British Prime Minister, Gordon Brown, has recently insisted. Globalisation and the policing of the new world order have strengthened the dynamic of Anglo-America. Britain's capabilities are uniquely dependent on the US, reinforced by the British government's recent decision to modernise the Trident weapons system, underpinned by privileged access to American intelligence and sophisticated military technology. The Atlantic alliance has always been susceptible to sporadic tensions, given American hostility to the British Empire and the later refusal of the British to give military support to the US during the Vietnam crisis. The special relationship in Britain has never been fundamentally imperilled, however, as parties and politicians that challenge it, whether on left or right, are widely regarded as unfit to govern. It has been accepted as part of the unquestioned framework of foreign and domestic policy.

Britain's entry into the European Community was influenced by the changing realities of the expanding European market, but it was also about the defence of western Europe and the maintenance of

British influence. The United States at that time strongly supported greater European unity. The United Kingdom staked its future on the maintenance of wider institutions and relationships designed to safeguard British interests, refusing to make the choice between Europe and America. Britain should be both Atlanticist and European, remaining close to both. That was Blair's transatlantic strategy, insisting that there is no contradiction in being a strong supporter of the United States and the advocate of a leading role for Britain in Europe. Although Blair consistently argued that Britain should never have to choose between Europe and America, it was nevertheless the choice he faced during the Iraq crisis.

This book seeks to understand the changing nature of global governance and security from the perspective of British politics. It is structured so as to assess the implications of the choice between Europe and America for Britain's foreign policy in the next decade.

- Chapter 1 explores what is meant by the concept of 'grand' or global strategy and the historical evolution of Britain's special relationship with Washington. Alan Milward has defined 'grand strategy' as the bipartisan view of where national interests lie.[7] The focus is Britain, but the chapter explores underlying perceptions of the special relationship in Europe and America, assessing the unresolved dilemmas confronting the states of central and eastern Europe.
- It is important to crystallise the historical perspective on British foreign policy set out in Chapter 2. This section examines how the Anglo-American alliance became central to British global strategy after 1945 and especially after the Suez crisis, achieving a strong consensus between all the major parties in the British state. In the early 1980s, the special relationship was rejuvenated by Ronald Reagan and Margaret Thatcher after both the US and Britain had suffered a serious recession, and their ability to counter the Cold War threat was being questioned. The chapter argues that the Reagan–Thatcher special relationship repudiated the frame-

work of British and US policy that had developed after the Second World War, elaborating a new set of neo-liberal principles to revive the Atlantic community. The contested interpretations of the special relationship on the right and left in British politics are also explored.

- The Blair premiership needs to be understood within this broader historical and cultural frame of reference. Chapter 3 analyses the development of Britain's global strategy under New Labour. Since 1997, the transatlantic alliance as a central pillar of British foreign policy has been consolidated and revived. This was understood as part of the mission of the British political class to break decisively with the legacy of post-war economic and imperial decline. It entailed the reconciliation of Britain's European and American commitments, instead of desperately clinging to the US in a bid to disguise the loss of global power. On the one hand, Blair acted like all modern British Prime Ministers: refusing to break with America and cultivating intimate ties in Washington. On the other hand, he marks a definitive break in that he sought to fundamentally challenge the politics of decline.

- The Blair era was about preparing Britain for the realities of globalisation. Chapter 4 explores how Blair's conception of global strategy became central to the revival of Britain as an influential industrial and military power in the global age. This meant that the UK would adapt to become a leading beneficiary of globalisation rather than resisting global markets and international competition through the creation of a fortress economy, as governments sought to do elsewhere in western Europe. Britain grew increasingly confident that it could exercise global influence, acting as the pivot of the international system and projecting its liberal enlightenment values. But the chapter concludes that sustaining the great balancing act of the transatlantic bridge was far tougher than it first appeared.

- Chapter 5 examines how the Iraq crisis stretched British foreign policy to breaking point, undermining the global strategy framed by the Blair government after 1997. The chapter examines detailed empirical evidence that charts the decline of support for America among British voters, and the loss of faith among the political class. It argues that the dramatic fall in support for the special relationship has reached a 'tipping point' in British politics. But enthusiasm for the European project in the UK has also ebbed away in recent years. This alters irreversibly the foreign policy choices available to parties and leaders, redefining British politics long into the future. Iraq was the symptom rather than the cause of a broader structural shift in the geo-strategic landscape. The traditional assumptions of British foreign policy have been the unwitting casualty.
- In Chapter 6 the wave of structural shocks that have recast the geo-strategic landscape of the West since 1989 is explored in greater depth: the end of the Cold War, the rise of new Asian powers including India and China, and the terrorist attacks on the US. This is coupled with growing tensions between the West and the Islamic world. Britain's traditional alliances – built on its Commonwealth links and forged in the post-war epoch by Clement Attlee and Harold Macmillan – are increasingly compromised or under threat. The US's reputation is badly tarnished by the pursuit of the ill-defined 'war on terror'.
- The US is far from a static or disinterested actor, as Chapter 7 demonstrates. It analyses American perceptions of Britain and the special relationship, and the growing antagonism in America towards western Europe. Europe and North America are more than continents, regions of the world economy, or structures of political organisation. They are what Benedict Anderson terms 'imagined communities', defined by their competing identities, values, cultures and models of capitalism.[8]

The transatlantic alliance has been transformed by the changing social, ethnic and geographic composition of the United States, the inexorable rise of the US conservative movement, and the emergence of unilateralism in US foreign policy, most recently encouraged by President George W. Bush.

- Chapter 8 argues that the new strategic challenges confronting British foreign policy can no longer be met through the traditional American nuclear shield and the security afforded by NATO. Instead, new forms of collective security are necessary in the twenty-first century, in which Europe has the opportunity to develop as an influential strategic actor. But the EU has a long way to go in building up genuine coherence and credibility. The opportunity for the UK lies in an EU agenda that increasingly reflects traditional British priorities: the drive to reform the European economy and the social model; the need for greater accountability and transparency in the workings of its political institutions; and the development of a common security and defence policy enabling it to project Europe's influence. The chapter contends that Britain will need to fully engage in making European governance effective if it wants to help shape the future destiny of the EU.

- In Chapter 9 the book goes on to argue that the UK cannot sustain its ambivalent and reluctant attitude to the next phase of the European project. The very success of Britain's global strategy since the late 1950s has delayed the British political class and the British electorate from acknowledging that the UK's future will increasingly depend on the growing salience of the EU. The great challenges of the new century include resolving the relationship between the West and Islam, developing a model for the effective inclusion of immigrant communities, and dealing with the enormous implications of globalisation. These challenges are common to all European countries, as well as the US. The close security and intelligence relationship with the US and NATO will still be significant for British governments. But Britain's political leaders should also acknowledge that the UK's position on major international issues, its perceptions of power and the nature of the international order itself will often be closer to Europe.

- The concluding chapter critically assesses the coherence of the British government's strategic vision of a post-Westphalian world order driven by the competing impulses of globalisation and national rivalries between existing and emerging powers. Until Iraq, Britain could credibly adhere to the special relationship as the central pillar of its post-Suez foreign policy, echoing the its status as a pivotal power. This approach is no longer strategically credible and needs to be updated. It fails to acknowledge that both Europe and America are increasingly complex partners. Both have reached different conclusions about the calculus of risk and reward in their use of 'hard' and 'soft' power, and there is little agreement on how to approach the 'war on terror'. The breach in transatlantic relations is not as visceral as it was immediately before the outbreak of the Iraq War, but deep divisions nonetheless remain.

The author would like to thank the following for discussions and comments concerning the themes explored in this book: Martin Albrow, Ronald Asmus, Katinka Barysch, Andrew Gamble, Anthony Giddens, John Glenn, Philip Gordon, Charles Grant, David Held, Mary Kaldor, Sunder Katwala, Denis Kavanagh, Jürgen Krönig, Roger Liddle, Denis Macshane, David Miliband, Alistair Murray, Jonathan Powell, Giles Radice, Peter Riddell, Gene Sperling, Philip Stephens and Helen Thompson. Particular thanks go to the Centre for the Study of Global Governance at the London School of Economics and the German Marshall Fund of the United States. My thanks also go to Policy Network, especially

Mark Day and Olaf Cramme. At Politico's, Jonathan Wadman copy-edited the volume with his usual mixture of flair and diligence, and special thanks are also due to Alan Gordon Walker for helping to move this project from conception to contract.

London
January 2008

Introduction

> In politics as in strategy, it is better to persuade the stronger than to pit yourself against him. That is what I am trying to do. The Americans have immense resources. They do not always use them to their best advantage. I am trying to enlighten them, without forgetting, of course, to benefit my country.
>
> Winston Churchill[1]

After Iraq, Britain's global strategy is seen as irreversibly altered. The contradictions and dilemmas of the UK's world role have been exposed at various critical turning points in post-war British history. There is nonetheless a constant danger of over-emphasising the discontinuities in British policy in the context of the Iraq crisis. Of course, Iraq threatened to severely undermine the Anglo-American special relationship while detaching Britain ever further from Europe. The transatlantic partnership based on the conception of 'hug them close' diplomacy visibly waned,[2] while Britain has remained deeply ambivalent about further political and economic integration in Europe.

At the very least, Britain cannot simply have the best of both worlds: a close relationship with the White House will have some political costs, not least at times the perception of closeness to an unpopular President; and stronger ties to Germany and France will require a coherent approach to EU integration and enlargement that may offend Eurosceptic elements within the British governing class.[3] To believe otherwise will undermine the credibility of Britain's global strategy and will rapidly prove unsustainable. The danger for the UK will be an ambiguous role in Europe combined with a lack of influence in Washington: a recipe for strategic confusion and disarray.

Along with the accession states in the European Union, Britain has felt the pain of balancing Washington and the major EU capitals ever more acutely since the Iraq crisis. The UK government singularly failed in its self-appointed role of providing a bridge of understanding between Europe and the United States. The turbulence across the Atlantic has been unprecedented in its scope and intensity. But the Iraq crisis has been the symptom rather than the cause of the structural dilemmas that are posed for British foreign policy. It is essential to examine the fundamental drivers of the new security context, such as globalisation and the emergence of the unipolar international system following the collapse of the Soviet Union. It is also wrong to extrapolate from current problems to suggest that these relationships will change fundamentally now.

It is likely that future Prime Ministers will have a similar conception of Britain's role in the world as the bridge between Europe and America. British foreign policy will combine European engagement with the Atlanticist instincts and reflexes that have traditionally enabled Britain to project global influence. It may no longer be described as a bridge, given the legacy of the Iraq War, but it will remain Britain's national strategy, as it has been since Suez. Nonetheless, this book argues that unless it is rebalanced, sustaining the relationship will not be easy. Both the US and Europe are more complex partners than at any point since the end of the Cold War.

Britain's apparently fraught relationship with George W. Bush's United States has reflected the changing contours of the post-Cold War landscape and the reluctance of the British to be engaged partners in Europe. In a multipolar world, the only alternative to a unilateralist US is a stronger EU. Even for pro-Europeans, the refashioning of the British transatlantic partnership does not mean the complete severing of ties with America. The bonds of moral and cultural affiliation are likely to remain strong. On both sides of the Atlantic, Britain feels close not only because of shared values and language, but because of its commitment to free trade, flexible capital and labour markets and a model of dynamic global capitalism.

British policy-makers must also confront the argument that the transatlantic relationship is inevitably becoming a smaller object on an enlarged strategic landscape. Globalisation has to be framed as a security issue as well as a question of trade and economics. A new strategic and security landscape is emerging as a consequence of the global communications revolution and the ease of mobility across borders. Power is shifting from West to East and between states and regions of the world.

Recent polls also illustrate the extent of the shift in British public opinion: 63 per cent believe that Britain is too close to the US and that the special relationship has become too special.[4] Only 14 per cent of British voters want London to be strongly aligned with Washington. There are constituencies within the British political class who argue that it is illusory to suggest there is no choice to be made between Europe and America. They insist that a generation from now Britain must no longer be the dependable ally of the US.[5]

The contrary view is that at the beginning of the twenty-first century, the Anglo-American special relationship has reached its apotheosis. The special security partnership has flourished since regime change in Afghanistan and since Iraq became the front-line of the global war on terror. For Americans still traumatised by the September 11 atrocities and bristling at querulous attacks from their ungrateful allies in Europe, Britain's unwavering commitment to its friend across the Atlantic was Tony Blair's finest hour.

Proponents of this view argue that it is misguided to suggest there will be an imminent breach in London's privileged relationship with Washington. The Anglo-Americans insist that

Blair and Bush found in one another remarkably similar instincts, like so many Prime Ministers and US Presidents before them. Inevitably, there were disagreements, from the US's refusal to adhere to international law for British detainees in Guantanamo, to Bush's reluctance to push more vigorously for a resolution to the Middle East peace process and the expansion of the United Nations' role in post-war Iraq. But the closeness forged by common historical and cultural ties, reinforced by the umbilical relationship between the American and British scientific and military establishments, encourages a special understanding of each other's priorities. It is the enduring dependence of the UK on the US for the last half-century that has enabled Britain to sustain the image of global influence. In a disorderly world, the special relationship is one of the few stabilising forces in the Western geo-political landscape.

The Anglo-Americans assert that the special relationship, far from descending into crisis, has fulfilled its historical purpose. Having withstood the demise of the Cold War, the transatlantic alliance has recovered its momentum in the light of the global terrorist threat. In fact, divisions over Iraq make it dangerous for Britain to rely on a common European approach, as France and Germany have repeatedly failed to prove themselves as reliable strategic partners.

The Anglo-American arguments deserve to be taken seriously. It is a mistake to extrapolate from current problems and argue that the relationship is set to change fundamentally in the immediate future. But the special security alliance between the US and the UK continues to evolve, and it will look very different two decades from now. The central premise of Britain's post-war national strategy, balancing the commitment to the US with the impetus towards European integration, has at times appeared unsustainable. The familiar landmarks of the geo-strategic landscape are being uprooted. The overarching triangulation of British foreign policy – the historical tensions between loyalty to the

Commonwealth, wariness of Europe and bonds with America – has arguably reached breaking point.

That is why the Iraq crisis alone does not explain why the special relationship appears increasingly fractious. Differences of opinion over Iraq have divided Europe and America, while exposing new divisions within the British political class and the British electorate. But Iraq alone is not the driver of a fundamental shift in the assumptions underlying Britain's view of the world.

There was of course a strong element of contingency in the failure of the Western allies to forge an agreed policy for tackling Saddam Hussein's regime. It is clear that personality, misguided diplomacy, weak leadership and inept presentation of the case for war were all culpable. It did not have to be that way. In the immediate aftermath of September 11, the Europeans and the Americans surprised each other positively. Bush confounded the Europeans' expectations with his careful and proportionate action in Afghanistan. In turn, the Europeans also broke with conventional stereotypes, strongly supporting military action against Al Qaeda. Europe's leaders pronounced 'unlimited solidarity' with the US. Yet relations between the transatlantic partners rapidly deteriorated, with Europeans accusing the US of a simplistic, Manichean approach to the conduct of foreign policy.

The personal unpopularity of Bush in Britain and the European continent does not offer an adequate explanation for the weakening of the special relationship either. Historians have long debated the role of structure and agency in determining the course of events. Yet there is a constant danger of over-emphasising the impact of individual personalities in setting the agenda of governments and mobilising political support.[6] Differences over global strategy between Europe and America are nothing new, although there is a belief among some analysts that we are now witnessing a fundamental structural shift in the transatlantic relationship.[7]

It is vital to assess the impact of long-standing historical and institutional forces. The strategic challenges governing Britain are perceptibly changing. The special relationship with the US originally reflected British anxieties about relative military and economic decline at the end of the Second World War. Yet as the era of decline draws to a close, Britain still seems stuck in the age of post-imperial trauma. Declinism no longer serves as a satisfactory rationale for Britain's relationships with either America or Europe.

The structural drivers of British foreign policy and Britain's global strategy are principally concerned with the geo-strategic environment after the Cold War and the rise of globalisation. To this should be added the growing importance of public opinion, which frames the choices open to parties and politicians. British policy has potentially reached a 'tipping point' because the electorate believe that the UK is too close to both America and Europe. The UK electorate are anxious and uncertain about the country's future direction. They do not have confidence in efforts by the US to win the war against Islamic fundamentalism. They fear that Britain has made itself the target of future terrorist attacks. Yet the desire for closer European co-operation has also waned over the last decade. The choices open to Britain look distinctly unattractive.

The governing approaches of the major political parties in Britain are in flux as they struggle to assess what this tipping point means for the future of British foreign policy. Future leaders on both left and right will seek to address how Britain redefines its troubled role as the bridge between Europe and America.

The Labour Party's strategy should be less defensive than in the Blair era. The party has secured three consecutive election victories, building its reputation as a competent governing party. The Conservatives are reflecting on the implications of their commitment to the special relationship, as well as Britain's membership of the EU. In the period leading up to the 2005 election, they appeared to distance themselves from the Atlantic alliance and adopted a more sceptical tone on the Iraq War.

Of necessity, the continent of Europe should seek to develop a stronger security capability in the next generation. That does not mean pushing for the creation of a federal superstate. But it does imply that as the US becomes more preoccupied with the challenges of the Middle East and central and south-east Asia, Washington will expect the EU to resolve more problems that occur in its own 'near abroad'. The dilemma is that stronger European defence will require British engagement, but Britain's enthusiasm for building up joint capabilities in the past has been limited.

The issue for the next decade is whether a new consensus in the political class about the desirability of further European integration and enlargement might be achieved that commands popular support. The alternative is that the balance swings towards a much looser association between Britain and the other nations of Europe. Britain might accept that a stronger EU will help to make Europe more influential in the world. But is it prepared to accept that this entails the extension of qualified majority voting as a mechanism of sovereignty-pooling, and an acceptance that intergovernmentalism alone has serious limitations as a framework for European governance?

The pro-Europeans must acknowledge that there are inevitably major strategic obstacles to enhancing Europe's role in British foreign and security policy. The present generation of leaders have taken the existence of the EU for granted, notwithstanding the recent debate about the European reform treaty. In the next decade, they will be required to articulate compelling arguments that justify Britain's participation in the development of the European Union itself. Too few British politicians have succeeded in conveying a sense of idealism about the historical purpose of European integration. This was brilliantly documented by the commentator Hugo Young:

For the makers of the original 'Europe', their creation was a triumph. Out of defeat, they produced a new kind of victory. For Britain, by contrast, the entry into Europe was a defeat, a fate she had resisted, a necessity reluctantly accepted, the last resort of a once great power, never for one moment a climactic or triumphant engagement with the construction of Europe.[8]

This study is not concerned with the future of the EU or the transatlantic relationship per se, but the implications of both for the future of British politics. To insist on a stark choice between Europe and America misconstrues the strategic options available to the UK. But to deny that there are dilemmas for British policymakers between Europe and America flies in the face of reality. In that sense the transatlantic bridge turned out to be a bridge too far for Tony Blair.

The unresolved dilemma between Europe and America is set to frame the narratives of British politics long after Blair's departure from office. It captures the defining question about British politics in the early twenty-first century and the domestic and geopolitical implications. As Andrew Gamble has emphasised, the choice between Europe and America is the major strategic challenge confronting today's generation of politicians and the governing class. How it is resolved will have profound consequences for the future of the British state.

There are several leading options available to the British political class in determining their strategic view of Britain's place in the world. The concern is that they are all wrong, or at least misguided. Pro-Europeans argue that since the UK is no longer a global power in its own right, it should deepen and widen its European alliances. But that would require the British people to reconcile themselves to a fundamentally European future. There is no clear evidence that they are yet ready to do so. Many of the setbacks since 1997 occurred in European policy and Blair largely failed in his repeated aim of ending decades of British distance and hesitation about

Europe; Britain remains the perpetual awkward partner.[9] Europe is one of the central failures of Blair's premiership.

Anglo-Americans argue that Britain should instead embrace the comfort blanket of the special relationship as a warrior satellite of the US.[10] The US remains the most reliable and trusted ally of the UK, as well as sharing an economic model based on the commitment to neo-liberal globalisation. Yet the Anglo-American special relationship is imperilled as never before; the US has never been more distrusted among the British electorate.

The third, 'British multilateralist', alternative is that the UK should avoid the dilemma of Europe and America altogether. Britain must become a third force, as some on the left urged after the Second World War, caught between the Atlantic alliance and Soviet communism.[11] Britain has long been thought of as an exceptional place with its own path of economic and political development that distanced it from American and European influences, both of which were seen as the enemy and a threat.

The homogeneity of Britain and British identity was one of the bulwarks of the British state, at least as perceived in England, if not elsewhere in the UK. Its role in the world has been shaped by the legacy of empire and the links between the UK and the Commonwealth countries. Given this sphere of influence Britain should have the courage to act on the basis of its enlightenment values. This reflects the nineteenth-century view of Britain as a beacon to the world.

Caught between Europe and America and feeling the dilemma acutely since the Iraq crisis, the British could hardly be blamed for adopting a more independent posture in foreign affairs. The belief in Britain standing apart has a long pedigree, from Shakespeare's 'sceptred isle' to Churchill's defiance, 'if necessary, alone', in resisting Nazism. The danger is, however, that Britain isolates itself at the moment when globalisation puts a renewed premium on interdependence.

There is also an underlying tension between a strong sense of Britishness and the commitment to a multilateralist foreign policy. The inclination towards independence and the focus on the primacy of British national interests sits uneasily with the desire to co-operate with other partners and allies in the EU and beyond. Equally, the world has never been more closely and intimately connected. Europe, for example, offers Britain a gateway to the global economy through the knowledge- and science-based industries and sectors, symbolised by the success of the City of London as Europe's leading financial centre.

Instead, Britain's world role must shift from one of transatlantic bridging to one of European partnership. Nation-states by themselves can exercise little effective sovereignty in the new world order. The world of the twentieth century was defined by the power of the state.[12] The world of the twenty-first is one where states are fast losing their monopoly of power – in part to a new set of global actors as well as through the awakening of a once-passive citizenry. It is a world where, as Jeremy Rifkin argues, 'geographic boundaries of all kinds are loosening or disappearing altogether'.[13] 'If the 19th century saw the state's development and the 20th century its apotheosis, the 21st may be the century of its decline.'[14]

This ongoing erosion of borders is characteristic not just of economic life. A recent study by Professor David Held and colleagues at the London School of Economics and Political Science on 'global transformations' includes findings on global trade, financial markets and multinational corporations, as well as global domestic politics, peace-keeping and organised violence, the rise of migration, new media and communication networks, forms of culture, and identity conflicts that arise from the 'disembedding' of the economy, culture and society. All these dimensions impinge on state systems constructed on the basis of the territorial principle. As Jürgen Habermas describes, 'states which are becoming increasingly *entangled* in the interdependencies of a global economy and global society are forfeiting their capacity for autonomous action, and with it their democratic substance' (original emphasis).[15]

The most promising response is arguably to pool sovereignty and establish new forms of trans-national governance and co-operation. A new British model of liberal internationalism is needed, rooted in the commitment to Europe but drawing on notions of global civil society: public spaces in the global polity based on networks and associations that sustain new forms of politics, complementing the nation-state. The EU is an example of what can be achieved, as it possesses stronger regulatory powers than many other regional bodies. But the British have historically shown great reluctance to fully engage with the EU because of the Atlanticist preferences and priorities of the governing class, underlining the deep post-war schisms and divisions that have beset British politics.

What seems certain is that the dilemma of how to balance Europe and America will be one of the most compelling debates for Britain in the post-Blair era. Historical circumstances as well as changing geo-political realities have meant that attempts by British governments to reconcile the competing attractions of Europe and America have created an unstable and uncertain context. This book explores the implications for the future of British politics, and the very survival of the British state itself.

1

Bridging the divide?
Europe, America and the future of Britain's global strategy

> The Anglo-Saxon race is infallibly destined to be the predominant force in the history and civilisation of the world.
> Joseph Chamberlain[1]

> Propagate our language all over the world . . . Fraternal association with the US – this would let them in too. Harmonises with my ideas for the future of the world. This will be the English speaking century.
> Winston Churchill[2]

The critical event in the shaping of post-war British global strategy was Suez. At the end of the Second World War, both Winston Churchill and Clement Attlee believed that Britain was still a great power, one of the 'big three', alongside the United States and the Soviet Union, that defeated Nazi Germany. Britain's leaders acknowledged that the country had been gravely weakened economically; Attlee's Labour Party openly accepted that the days of empire were over. With the decline of empire, the attempt to bridge Europe and America became increasingly central to British identity and British political economy. But as diplomatic ties with Stalin's USSR steadily deteriorated, the relationship with the US was increasingly seen as fundamental to safeguarding British national security. The pretence was sustained that Britain and the

US were on the same level as great powers. This mind-set had been frozen in the image of the peace conferences at Tehran, Yalta and Potsdam. But the Suez crisis shattered those illusions.

Suez is traditionally seen as the great dividing line in post-war British history since it highlighted the need to adjust to a less influential role in the world. The debacle occurred eighteen months after Churchill's retirement as Prime Minister. It was a clear demonstration that the special relationship with the United States – if it still existed – was that of a subordinate to a superior. It was also a brutal lesson in highlighting the limitations of Britain's ability to act without the US's backing, as the hostility of Washington and its refusal to support sterling forced Anthony Eden to withdraw from the operation to seize back control of the Suez Canal. The ignominious retreat shattered the illusions of empire, and reminded the governing class that Britain could no longer act without the prior agreement of Washington.

This compelled British governments to begin to come to terms with post-imperial decline and the reality of a reduced status in world affairs. The Suez experience demanded a full-scale reassessment of British foreign policy. The UK's status as a global industrial and military power in the post-war age had been thoroughly undermined, but there seemed to be no alternative alignment that could sustain Britain's role as a major power. By the early 1960s Harold Macmillan was able to comment: 'Our whole position in the world was in the nature of the rearguard action.'[3]

It fell to Macmillan as the post-Suez Prime Minister to initiate a crucial phase of adjustment to Britain's diminished world role. This meant reconciliation with the US, the shrinking of the British Empire – notably in Africa and the Caribbean – and rapprochement with Europe. The renewal of the special relationship would also make it possible to retain an independent nuclear deterrent. The British Cabinet drew its own conclusions, as the minutes of a discussion in January 1957 reveal:

> There must be a sea-change in the basis of Anglo-American relations. It was doubtful whether the US would now be willing to accord to us alone the special position which we had held as their principal ally during the war. We might therefore be better to influence them if we were part of an association of powers which had greater political, economic and military strength than we alone could command.[4]

That effort was about weaving a less grandiose but more viable and coherent future for Britain. Yet the conclusions inevitably appeared ambiguous and uncertain. It became an article of faith that never again could British policy come into open conflict with the United States. The British hoped this would secure US support even where their interests were less immediately threatened.

The major and urgent response of Macmillan to Suez was the restoration of close ties with Washington. The historian Paul Addison argues that 'from the point of view of people who were in charge of the UK government, the special relationship was simply necessary in order to keep the show on the road'.[5] This concept of the special relationship was, of course, not uniquely Anglo-American. The term has been applied to other US allies, notably Israel, Brazil, pre-communist China, and the Federal Republic of Germany.[6] After 1956, it meant that the British did not intervene anywhere without US approval. Yet the French had drawn the opposite conclusion. Even before Charles de Gaulle returned in the spring of 1958 they had refused to subordinate their foreign policy to the US. Instead, France grew closer to West Germany, strengthening the momentum towards the launch of the European Economic Community following the treaty of Rome in 1957.

As Henry Kissinger later observed, Macmillan tied Britain into US policy, conceding pre-eminence to Washington in return for the appearance of influence in the White House. But major events in the early 1960s, from the Berlin crisis to the Cuban missile confrontation, only served to underline Britain's marginal role. Numerous historical monographs have also exposed the friction and controversy beneath the surface of Anglo-American co-operation – although, of course, there are elements of tension and hostility in any diplomatic relationship.

When in the late 1950s Britain took the first hesitant steps towards European integration, it was a gesture to where Washington felt Britain should be as much as a rational calculation of Britain's economic interests. Britain did not join the Schuman plan negotiations in 1950, and Dean Acheson, US Secretary of State at the time, later expressed profound irritation at this, suggesting in 1969 that it was our 'great mistake of the post-war period . . . It was not the last clear chance for Britain to enter Europe, but it was the first wrong choice.'[7] In a pamphlet aimed at reassuring the many critics of Britain's application to the EEC, Macmillan argued that the US would inevitably attach greater importance to the continent of Europe, paying progressively less attention to British interests. The European dimension had occupied a low priority.

During the 1960s, the American progressive constituency clearly and unequivocally backed the cause of European unity. President John F. Kennedy was an enthusiastic supporter of European integration, encouraging the emergence of a united Europe as a trusted strategic partner of the US. These are the origins of the transatlantic bridge championed by Tony Blair. The cornerstone of that strategy is the United Kingdom's role as a bridge across the Atlantic, reconciling contrasting, even conflicting, attitudes and interests. But the Suez debacle has bedevilled Anglo-French relations for the last fifty years, preventing the emergence of a coherent European foreign policy.[8]

It also became apparent to many observers that the strategy has some inherent contradictions and unresolved dilemmas. It was simply not credible for the UK to act as both an Atlantic and a European power, playing a separate role through the special relationship. In the winter of 1962–3, the Kennedy administration threatened to abandon the Skybolt stand-off missile system, ending Britain's status as an independent nuclear power. Although Kennedy relented, agreeing that the UK could have the Polaris submarine-based system, in practice Britain's dependence on the United States grew further as the Royal Navy became increasingly reliant on US technology and expertise.

There was also a direct conflict between Britain's worldwide strategy – which still had many powerful adherents in the Conservative Party – and the necessity of basing its economic and political future on European preferences.[9] This was despite the clearly demonstrable evidence that British trade was growing very rapidly with other leading capitalist economies in western Europe, rather than in the Commonwealth. These apparent conflicts of interest famously led de Gaulle to veto British entry to the EEC in January 1963, fearing that Britain did not share France's strategic view of Europe.

Despite this every British Prime Minister since Macmillan has fought to sustain the balancing act between Washington and Europe's leading capitals. This particular conception of global strategy has proved to be one of the most contested and controversial themes in contemporary British politics. It is captured in the common jibe that the UK is merely the fifty-first state, a satellite of America. At the height of the Iraq crisis, the former South African President Nelson Mandela referred to the British Prime Minister as 'no more than the foreign minister of the United States'.[10] The decision of the British political class to link its fortunes so consistently with the US has been the source of some of the great debates in British national life.

Controversies aside, how are the qualities or characteristics of the special relationship best described? The special relationship is principally a British concept since it is intended to emphasise the closeness of the UK to the world's leading economic and military power. It has often been invoked to suggest that Britain's relationship with Washington offers an alternative to the post-war project of closer European integration.[11]

In one sense, pro-American ideology in the UK reflects a richer set of cultural, linguistic, institutional and historical ties that have always bound together the two nations of Britain and the United States. That ideology embodies the imagined community of Anglo-America. It is often framed as a story of 'those great days of Britain and America standing together' in the Second World War. It turns on a visit by President Franklin Roosevelt's adviser Harry Hopkins to assess Britain's chances of survival in 1941, a story recounted by Tony Blair to Bill Clinton in 1998:

> On the last evening before he left to take home a message to America he gave a speech to the dinner and sitting next to Churchill he said: 'I suppose you wish to know what I am going to say to President Roosevelt upon my return.' And then Harry Hopkins said he would be quoting a verse from the Bible: 'Whither thou goest, I will go, and whither thou lodgest, I will lodge. Thy people shall be my people and thy God my God.' And then Hopkins paused and then he said: 'Even to the end.' And Churchill wept.[12]

The Atlantic alliance that emerged during the war has to be set in a wider historical frame of reference, dating back before the American Revolution. It includes not only the United States but the other colonies of settlers, including Canada, New Zealand and Australia: the English-speaking peoples of the English-speaking world that Churchill romanticised. 'Anglo-America', as Andrew Gamble defines it, is 'a complex set of interlinked narratives and institutions'[13] with a long history, at once a military alliance, a model of capitalism, a form of government and a popular culture.

This should not imply that the unification of 'Anglo-America' was ever guaranteed. At the outbreak of the Second World War, the emotional bond between Britain and America was not sufficiently strong to allow Roosevelt to take the US to war in defence of its ally. In the early twentieth century, the struggles between Europe's powers and the swift rise of the United States led some to predict that the military contest between Britain and the US would lead to the next round of imperialist conflict as the First World War ended.

The United States became particularly antagonistic to the British Empire in the inter-war years.[14] In part, this was a reflection of naval rivalry, but it was also an economic struggle as the US wanted the empire to be opened up to trade with it, neutralising a commercial rival. Even in the post-war negotiations over financial institutions, John Maynard Keynes struggled to persuade the Americans to lift the burden on the British economy. British historians have also revealed how Churchill's imperialism frequently annoyed the Americans, strengthening their resolve not to help Britain in any way that would sustain its empire.[15]

Yet there were broader strategic considerations that made war between the two powers unlikely. The governing class in Britain knew that the empire was sustainable only if it avoided costly wars with rival powers. But there was also little appetite to fight the US, so potent was the ideology of Anglo-American unity in domestic politics. This was reciprocated to some extent in the US: pro-British feeling was especially strong in Wall Street, where financiers such as J. P. Morgan were ardent Anglophiles who spent half of each year in Britain.[16]

An alternative explanation for the special relationship is that the transatlantic alliance was purely a 'marriage of convenience', evolving as a strategic alliance after 1945. In that sense it was consistent with balance-of-power politics and realist diplomacy, since Britain and the US had their own strategic interests and imperatives. Yet if the origins of the contemporary alliance are traced to Churchill's speech on the 'sinews of peace' at Fulton, Missouri in March 1946, the myth of Anglo-America looms large.

Britain's wartime leader called for a 'fraternal association of the English-speaking peoples' and 'a special relationship between the

British Empire and Commonwealth, and the United States'. Churchill drew the battle-lines of the Cold War, arguing famously that an iron curtain had descended across Europe, setting the stage for Anglo-American agreement on the need to contain the Soviet threat in Europe. He elaborated a conception of 'England' at the heart of three key historical relationships or concentric circles: the British Empire, Europe and Anglo-America, which continues to influence sections of the British political class in the twenty-first century.

Churchill's ideas were subsequently criticised, for they appeared to permit the avoidance of a choice about Britain's role in the world after 1945, propagating the myth of equal status with great powers such as the Soviet Union and the United States. The Fulton address does reinforce the image of Britain clinging on to the sense of itself as an influential power. Yet the disparity between Britain's post-war situation and its colonial responsibilities was enormous.[17] It suggested that the political class was often incapable of comprehending the extent of Britain's economic decline, while distracted by loyalty to the Commonwealth and unable to put itself at the heart of the European project. This reinforced the self-image of Britain as a 'world island',[18] a 'cradle of democracy', as a model that others should emulate. For Churchill's generation, Britain was a special place with its own path of development through the twin empires of territory and trade. It deserved to maintain a distinctive identity and inviolable political sovereignty.

This historically constructed notion of Britishness was based on several attributes.[19] The first was the idea of the British as innovators and pioneers who led the world. The industrial revolution, creativity in science and culture as well as parliamentary democracy made Britain 'the workshop of the world'.[20] Another attribute was the capacity of the British for leadership in the global economy and the international state system. The strength of British institutions was that they should serve as a model to others. Britain stood for political stability and institutional continuity, having established its constitutional state in 1689. It has survived for more than 300 years without overthrow or external invasion. The historian Andrew Roberts argues this is necessary to understand why the 'English-speaking peoples' have been so successful in exporting their political culture, especially after 1900.[21]

What the Anglo-American alliance apparently offered was the opportunity to sustain the strategic relationships through which the UK could project global power and influence, but without undermining this hegemonic conception of British identity. Europe on the other hand always seemed to pose a threat. That sense of British identity embodied in the history and founding rituals of England and subsequently the British state itself held that Britain should remain a global and imperial power, fundamentally oceanic, not continental.

The British political class remained wedded to the idea of the special relationship with the US. But the relationship became very different to how it was envisaged in the 1940s, when it was forged by Roosevelt and Churchill to defeat Nazi Germany. Then it naturally demonstrated Britain's status as a great power and the leading role that Britain had assumed in the fight against Hitler. After Suez, the political class held on to the special relationship, but it was merely a reflection of Britain's growing vulnerability as influence and power became increasingly elusive.

Harold Macmillan in particular sought to position the UK as playing the role of 'Greece to America's Rome'. He developed his own ideas about how American power might be manipulated. Suez taught that Britain could never be in open confrontation with the US, but that it should revert to the more subtle practice of covertly reshaping American interests. It would act as a civilising and restraining influence that educated and guided the new superpower in the intricacies of leadership in the free world. This aspiration faded in the 1960s, but was revived again in the 1980s by Margaret Thatcher and Ronald Reagan, reaching a new intensity in the era of Bill Clinton, George W. Bush and Tony Blair.

The predicament in Britain's global strategy is that the strategic choice between Europe and America, while not exclusive, grew starker in the second half of the twentieth century. The UK has not been alone in struggling to perform a precarious balancing act between Washington and other EU capitals, especially Paris and Berlin. Many accession countries in central and eastern Europe have felt it acutely too, notably as the Iraq crisis has unfolded. Traditional Atlanticist countries such as the Netherlands and Portugal have felt increasingly marginalised from the transatlantic alliance. For decades, West Germany balanced the pursuit of Franco-German reconciliation through the European Union with vigorous support for the transatlantic relationship. But Chancellor Gerhard Schroeder challenged this tenet of German foreign policy by confronting President Bush and refusing to accede to the invasion of Iraq.

Nor is it the case that the special relationship has remained frozen across the post-war era. Britain's world role was drastically redefined after the Second World War. But there has been widespread agreement among the governing elite about global strategy. The attractions of influence in Washington have been enormously seductive for British Prime Ministers. The special relationship has often felt like an emotional comfort blanket for a declining power. The need for British governments of both right and left to construct a credible security partnership in order to remain serious contenders for power has served to buttress the transatlantic bridge. The post-war years have seen continuing ambivalence in attitudes to America and Europe among the British electorate. But the fundamental commitment to the special relationship has never really been in doubt despite so many unresolved contradictions and dilemmas.

Britain's predicament now is that the familiar landmarks have been uprooted. The British state and the British economy have moved beyond decline since the late 1970s. But the UK now confronts an unstable, rapidly changing geo-political landscape. Globalisation presents myriad challenges, from competition over energy resources to the perception of growing cultural conflict between the West and Islam.

The inherent asymmetry of power between Britain and the US has also created persistent tensions in the special relationship. The end of the Cold War and the rise of unilateral foreign policy in the Bush administration – rather than Iraq per se – have shattered the traditional Atlanticist pillar. Britain's emphasis on sustaining the transatlantic bridge signified that America rather than Europe would remain the priority, but in future, no British Prime Minister will endorse unilateral military action by the US as Blair did in Iraq. A fundamental and far-reaching reassessment of Britain's place in the world is now long overdue.

2

The Anglo-American alliance and British global strategy since 1945

> After the detour of Empire, the Saxon is now back ploughing his field.
>
> Tom Nairn[1]

This chapter explores in greater depth why the special security relationship with the United States became a fundamental pillar of British foreign policy at the end of the Second World War. All British leaders from Churchill to Brown have resorted to the belief that Britain's security and defence interests lie with America rather than Europe. As the previous chapter argued, the bridge between Europe and America always meant giving primacy to the partnership with the US. That was apparently Britain's best hope of projecting power and influence after the loss of empire.

The permanence of the alliance with the US has been something of an anomaly in British history. For centuries, Britain practised balance-of-power diplomacy and tended to avoid alliances with other states. British foreign secretaries proudly acted in accordance with Lord Palmerston's dictum: 'We have no eternal allies and we have no perpetual enemies. Our interests are eternal and perpetual, and those interests it is our duty to follow.'[2] The transatlantic partnership breached this sacred principle of pragmatism since Britain had apparently found an eternal ally.

As the previous chapter argued, the origins of the special relationship lay in Britain and America's military alliance in the Second World War. This was relaunched in 1949 in the form of the North Atlantic Treaty Organization (NATO). But the ties extended into many other fields of co-operation. At the outset it was presented as a genuine partnership of equals, although the significant disparity of power between the US and Britain led some to question whether there was anything special at all about the 'special relationship'. David Reynolds argues that what is considered 'special' cannot be judged against an idealised standard of international amity. It is also necessary to consider how the co-operation – whatever its imperfections and flaws – differs in degree and extent from other diplomatic alliances.[3]

One influential interpretation of the Anglo-American relationship has emphasised Britain's desire to sustain global influence despite the devastation of war and the imminent decline of the British economy. In 1945, Britain was the world's third largest power after the United States and the Soviet Union. But the nation had almost been destroyed after six gruelling years of conflict. The reputation of Britain was higher than at any time in the twentieth century, as historians such as Christopher Coker have noted,[4] since no one fought Hitler for as long or as courageously as the British.

But the country had been exhausted by its efforts. In the closing months of the war, British strength was visibly declining. By March 1945, only a quarter of the troops under the command of the supreme Allied commander in Europe, Dwight Eisenhower, were British forces. The UK economy had been almost destroyed by the war effort, with a gross debt of more than £22 billion. The collapse of industry threatened to permanently destroy Britain's wealth and standard of living.

Despite the devastation in the domestic base of the British economy, successive governments were not yet prepared to relinquish global influence. This would enable Britain to play a larger role than its national territory would usually afford. The governing elite viewed the special relationship as the means of recreating Britain's status as a global power as well as ensuring collective security. If the UK projected this global role onto America, it could influence its most powerful ally, acting as a proxy for great power status. Britain would remain one of the three great powers with the United States and the Soviet Union, at the intersection of three overlapping circles of influence: empire, Europe and Anglo-America.

British governments were also prepared to assist the Americans in their new global role as the dominant capitalist power because of their view that the country's economy depended on an open, liberal trading network, as well as ensuring the security of the capitalist world against the Soviet Union. This enabled Britain to prolong its traditional world role.

But the Suez crisis forced a rapid adjustment in British national strategy. After 1956, the British political class were forced to contemplate an unpalatable fact. Britain could no longer act independently without the support of the US. This also meant that disengagement from the former colonies should be speeded up, as Suez hastened both Britain and France's protracted withdrawal from empire. The historian Tony Judt has observed that 'the retreat from Empire contributed directly to a growing British anxiety about the loss of national direction'.[5] The long-term economic vulnerability of the UK was becoming apparent in the early 1960s, given the loss of competitive advantage suffered by British industry.

Nonetheless, the Anglo-American special relationship held out several advantages for the governing class in determining Britain's global strategy after 1945. The UK government drew great strength from its perception of being the US's closest ally. In defence, it included a direct input into the strategic thinking of the US military establishment. 'There was no other government', the US Secretary of State Henry Kissinger later recalled, 'with which we could have dealt with so openly, exchanged ideas so freely, or in effect permitted to participate in our deliberations.'[6] In contrast to France, Britain had a defence identity that was wholly compatible with membership of NATO, through which it could sustain close collaboration with the US.

Harold Macmillan in particular was able to capitalise on Eisenhower's own instinct to strengthen Anglo-American relations, extracting significant commitments from the President in the fields of nuclear co-ordination and in solving Cold War challenges in the Middle East, Hong Kong and Algeria. Eisenhower's Secretary of State, John Foster Dulles, felt that any intensification of Anglo-American relations should be the starting point for reinvigorating America's alliances worldwide, but it was a 'unique high point' in the special relationship.[7]

The intelligence relationship between the UK and the US grew steadily closer during the 1950s. The GCHQ command centre and the National Security Agency (NSA) in Washington collaborated extensively. The NSA had a presence at GCHQ in Cheltenham and Menwith Hill. James Woolsey, a former director of the CIA, has remarked: 'Although no one is a complete friend in the intelligence world, with Britain and America it is as close as it gets.'[8] Britain passed intelligence to the US and other English-speaking countries that it did not share with its European partners.

Although until the end of the 1950s Britain sought a genuinely independent nuclear deterrent, the subsequent Polaris and Trident submarines were powerfully dependent on American technology. At the height of the Cold War, the British enjoyed privileged access to nuclear research conducted in the US as a precedent of the 'dual key' operating system established in the late 1950s. In 1958, Macmillan had sought to emphasise the importance of the special relationship by securing the repeal of the McMahon Act, enabling useful nuclear information to be shared with Britain. Even today, Britain's Trident missiles are leased from the US, and the UK's nuclear forces are configured in accordance with US strategic doctrine. The UK is the only European power that is committed to developing military capabilities that remain technologically interoperable with US forces. That has been the product of its special security partnership with the United States.

The sharing of intelligence and the interoperability of nuclear forces are naturally complemented by a third element: close co-operation between Britain and the US as allies within NATO extending into trade and the governance of international institutions. The Atlantic alliance envisaged intensive collaboration between Britain and the US in promoting a particular conception of the global economy, governed by free trade, sound finance and universal respect for property rights.[9] The US helped to ensure that Britain was able to participate fully in the post-war economic system as a powerful commercial and financial player, maintaining sterling as one of the world's leading currencies.

The US establishment also knew that it could depend fundamentally on its alliance with Britain, since it was a core premise of the governing consensus between the major political parties in the British state. One of the striking features of British national life after 1945 was the extent to which both Labour and Conservative governments succeeded in maintaining a solid bipartisan agreement on security, in contrast to the fierce disputes of the 1930s. The Atlantic partnership was the linchpin of all subsequent post-war governments.

It fell to the Labour government elected in 1945 to shape British policy in the immediate post-war era. Under the Foreign Secretary, Ernest Bevin, the administration chose to sustain its wartime alliance with the US. Bevin vigorously persuaded the Americans not only to remain engaged in Europe, but to assume the global responsibilities that the US's power and status warranted. The Attlee government accepted the need for greater European unity. But it remained wary of the implications: Clement Attlee and Bevin were determined that Europe should be based on intergovernmentalism alone. Labour was instinctively suspicious of European integration and the European project, believing in the uniqueness of British socialism and the ability to build socialism within the bounded territory of the British Isles.

It was Labour that established the path subsequently followed by Conservative governments in the 1950s, despite the opposition of the Labour left and demands for a socialist foreign policy fulfilling the traditional ideals of internationalism and antimilitarism. There was a strong belief in the Atlantic alliance as the bedrock of collective security. Such pro-Americanism was also based on the experience and interpretation of the Cold War, but it was encouraged by the election of John F. Kennedy as President in 1960.

Bevin strongly believed that the US alliance was necessary to contain the Soviet threat in Europe. Communism and its sympathisers were common enemies both at home and abroad. America's influence helped to provide Labour with a credible strategy for domestic modernisation: class harmonisation and the new techniques of Fordist industrial production would provide the springboard for stronger economic growth.

The commitment to America on the British centre-left was strong since the Labour leadership identified Atlanticism as a means to marginalise the left in the Labour Party and the trade union movement. The reconstruction plan launched through Marshall Aid in 1947 enabled the party to discipline the demands of labour, restraining wage rises and containing unrealistic expectations of radicalism. As Rhiannon Vickers has outlined elsewhere, the Labour government used Atlantic influences to persuade its own supporters of the need for moderation, equating attacks on the Marshall plan with communism and treachery.[10] The preference given to Anglo-America also reflected an inherent scepticism among British socialists about the European project and the commitment to European integration. Europe was initially regarded as anti-socialist, a threat to Labour's domestic achievements in nationalisation and the welfare state.

On the right of British politics, giving priority to America over Europe was the guarantee of preserving Britain's global economic role and the importance of the sterling area represented by the City of London. There were still stark divisions within the coalition of Conservative support. British industrialists, for example, wanted to retain imperial trade preferences. But in general, Labour and the Conservatives agreed to maintain the special relationship as part of what has subsequently been termed the post-war consensus.

As the Cold War intensified, the Anglo-American relationship held out other obvious advantages for the British governing class. It provided a soft landing after empire, the means by which the United Kingdom would retain the appearance of a great power and protect its global interests. Sterling would remain an international currency as the Americans underwrote key aspects of Britain's world role, enabling parts of the empire to be retained even after India and Pakistan were granted independence. Britain could still project itself as a world power. But the Atlantic partnership offered strategic advantages to both sides. The US was able to command a high price for continuing engagement in Europe after 1945. Britain was a reliable ally in fashioning multilateral institutions such as the United Nations, NATO, the International Monetary Fund, the World Bank and the General Agreement on Tariffs and Trade (GATT), which developed into the World Trade Organization.

The war had also led to an enormous expansion of aggregate demand in the American economy, which threatened to fall back as the conflict ended. The launch of Marshall Aid enabled demand for US exports to be stimulated in foreign markets, greatly strengthening the dollar as a reserve currency and sustaining the buoyancy of the US economy. The urgency of restraining the Soviet Union also led to higher levels of military expenditure, encouraging a bipartisan consensus between the Democratic and Republican parties during the Cold War era with obvious advantages for the military establishment in Washington.

In the 1950s and 1960s, the terms of the Anglo-American special relationship were gradually consolidated. This led to the construction of a new world order based on an open economy, multilateral trade and the North Atlantic military alliance. It promoted the idea of the 'free world' as a global ideology: the special relationship between Britain and the US was the most visible expression of the West's commitment to capitalism and freedom. In some circles, this vision of Atlantic community was the product of a new compatibility between capitalism and the institutional and military architecture of the Cold War. To thrive in a world where communism represented a continuous threat, capitalist markets had to be underwritten by the transatlantic alliance, guaranteeing security. Dominion over material goods and energy is intertwined with the capacity of states to mobilise resources and to project power globally. The Anglo-American alliance was the means of sustaining an open, capitalist trading economy, but also of guaranteeing the future security of the British state itself.

This encouraged the continuous refashioning of an Atlantic identity to which the notion of the imminent threat of Soviet communism and the assumption of an exhaustive conflict between it and American capitalism were both critical. Atlanticism also implied the collective commitment to parliamentary democracy and managed capitalism, combining a liberal international economy with state intervention at home. The post-war system based on the strength of the dollar was underpinned at home by this combination of the liberal international economy with state intervention, and abroad by global financial institutions.

The special economic and security partnership between Britain and the US was not without its opponents in the political class. Influential strands of opinion in both main political parties held out against what they saw as the forced liquidation of British power and its unique spheres of interest in the empire and the Commonwealth. There were elements on both right and left that were not prepared to see Britain abandon its aspirations for global power, placing serious constraints on the capacity of governments to pursue active demand management of the national economy. On the right were those who refused to give up Britain's independence of action, on the left those who argued that 'socialist Britain' should not ally with capitalist America.

One of the most prominent themes of British historiography since the 1960s has been the argument that Britain made the wrong strategic choices after the Second World War. In choosing to align itself explicitly with the US, it was forced to cling to a set of costly great-power assumptions that damaged its post-war economic performance, and postponed the acknowledgement that Britain's role as a world power was finally over.

The most sophisticated version of this critique focuses on the tendency of the Atlantic partnership to deceive British policy-makers, continuing to hold out the possibility that a non-European future was still viable. This was combined with the UK's deep-seated reluctance to surrender or dilute national sovereignty. Such fears contributed to Britain's dysfunctional attitude to the process of European integration, weakening the country economically by preventing it from taking full advantage of the European market.

It was claimed that the special relationship distorted British priorities, forcing it to commit to much higher defence expenditure than it could afford while inhibiting post-war recovery. There was a basic conflict between the needs of the domestic economy and the international priorities of British politics. Britain had sought to recapture its former position in the world, re-establishing the British Empire instead of investing in its domestic industrial base. By 1950/1, more than 8 per cent of GDP was still being committed to defence expenditure despite the heavy demands of domestic reconstruction and the development of the welfare state.

Successive defence reviews failed to resolve the problems of military over-stretch. Even in the late 1950s, Britain still had extensive commitments in Malaya, Indonesia, Kenya, the Middle East and the wider Gulf region. In 1968, the Wilson administration was forced to downgrade British commitments east of Suez following the devaluation crisis the previous year. It forced through the shift in policy by a Cabinet majority of just one vote, demonstrating the reluctance of the governing class to accept that Britain should surrender its global role. The divisions within the Labour government illustrate the dilemma at the heart of British politics between sustaining Britain's role as a global power and effective domestic economic management and modernisation.

This critique concluded that the Anglo-American special relationship had diverted governments in the 1950s and 1960s from the urgent task of modernising the British economy in the face of intense international pressure, with Japan and West Germany emerging as tough global competitors. The policies of liberal, outward-looking economic management were not the only cause of Britain's slow growth rate, but they made it much more difficult to tackle the internal weaknesses of the British economy – renewing domestic industry for the international challenges that it now faced.

The Americans' policy itself was also imposing massive pressures on British economic performance. This included the immediate end of the Lend-Lease scheme on the cessation of hostilities in 1945, and tough conditions for the post-war loan that John Maynard Keynes was sent to negotiate from the US. It led directly to the 1947 convertibility crisis, which fatally damaged the Attlee administration's reputation for economic competence and set the terms for post-war under-performance.

Harold Macmillan was also forced to acknowledge the limitations of his 'Greeks and Romans' approach to Anglo-American relations. He completely failed to influence President Eisenhower's dealings with Nikita Khrushchev and the Soviets. The Americans also let Macmillan down over Skybolt, abandoning any independent British means of nuclear delivery. The unravelling of Anglo-American interdependence then forced Macmillan to pursue an alternative strategy of joining the European Economic Community, but this was infamously blocked by the French President, General Charles de Gaulle.

In 1962, Dean Acheson famously argued that 'Great Britain has lost an empire and has not yet found a role'. He added in his brutally honest assessment:

> The attempt to play a separate power role – that is, a role apart from Europe, a role based on a 'special relationship' with the United States, a role based on being the head of a 'Commonwealth' which has no political structure, unity or strength and enjoys a fragile and precarious economic relationship by means of the sterling area and preferences in the British market – this role is absolutely played out.[11]

Despite this strong opposition to the choices underlying Britain's post-war national strategy, the basic consensus for the special relationship between all the political parties was never fundamentally challenged. Other commentators have queried whether early British involvement at the launch of the Schuman plan in 1950 would necessarily have fulfilled the national interest more successfully than the Atlantic alliance.[12] They argue that the unwillingness of British policy-makers to sacrifice trade preferences within the sterling area and the Commonwealth was a rational choice, although the evidence about the potential for trade with other advanced capitalist democracies in western Europe does not necessarily support this view.

Inevitably, Macmillan's retirement and the shock of President Kennedy's assassination in 1963 meant that the special relationship appeared to cool markedly during the 1960s. Some of its functional and psychological impetus was lost over the following decade in the face of growing diplomatic friction.

There were several reasons for the temporary waning of the alliance during the 1960s and early 1970s. The first was the Vietnam conflict. The use by the US of napalm and gas, and the heavy bombing of North Vietnam, encouraged a wave of anti-American feeling in Britain.[13] The disagreement over Vietnam coupled with the rise of new social movements threatened to undermine the Atlanticist pillar of British foreign policy.

Although Harold Wilson and his strongly pro-American Foreign Secretary, Michael Stewart, continued to support US policy, they refused to commit British troops. This illustrated that Britain and the US still had divergent strategic interests despite the need for transatlantic unity in the face of the Soviet threat.

The British government had sought a security partnership with the US, which would enable it to readily acquire nuclear information, thereby ensuring the continuation of the UK's global role. Another reason for the cooling of the special relationship, however, was that within the US establishment policy-makers were divided between those who favoured maintaining close ties with the UK and those who argued for stronger bilateral relationships with France and West Germany. Numerous commentators have described the internal divisions in Washington between pro-British Presidents such as Eisenhower and Kennedy and 'Europeanists' in the State Department who fought to put an end to the special relationship altogether.[14]

Another important factor in the dynamics of the special relationship was the nature of the personal connection between US Presidents and British Prime Ministers. It is, of course, dangerous to over-simplify complex relationships, but the warmth of bilateral ties and personal friendships in moments of international crisis can often be decisive.

Wilson calculated that the Labour Party and the British electorate would never accept British military involvement in Vietnam, but he faced an acute dilemma. Wilson's policy openly contradicted the post-Suez spirit of Anglo-American cooperation. At a White House dinner in December 1964, Wilson defined the special relationship in terms that were very different to those that shaped Macmillan's thinking a decade earlier:

> Some of those who talk about the special relationship, I think, are looking backwards and not forward. They talk about the nostalgia of our imperial age. We regard our relationship with you not as a special relationship, but as a close relationship, governed by the only things that matter, unity of purpose and unity in our objectives.[15]

There was self-evidently no unity of purpose over Vietnam, despite Wilson's efforts to defend US policy and resist anti-American gestures from the British left. The Prime Minister fought to prevent a major schism within his own administration, retaining Britain's special relationship with the US without causing further anger and disillusionment throughout the Labour Party. Wilson was relatively successful in achieving these aims. The underlying theme of a Labour Prime Minister resisting the pressures of a superpower leader in a misconceived war is rich in contemporary resonance.[16]

In fact, Vietnam was a unique moment in the Cold War. The psychological impetus that urged the preservation of the special relationship suddenly became far stronger on the American side. Senior officials in Lyndon Johnson's White House argued that a significant British presence in Vietnam 'would make a considerable psychological difference particularly in liberal circles where the main criticism of the war comes from'. Only a symbolic commitment was necessary: as Johnson told Wilson in 1966, 'a platoon of bagpipers would be sufficient – it was the British flag that was wanted'.[17]

Under Richard Nixon's tenure, the special relationship still struggled to recover its post-war momentum. Edward Heath was the post-war British Prime Minister who more than any other challenged the idea that the Anglo-American alliance had definite functional value. During the Macmillan era, the British Conservatives had transformed themselves from the party of empire to the party of Europe. The motives for this shift were in part political, enabling the Conservatives to present themselves as the party of modern Britain, looking to the future. But they were also motivated by economics, hoping for more rapid British growth as a result of joining the dynamic European market, as well as security, preserving British influence and defending western Europe from the threat of incursion by the Soviet Union.

Heath's premiership nevertheless came to highlight a persistent dilemma in British politics. His approach sought to break with the era when Britain's leaders were compelled to align themselves with American power and American interests. In 1970 on a visit to Washington, the British Prime Minister explicitly warned that he would not be prepared to act as the US's Trojan horse in Europe. Instead, Heath sought to make complete engagement in the process of European integration the feasible objective of national strategy. He wanted harmonious ties with the Nixon presidency, but not a special or privileged relationship. The Heath government thus developed a modernisation strategy focused on British membership of the EEC. Europe was framed as the solution to relative national decline involving a major reassessment of British policy and Britain's role in the world. It also meant a tacit recognition that the era of imperial and economic expansion was over, that British economic security could only be guaranteed by joining a regional bloc within the wider world economy. For Heath, the strength of Europe was preferable to the American special relationship. David Dimbleby and David Reynolds conclude that by 1973, the special relationship seemed to be a thing of the past.[18] The Conservatives opted overwhelmingly for Europe, negotiating British membership of the EEC with effect from 1 January 1973.

This characterisation of the Heath period nonetheless underplays the extent of the ongoing collaboration between the British and American military and intelligence establishments. The special relationship always functioned at several levels. The British had been forced to withdraw from east of Suez due to the weakening economy and the collapse of sterling. Britain's world role was now restricted to areas where the United States could provide protection, reinforcement or the promise of assistance if required. The UK was gradually displaced by the US as the major Western power in the Middle East, a region where it had formerly exerted the greatest influence.

In the 1974–9 period, relations between Wilson and James Callaghan in London and Gerald Ford and Jimmy Carter in the White House were naturally cordial. Both the US and Britain experienced a more cautious phase in their foreign policy. Politics, society and culture in America were still absorbing the shockwaves of defeat in Vietnam and the aftermath of the Watergate scandal. Meanwhile, Britain was gripped by domestic turbulence. The British economy was convulsed by external forces, notably the oil crisis and the rocketing trade deficit. This inflicted successive structural shocks on Britain's industrial base, leading to soaring inflation and mass unemployment. During this period there was a discernible shift as West Germany assumed the role of leading the western European axis of the Atlantic alliance, especially under Helmut Schmidt, who requested that the US locate cruise missiles in Europe.

The final decade of the Cold War altered the dynamic of the Anglo-American alliance still further. Under Ronald Reagan and Margaret Thatcher, this meant a strong repudiation of the British and American approach to transatlantic unity dominant in the first quarter-century after 1945. Instead of relying on old-fashioned state intervention and the corporatist power of national governments, the Cold War would be won by reviving the myth of Anglo-America. What held Britain and the US together were special qualities of entrepreneurship, innovation and economic dynamism. What Britain needed, according to Thatcher, was a viable model of political economy that would enable it to assume a global role after decades of retreat. Clear parallels were to emerge between the special relationship, the Anglo-American model of capitalism and the growing importance of globalisation.[19]

As James Cronin has elaborated, this neo-liberal paradigm was not invented all at once, but its key principles began to cohere in the late 1970s.[20] It had three central pillars:
- the resolve to enhance the military superiority of the United States through continuing reliance on nuclear weapons and technologically sophisticated conventional weapons, but a cautious stance on the exercise of military force;
- the commitment to neo-liberalism domestically and internationally, implying a shift away from Keynesian demand management policies towards open, liberal world markets predicated on the free movement of labour and capital;
- the increasing emphasis on human rights and democracy, with a growing insistence on the market as the precondition of democratic institutions.

The rekindling of the special relationship was initially the result of the close friendship between Thatcher and Reagan. Ideologically, Prime Minister Thatcher believed that priority should be given to America over Europe, because this was the best guarantee of preserving a liberal capitalist economy with commitments across the world, not merely in Europe.

Thatcher's warm relationship with Reagan was both unlikely and complex,[21] but it was driven by several factors. The first was Reagan's willingness to stand up to the Soviets at the height of the Cold War. Central to the Conservative New Right that Thatcher represented was the perception of renewed danger from the Soviet Union, arguing that what was required was not merely military rearmament, but ideological and political rearmament, restoring unity to the Western alliance.[22] Second, Thatcher recognised that a convivial relationship with the US President satisfied her own domestic political constituency. Finally, Reagan was genuinely interested in what Thatcher had to offer while Britain gained a privileged standing in influence over Washington, maintaining the UK as a nuclear power of the first rank.

The Thatcherites insisted that the most favourable approach for Britain, if it was to survive the encroachment of European integration, was to preserve its ideological and institutional alignment with Anglo-America. They insisted that the UK should resist becoming entangled with the protectionist and inward-looking economies of continental western Europe, where political debate was shaped by consensus and increasingly influenced by pacifism and growing antipathy to nuclear weapons.

The market liberal framework that underpinned the latest revitalisation of the Anglo-American alliance was the product of crisis and failure in economic policy and foreign affairs during the 1970s. Post-Vietnam, the US's ability to project global influence had diminished markedly. The Carter presidency was derailed by the Iranian hostage debacle, and the strategy of détente initiated by Henry Kissinger after Vietnam seemed to produce a sudden and perceptible loss of confidence in the West. The post-war economic boom was clearly over: the US industrial manufacturing sector, like the UK's, was forced to confront the reality of 'rust-belt' decline in the face of growing international competition.

That was the basis of the new special relationship. Reagan pursued an increasingly unilateralist, anti-Soviet, anti-communist approach to foreign policy. The value of Britain to the US perceptibly grew. The UK would become its leading ally, policing the new world order as the Cold War was ending. But it was clear that the British would be involved in global security only as the partner of the United States. At Sinai in 1981, British forces underwrote the US-negotiated Camp David agreement and in Lebanon in 1984 they were engaged as part of a five-power peace-keeping force.

Despite the revival of the special relationship, tensions inevitably continued during the Thatcher period, emphasising that the US's and Britain's strategic interests were rarely symmetrically aligned. In the late 1980s, the US supported the reunification of Germany despite Thatcher's deep reservations, underlining its determination to pursue its interests in Europe rather than subordinating them to British influences. The Russian pipe-line dispute in 1981 was another fracture in Anglo-American closeness.[23]

Military incidents also occurred during the 1980s in which there were serious disagreements between the British and US governments. The most notable was the Falklands conflict in the spring of 1982, in which the United States was faced with an acute dilemma over Argentina's decision to invade the British dependency. Should the US support the UK government, given the special relationship and its NATO obligations, or should it side with Argentina on the terms of the Monroe doctrine, which promised military co-operation between the two countries? Argentina had been crucial to the US's efforts to gain greater leverage in Central America.

The State Department initially recommended against supporting their British ally after the invasion of the islands. If that had been accepted the Anglo-American special relationship might never have recovered. The Reagan administration finally backed the UK, but its promise of 'material support' was by no means automatic or immediate. The Americans came to the conclusion that they could not afford to see a NATO ally defeated at the height of the Cold War, but it was the subject of heated argument in Washington.

The US decision to invade Grenada in 1983 also caused intense embarrassment to the British government. The UK's closest ally launched a massive military offensive against a member of the Commonwealth which had the Queen as its head of state. The shadow Foreign Secretary, Denis Healey, castigated Thatcher as the 'obedient poodle' of America for failing to stand up to President Reagan. When the US was determined on a particular course of which the British did not approve, Thatcher enjoyed no more success than her predecessors in changing American minds.

Controversially, the British also agreed in 1986 that the Americans should be able to use their UK bases to attack Libya. In 1973, Edward Heath had refused a request from Richard Nixon to use British bases during the Yom Kippur war. But the Thatcher administration was far more enthusiastic about preserving Britain's privileged relationship with Washington than co-operating more closely within the wider European political community.

Reagan's electoral success enabled Thatcher to project her government's national strategy as part of a new transatlantic hegemony of market liberal ideas. On departing office in November 1990 she declared that the great lesson of the twentieth century was that when Britain and the US stood together in the interests of prosperity and democracy, they were ultimately victorious. The intensive efforts of Reagan and Thatcher to add fresh impetus to the special relationship are less surprising in retrospect, as the Cold War was reaching its final phase.

Reagan and Thatcher were close ideological affiliates with a common project to restore the competitiveness of their economies, breathing new life into Britain and the US by breaking the economic cycle of despair and decline. After their first meeting in April 1975, Reagan, then the retired governor of California, declared: 'We really were akin with regard to our views of government and economics and government's place in people's lives and all that sort of thing.'[24]

This laid the foundations for the high point of the special relationship between the UK and the US during the first Gulf War in 1991. For commentators on both sides it was the finest hour for the Atlantic alliance. This is partly because Britain was increasingly perceived as a more equal partner. It is striking to compare British efforts in the Gulf during the early 1990s with the Korean War in the 1950s. In Korea, British forces had been astonishingly under-equipped. Historians have recorded that British forces amounted to only a handful of almost obsolete military vehicles. UK troops were entirely subordinate to American command. It is notable that on reading a State Department memo in 1950, Dean Acheson insisted on striking out a reference to Britain as a partner of the US.[25]

But in the first Gulf War forty years later, Britain was able to contribute fully to allied forces, filling gaps that other countries could not meet. The British had their own independent command, and they were able to significantly influence the US's strategic thinking. This included the commitment not to pursue regime change in Baghdad, but to limit the operation to the liberation of Kuwait. The twentieth century ended with continued British support for US actions in the Gulf. The two countries vigorously pursued a strategy of containment against Saddam Hussein, launching the Operation Desert Fox joint air strikes against Iraq in December 1998, and policing the 'no-fly zones' over northern Iraq.

The alternate aspect of this national strategy was that during the 1980s, Thatcher had significantly reversed the pro-European bias of British Conservatives. She argued explicitly that there was a choice to be made between Europe and America. One of the successes of the Conservative Party in the twentieth century was the ability to project itself as a national party, while at the same time accepting the UK's involvement in wider institutions and relationships designed to safeguard British interests.[26] Many in the Conservative leadership had become convinced by the late 1950s that Britain's future economic security was best achieved by joining the EEC. But for Thatcher, America, not Europe, had become the model that Britain should embrace. In economic policy, the Thatcher governments sought to emulate the American experiment with supply-side economics, adopting policies based on monetarism, shareholder value, privatisation, deregulation, flexible labour markets, reductions in taxation and public spending, and so on.

The transatlantic partnership was about developing a new model of capitalism, as well as maintaining a military and defence alliance in the final stages of the Cold War. Yet the issue of defence still played to the Conservatives' advantage, as the party put the Atlantic alliance at the heart of its appeal in the 1983 and 1987 general elections. This did great damage to the Labour Party, which was still committed to a non-nuclear defence policy, and was therefore viewed as unelectable by the majority of British voters. In confronting the challenge of framing British foreign policy in the mid-1960s, Harold Macmillan concluded:

> All our policies at home and abroad are in ruins. Our defence plans have been radically changed, from air to sea. European unity is no more; French domination of Europe is the new and alarming feature; our popularity as a government is rapidly declining. We have lost everything, except our courage and determination.[27]

Yet despite some underlying shifts and adjustments during the 1950s and 1960s, the parameters of British policy have remained fixed since Macmillan's premiership. Today, a new set of geo-political priorities urges a major reassessment of Britain's role in the world.

At the end of the Cold War and in the light of the Iraq debacle, Britain needs to update the strategic priorities that have served as a compass for its foreign policy since the Second World War. That means developing a more sophisticated resolution of the complex choice between Europe and America. The commentator Philip Stephens has eloquently spoken of the transatlantic relationship as merely a fragment on a far larger canvas as the centre of geo-strategic gravity shifts to the south and the east. It is ironic that the Blair era appears to have entrenched even further the traditional pillars of British post-war foreign policy, at precisely the moment when major structural adjustment is arguably most required.

Negotiating the special relationship has been an uncomfortable act for every British Prime Minister, including Thatcher and Blair. One of the enduring problems since 1945 has been the scope for mutual incomprehension on both sides. This is brilliantly captured in Ian McEwan's novel *The Innocent*, in which a CIA agent and an MI6 agent are collaborating to build a tunnel under East Berlin in the 1950s.[28] The British are exasperated by the self-confidence and ignorance of the Americans: 'What's worse, they won't learn, they won't be told. It's just how they are.' The Americans, for their part, find the British amateurish and proud of their amateurism: 'They're so busy being gentlemen.' The real source of irritation, however, is the hard slog of collaboration that 'leads to errors, security problems, you name it'. The British have invested the special relationship with great significance, seeing it as their historical right after fighting Hitler's Germany for longer than any other power. The Americans, however, have been more pragmatic in making calculations about the relationship in terms of strategic interests. That basic structural imbalance has been one of the defining features of the post-war era, and was still prevalent as the twentieth century drew to a close.

3

British global strategy in the Blair era
Managing the forces of globalisation

> We are the ally of the US not because they are powerful, but because we share their values ... There is no greater error in international politics than to believe that strong in Europe means weaker with the US ... We can help to be a bridge between the US and Europe.
>
> Tony Blair[1]

According to New Labour's narrative, the conception of Britain's role in the world as the bridge between Europe and America has enabled the UK to tackle the major strategic challenges of globalisation. In Labour's governing model, states had to either work with global economic forces or be overwhelmed by them. The apparent success of the Anglo-American model of global capitalism by the late 1990s was a vivid reminder to the British of their strong links with the United States, and the dangers of absorption into Europe.

In 1997, Tony Blair was elected Prime Minister with the largest majority in modern British history. Blair was a very traditional British Prime Minister in that he sought to act as the bridge between America and Europe. He pursued the most familiar foreign policy approach towards the US, seeking to be on the inside in Washington's power games. Furthermore, Blair's strategic judgement was that the US should never be left to fight alone.

Like all British leaders, Blair was quickly drawn into foreign affairs despite the obvious lack of previous knowledge and experience. His capacity for improvisation was suited to the twists and turns of international events: foreign policy has always been a combustible mixture of instincts and reactions. The new Prime Minister quickly cultivated relationships with leading foreign policy intellectuals including Robert Cooper, Timothy Garton-Ash and Lawrence Freedman, but combined them with the expertise of political advisers such as Jonathan Powell, as well as military strategists such as Charles Guthrie. This activity represented a sharp break with the traditionally pragmatic approach to foreign policy-making in Britain.[2]

The new Prime Minister quickly developed what was to become the 'doctrine of international community', first enunciated in his speech at the Chicago Press Club on 22 April 1999. He described the NATO bombing of the former Yugoslavia as 'a just war, based not on any territorial ambitions but on values',[3] even though it did not receive explicit authorisation from the United Nations Security Council. Blair also set out the five major considerations to determine whether or not to intervene:

> First, are we sure of our case? War is an imperfect instrument for righting humanitarian distress; but armed force is sometimes the only means of dealing with dictators.
>
> Second, have we exhausted all diplomatic options? We should always give peace a chance, as we have in the case of Kosovo.
>
> Third, on the basis of a practical assessment of the situation, are there military operations we can sensibly and prudently undertake?
>
> Fourth, are we prepared for the long term? In the past we talked too much of exit strategies. But having made a commitment we cannot simply walk away once the fight is over; better to stay with

moderate numbers of troops than return for a repeat performance with large numbers.

And finally, do we have national interests involved? The mass expulsion of ethnic Albanians from Kosovo demanded the notice of the rest of the world. But it does make a difference that it is taking place in such a combustible part of Europe.

The concept of community was at the core of Blair's political beliefs, but as the justification for military action it sat uneasily with the lack of agreement from a formally constituted public authority, 'a key requirement of the just war tradition'.[4] The closest parallel to Blair's belief in moral interventionism was William Gladstone's reaction to the Bulgarian horrors of the 1870s. He judged that the prevention of human suffering was a moral obligation incumbent on Britain as the superpower of the day, rather than continuing with a foreign policy based on narrow calculations of the national interest. In a speech at the Bush Presidential Library in April 2002 Blair argued:

> The only purpose of being in politics is to strive for the values and ideals we believe in: freedom, justice, what we Europeans call solidarity but you might call respect for and help for others. These are the decent democratic values we all avow. But alongside the values, we know we need a hard-headed pragmatism – a realpolitik – required to give us any chance of translating those values into the practical world we live in . . . I advocate an enlightened self-interest that puts fighting for our values right at the heart of the politics necessary to protect our nations. Engagement in the world on the basis of values, not isolation from it, is the hard-headed pragmatism for the twenty-first century.[5]

There are some parallels between Blair's doctrine and neo-conservatism in the US, but there are also significant distinctions. Blair was an instinctive multiculturalist who believed in a set of universal human values rather than the hegemony of American democracy and culture. He was also an avowed multilateralist who did not believe that the assertion of unilateral power was legitimate in any circumstances. Blair believed that multilateral approaches should be pushed to the outer limit before unilateral action was contemplated.

Alongside the evolving discourse of liberal interventionism in foreign policy, Blair arrived in 10 Downing Street as an instinctive pro-European. In one of his few foreign policy speeches as opposition leader, he argued that the two main partnerships for Britain were the European Union and the transatlantic relationship. He insisted that to be effective, the UK had to participate fully in each. In so doing, he consistently followed what is commonly referred to as a grand strategy for Britain's role in the world.

That national strategy is more than just the conventional wisdom of the age. It refers to a set of underlying assumptions about Britain's global strategy shared by policy-makers and the leaders of the major political parties. The strategy can change and has done so, but the shifts have little to do with the results of national elections. They reflect deeper currents of opinion and external shocks that profoundly alter existing understandings of a nation's position in the world system.

Such a debate about Britain's role in the world has been underway within the political class for several years, but not until the Iraq War and its aftermath did it become the subject of open controversy. Those who want Britain to become ever closer to America are ranged against those who would like to forge closer links with Europe. At the same time, there are some who are critical of US hegemony and would prefer to disengage from global affairs altogether.

The mandate that Blair sought in 1997 was intended to resolve the big strategic dilemmas confronting the British state while equipping the country for the new realities of the twenty-first century. Blair's confident assertion was that Britain would emerge as a pivotal power. This was the latest attempt by a British Prime Minister to coherently define the UK's role in the world after the demise of empire. It reflected an innate belief that Britain could act as a unifying force in the world, forging new global agreements on the basis of shared values and priorities. Blair also believed that in its economy, politics and culture Britain is a very globalised and globalising country.[6]

This vision enabled Blair's Labour Party to overcome major obstacles in its re-emergence as a serious contender for power in the British state. In the 1980s, Labour's policy on unilateral nuclear disarmament and the commitment to withdraw from NATO threatened to destroy it as a credible governing party. Like his modernising predecessors, including Hugh Gaitskell, Ernest Bevin and James Callaghan, Blair used America's disapproval of Labour's unilateralist policies after becoming leader in 1994 to persuade his own base of support that a change in the party's foreign and defence policy was necessary.

This challenge to anti-Americanism and the explicit support for the US was reinforced constantly by the leadership, desperate to distance New Labour from the extremist image of the early 1980s. The party's reputation of being too extreme and incompetent for office had caused it to lose four successive elections in 1979, 1983, 1987 and 1992. This was partially a reflection of its image as overtly hostile to America and prepared to give away Britain's defences.

The emergence of the Clinton Democrats after 1992, and the forging of a progressive strategy for economic and social modernisation in the aftermath of the Thatcher–Reagan hegemony, also provided the basis for a strong revival of Atlanticism under New Labour. This underscored the importance of the Atlantic alliance for Labour's politics since 1945.

That shift and the embrace of America by all parties expressed the desire of the British political class to move decisively beyond economic and imperial decline. For more than a century, the collapse of the British Empire and the eclipse of Britain as a major power in the world loomed constantly on the horizon. But from the 1980s there were important changes that appeared to make the shift beyond decline possible.

The first was the economic reforms inaugurated by the Thatcher governments and augmented by the constitutional reforms of the Blair era.[7] Both these phases of modernisation sought to restore the pre-eminence of Britain as a major force in European and world affairs, but did so on post-imperial terms. Blair described the challenges facing Britain as in essence four-fold:

- First, what was required for the UK to prosper in an era of growing international competition driven by the intensive globalisation of world markets and the decline of traditional industries?
- Second, how should the crisis of the union finally be resolved, defining a United Kingdom that is fully inclusive of Scotland, Wales and Northern Ireland, while determining the future of British national identity and managing the decline of traditional British institutions?
- Third, is it possible for Britain to play a leading role in the future development of the EU after decades of ambivalence?
- Fourth, how should Britain balance its ties with Europe in order to sustain the special relationship with America?

The Blair government was elected in exceptionally benign circumstances with a large parliamentary majority and a stable economy. Blair also had the advantage of close personal and ideological ties with President Bill Clinton, who saw mutual advantages in consolidating the Atlantic alliance but on new terms. This drew on a long heritage of mutual admiration between the British Labour Party and progressive forces in the United States. The 'Third Way' became a defining ideological choice that appeared to separate British Labour from other European social democratic parties.

Some commentators have chosen to emphasise that the early attitudes and policies of the Blair administration revealed a strong preference for American over European models. New Labour policies such as the working families' tax credit, the Financial Services Authority, the New Deal welfare-to-work programme, elected mayors in Britain's major cities, and the incorporation of choice and competition in public services were held to be Atlanticist in origin. Despite the influence of the US Democrats, this interpretation tends to regard the Blair premiership as the consolidation and continuation of Thatcherism by other means.[8]

Others have countered that while the Blair governments have adopted some of Margaret Thatcher's free market reforms, the agenda of equal citizenship within a modernised but universal welfare state coupled with the reform of the British constitution draws inspiration from Europe as much as America. In the early 1990s, as the Labour Party reframed its economic policy, it was able to draw on the success of European capitalist regimes, especially those of the Nordic countries.

It is important to put the Blair government's strategic choices on domestic policy in their broader context. By the mid-1990s, it was self-evident that the Franco-German engine of European integration had lost momentum. Similarly, the Rhineland model of social market capitalism was struggling to compete with its American and Asiatic counterparts. The British electorate had decisively rejected the Eurosceptic agenda of the Conservative Party in the 1997 election because of the perception that John Major had left the UK weak and isolated. Blair's premiership was intended to mark a new phase in Britain's relations with the EU.

The newly elected Prime Minister was quick to seize on what he saw as a favourable sequence of events. He understood immediately that it was possible to establish a new balance or partnership between Europe and America, with the UK as the pivot of the transatlantic community. Blair's insight was that Britain's isolation from Europe was weakening its global influence, but ironically it had also diminished its weight in the special relationship with the United States.

This pattern of British disengagement from Europe was encouraged by the uneasy relationship between Britain and France. Unlike most western European states, the UK and France aspired to sustain a leading role in global security, but each chose different means to do so.[9] After the Suez debacle, France under Charles de Gaulle had been determined to sustain its independent role and status as a great power. It sought to build Europe as an independent force in global affairs. In Britain, there were always some in the political class who favoured Europe over the United States. Yet the basic asymmetry between a unified American superpower and the EEC – still a loose confederation of nation-states whose members were often reluctant to project their power globally – meant that Britain inevitably prioritised America. Despite the post-imperial traumas of the 1950s and 1960s, the UK aspired to play a leading role in international security. The British viewed Europe as an economic project, arguing that foreign policy should be left to NATO. Meanwhile, the governing class decided that never again would they find themselves on the wrong side of the United States. As Philip Stephens has argued, 'almost every Prime Minister since [Suez] has followed the path mapped by Harold Macmillan after Suez. For all that Blair is often seen as a foreign policy radical, he has been true to the post-Suez conventional wisdom.'[10]

After his 1997 election victory Blair wanted to commit Britain to Europe, but several historical problems quickly re-emerged. In 1958 de Gaulle had sensed an opportunity for European co-operation to displace American dominance in western Europe. But this meant embracing a conception of Europe as a distinct political and security entity, and the French President's vision was apparently at odds with British values. Four decades later, the Blair administration immediately faced the problem of the euro as a test of its commitment to Europe. The European Security and Defence Initiative (ESDI) was also high on the agenda, but the British feared that it would antagonise the Americans by appearing to undermine NATO.

Nevertheless, there was still a major shift in British policy at the St Malo summit in the autumn of 1998. To reinforce Britain's intentions of playing an active role as an engaged European partner, the UK led the push for ESDI. The Blair Cabinet believed that the UK would play a leadership role in Europe, ensuring the development of an independent command capability, while encouraging the United States to accept such a shift as complementary to its own interests. Blair had also witnessed the all-too-apparent political and military weakness of Europe in the Balkans, reinforcing the case for increased foreign and defence co-operation.

The historical context underlines why such strategic adjustments were necessary. The decline of Britain's power and the relative isolation of the UK from the EEC had threatened to terminate London's privileged relationship with Washington in the 1960s. President George Bush Sr had clearly signalled his intention of strengthening the US's links with Germany, newly unified after the fall of the Berlin Wall. Blair acknowledged that only a firm commitment to share the military burden in pursuit of common interests would enable the UK to influence US strategic thinking, encouraging Britain to punch above its weight in international affairs.

Blair concluded that the UK should perform a leadership role in Europe, shedding its long-standing ambivalence towards the project of a cohesive EU and endorsing moves towards further integration and enlargement. More fundamentally, Blair argued, this would enrich the Anglo-American alliance rather than undermine it, as Eurosceptics in Britain feared. That has been the conventional wisdom in policy-making circles across the Atlantic for half a century, as Joseph Nye, professor of international relations at Harvard and a former Clinton administration official, suggests: 'The role of Britain in Europe remains a unique asset to the cause of European–American community. A Europe in which Britain continues to look both across the Channel and across the

Atlantic, which emphasises outward-looking aspects of the EU . . . helps to reinforce overall US–European relationships.'[11]

Yet Blair's bridge strategy was under immediate pressure even in the early phase of his premiership, an argument affirmed in Peter Riddell's account of New Labour's foreign policy.[12] The Prime Minister believed that Europe required a credible joint military capability, and was also keen to launch a fresh pro-European initiative after the UK's decision to rule out joining the euro in October 1997. Blair did not see why this should imperil his privileged relationship with Washington, since the Clinton administration, like its predecessors, was believed to favour European integration and stronger European defence capabilities.

But the St Malo declaration alarmed policy-makers in the Pentagon, who were surprised by its strident tone. They feared that the St Malo text was more French than Atlanticist with its repeated references to 'autonomous action'. The then British ambassador in Washington, Sir Christopher Meyer, reported that Sandy Berger, the US National Security Advisor, and Strobe Talbott, the deputy Secretary of State, were 'very upset indeed', fearing that St Malo would undermine NATO's decision-making structure.

The governing model of the 'Blair Bridge' was undermined further when, having underlined its European aspirations at St Malo, the UK joined the Americans in launching air strikes against Iraq in December 1998. This followed repeated refusals by Saddam Hussein to comply with UN weapons inspections, and growing fears in London and Washington that the Iraqis posed a clear and immediate threat to their neighbours in the Gulf region. But the diplomatic costs for Britain were considerable as the UK stood alone with the US. Operation Desert Fox marked a return to the familiar British way of merely following Washington's lead.

Nonetheless, the Blair government had restored the transatlantic bridge as a central premise of British foreign policy and global strategy. Blair insisted that there was no contradiction between these approaches. The notion of the bridge offered a coherent response to the strategic challenges facing the UK at the end of the twentieth century. Blair's bridging strategy reached its climax after the terrorist attacks of September 11 2001, as he sought to demonstrate that close relations with Europe were fully compatible with the Anglo-American special relationship.

George W. Bush and Blair were two of the unlikeliest partners, with little apparently in common ideologically. President Bush was a committed right-wing Republican and former governor of Texas. Prior to his presidency, he had emphasised his determination to assert the primacy of US national interests, but he demonstrated little interest in foreign affairs, appearing to embrace his father's cautious, moderate conservatism. The Prime Minister in contrast was a liberal internationalist, a close ally of President Clinton who believed in the importance of multilateral agreements as a pretext for international action, but also in assertive foreign policy informed by clear moral values.

The irony is that Bush and Blair both negotiated the special relationship through one of its most intense phases, particularly after September 11. The Labour government had been involved in several military conflicts since 1997, notably in Kosovo, Sierra Leone and Afghanistan. These actions were undertaken with the explicit support of the international community. In contrast, the war in Iraq was a unilateral exercise that lacked the explicit authorisation of the UN Security Council.

From Blair's perspective, the principal reason for seeking to revive the special relationship as a means of bridging Europe and America was to pre-empt a new strain of post-Cold War bipolarity. The danger as he saw it was that the US and UK would be set against Europe if they could not agree on terms of military intervention in countering international terrorism and rogue states, especially in the period after the 9/11 attacks. But Blair's approach had deeper historical roots and has to be understood as a product of British global strategy since the Second World War.

Blair's endorsement of the special relationship reflected his strong belief that US unilateralism posed grave dangers to the British national interest, and that the UK's influence would help to keep the United States on a multilateral course. This was particularly important if the hawks in Washington saw Iraq as only the first target in their war against the 'axis of evil', as Bush famously described it in his 2002 State of the Union address. Blair strongly believed that while there were many rogue states including Iran and North Korea, they should be confronted by the international community, not pursued unilaterally by an ad hoc 'coalition of the willing'.

The motives, world-view and historical forces shaping Blair's Iraq policy will be subject to more rigorous analysis later in this study. What is self-evident is that the strengthening of the special relationship during Bush's presidency has revived major strategic dilemmas for the British political class. The emphasis in Britain's global strategy after 1945 was on maintaining the familiar balancing act of Europe and America, a long-stated aim of all post-war governments. Shuttling between Washington and Brussels would preserve Britain's status as a pivotal power.

But as the previous chapter suggests, fundamental problems soon emerged. Andrew Gamble describes it succinctly:

> Many of the tensions in British politics, and the travails of the political parties, are because Britain has been drawing ever closer to Europe, but this has been resisted by a significant part of the political class which prefers America, and also by a large part of the electorate, which is hostile to both Europe and America and would prefer to remain detached from both.[13]

The Iraq crisis threatened to destroy the bridge between America and Europe, undermining the long-standing resolution of the UK's post-war dilemma that Blair too had endorsed. The Blair era in fact further entrenched the traditional pillars of Britain's global strategy, especially the desire to maintain a privileged relationship with Washington.

This is a curious paradox, since Blair came to power as an avowed moderniser who wanted to embrace the interdependence of the modern world and believed in upholding a values-based foreign policy infused with liberal mores. In reality he was a very traditional British leader, strongly Atlanticist, often cautious about European integration, yet ready to assert military power as a willing accomplice in the war on terror. Instead of transforming British foreign policy, the verdict of history may be that Prime Minister Blair became the unwitting victim of its contradictions, more a foreign policy traditionalist than a foreign policy reformer.

4

Is Britain back?
Beyond decline

> It is absurd to imagine that, for Britain, there is a choice between the relationship with Europe and that with America. On the contrary, the real value to the US of the British role in Europe lies in the influence we can and will exert to keep Europe firmly linked to the US in defence, outward-looking, open to trade and investment, and open also to the inclusion of the new democracies in central and eastern Europe.
>
> Tony Blair[1]

This chapter explains why the special Atlantic relationship as the bedrock of Britain's post-war global strategy was carefully refined and consolidated during the Blair era. This particular conception of the UK's strategic interests was not merely about British foreign policy. It was intended to revive Britain as an influential industrial and military power, enabling it to carve out a coherent role in world affairs.

There are numerous critics of the transatlantic alliance on both the left and the right of British politics. Later chapters will attempt to explain the nature of such criticism and underlying hostility. What these accounts implicitly assume, however, is that there was an alternative strategy that would have been more successful in fulfilling Britain's strategic interests. Some critics cite fuller engagement in Europe as the solution to Britain's dilemmas, where others would have preferred the UK to stand apart, sustaining alliances all over the world in the manner of Churchill's three intersecting circles of influence.

Yet it was far from clear that any coherent alternative to British Atlanticism existed, such that after Suez the UK could have pursued Charles de Gaulle's strategy of refusing to subordinate foreign policy to the United States. Another line of argument emphasises that the British economy and British security were strengthened during the post-war years by the decision to align the UK closely with the United States.

Taking a longer historical perspective, Britain ended the twentieth century as the fifth largest economy in the world. Britain's growth and productivity performance was finally outpacing those of most European economies. The Thatcher government had vigorously restructured capital and labour markets, strengthening Britain's ability to compete with the rest of the world while ensuring that the UK could become a leading beneficiary of globalisation.

This combination of institutional reforms and structural changes fundamentally altered the underlying trajectory of the British economy, enabling successive governments to maintain fiscal stability and steady growth, in stark contrast to the 1960s and 1970s. By 2000, the UK had the highest rate of employment in history, and the lowest inflation and interest rates for forty years. The Blair government's economic policy also achieved a substantial and sustained increase in spending on public services from 36 to 42 per cent of GDP, as well as modest redistribution that helped to boost the real incomes of the poorest. Britain's political settlement was also modernised with major reforms that breached the old constitutional state, paving the way for a period of sustained experiment and innovation in how the country is governed.

These constitutional changes sought to deal with the precarious nature of Britishness and the British nation, concerns that emerged in the latter half of the twentieth century. Of particular significance were legislation establishing a separate Scottish Parliament and a Welsh Assembly, and the first stage of House of Lords reform with the removal of all but ninety-two hereditary peers from the second chamber.

In the immediate post-war years, the UK also successfully restructured its military capability. As earlier chapters note, it is instructive to compare Britain's engagement in Korea in the early 1950s with the Falklands conflict in 1982 and the first Gulf War in 1990–1.[2] The exceptional performance of British forces in the Falklands illustrates the superiority of a regular, professional, well-led army. In the Gulf, the British were able to carve out an independent command and influence the tactics of their US partners.

This serves as a powerful antidote to the claims of the declinist school in contemporary British historical studies. By aligning themselves with the US and sustaining an alliance markedly less equal than it appeared at the end of the Second World War, successive British governments arguably laid the foundations for an astonishing period of strategic success.

The economic and constitutional changes introduced in the last twenty years have inevitably reinforced the preference in Britain's national strategy for the Anglo-American special relationship. That relationship has served as the central pillar not only for British foreign policy, but also for Britain's choice of economic and social models and its wider cultural and institutional relationships, notwithstanding the growing influence of European integration. Those choices were carefully consolidated and strengthened during the Blair years.

Such developments suggest that Britain has moved beyond decline, signalling a new era in which the contraction of British power is no longer the dominant preoccupation of the governing class and the political parties. Instead, the strategic tension lies in how to maintain the new balance between Britain's relationship with Europe and its ties with America, extending and deepening British influence. The UK under Tony Blair became increasingly confident of its ability to act as a pivot of the international system and to project global influence. Yet this era of revival has itself created new dilemmas: the fundamental question is whether what proved successful in the past is now the most credible strategy for the future. It could also be argued that those very achievements have diverted the British political class from engagement with the new realities of the post-Cold War landscape. The success that Britain attributed to its strategic alliance with the US has delayed it from coming to terms with new strategic realities in a globally interdependent world.

The fundamental drivers of globalisation together with changes in geo-politics have transformed the strategic context. This has coincided with significant underlying shifts in public opinion. It is unlikely that merely sustaining the special relationship on traditional terms with the US will be adequate. British foreign policy could of necessity become more European in the future, but there are significant structural obstacles, as later chapters will explore.[3]

Arguably, Britain's privileged relationship with Washington inhibited it from pursuing the strategic adjustments that became necessary in the early 1990s. The starker truth is that Britain's political and foreign policy establishment has often appeared to be trapped in the frozen Cold War landscape.

Today's world is evidently very different from the divisions between East and West that carved up Europe during the post-war era. Since 1989, the geo-political landscape has been torn up and remade by successive structural shocks: not only the end of the Cold War, but the rise of new powers in Asia and Latin America, and the wave of terrorist attacks against American and western European targets before and since September 11. The peculiar certainties of old have given way to a new set of contingencies and risks in global politics, 'a world of more shadowy and distant threats'.[4] The points in the landscape where the UK remains vulnerable are inherently more difficult to identify and predict. This should cast doubt on the traditional pattern of alliances that were engineered to protect Britain's security.

Another less considered shock concerns the resistance to market liberal approaches to globalisation that have framed the Anglo-American model since the early 1980s. Although not a monolithic doctrine, all narratives of globalisation have sought to stress its necessity and inevitability. Yet alternative models of capitalism, particularly those in the Nordic countries and Asia, have highlighted fundamental weaknesses in the globally orientated Anglo-American economies. The UK's economic model and its security choices are under scrutiny as never before.

The US will inevitably remain important for Britain in both strategic and military terms. Co-operation over intelligence is crucial in countering international terrorism, and collaboration on homeland security remains vital for both countries. The reality is that Britain's strategy has been to make its forces interoperable with the US and NATO. This will not be unbundled overnight, nor would it necessarily be desirable to do so.

Nonetheless, British policy-makers should reflect that the strategic advantages conferred by Britain's post-war foreign and security policy – solidly predicated on the Anglo-American relationship – delayed it from coming to terms with the end of the Cold War. It is very unlikely that the collective security of NATO and the conventional US nuclear shield will provide sufficient leverage and protection against the new threats. There is also the divergence of strategic interests across the Atlantic. The US adopts the mind-set of a hegemonic power in which multilateral institutions are seen as inherently prohibitive and constraining. For Britain on the other hand, nation-states exercise little sovereignty on their own in the new world order, so the onus is on establishing new forms of trans-national co-operation.

The British governing class self-evidently has difficulty in fully acknowledging the extent of this transformation in the geo-political order. Historically, the governing 'elite' was deeply reluctant to adjust to its reduced status in the world. The self-image of 'Empire' and 'Great Britain' has continued to shape so many British ideas and attitudes over the last 200 years.[5] That myth of empire still provides the framework within which many contemporary issues are debated and discussed, from immigration and multiculturalism to Britain's relationship with Europe, resonating as it does in popular culture and still dominating the thinking of many British politicians.

The balancing of the UK's ties in Europe with the special Atlantic relationship marks a continuation of national strategy since Suez. This has been largely successful in sustaining Britain as an influential industrial and military power punching above its weight in the world, especially during the Blair era. Britain's world role has been transformed since the end of the Second World War. The British state and the British economy have avoided further relative decline, but the familiar landmarks are once again being uprooted. The UK is merely one of several leading European powers.

That success has also delayed British adjustment to changing geo-strategic realities: first by postponing serious engagement in Europe, and second by failing to come to terms with the far-reaching implications of the Cold War's end. In different ways, that approach still reflects the legacy of empire and strong conceptions of English and British exceptionalism that perished in the course of the nineteenth and twentieth centuries, but whose influence lives on.

Iraq has brought home many of the tensions and dilemmas posed by these long-term historical trajectories. The transatlantic bridge was temporarily destroyed as the Iraq crisis unfolded. Iraq severed the UK from France and Germany, fatally weakening its European alliances. This was a turning point since it contradicted the key premise of global strategy, that Britain could act as a bridge across the Atlantic. It thwarted Tony Blair's aspiration to recast Britain as a pivotal power, leaving the UK to fulfil its traditional role as America's faithful ally. It also gravely damaged the Anglo-French alliance cultivated by Blair in the late 1990s, while it brought under public scrutiny the wisdom of the special relationship with the US. It seems unlikely that the traditional Atlanticist principles that have for so long informed Britain's national strategy will survive the catastrophic impact of Iraq, but we should be wary of overstating the impact of the Iraq War alone.

Such crises epitomise the ambiguities and contradictions in Britain's position. In the early 1960s the abandonment of Skybolt and General de Gaulle's veto on UK membership of the EEC led to a feeling that Britain had been isolated from both Europe and America; it found itself in a similar position after the St Malo declaration and Operation Desert Fox in 1998 (see Chapter 3), which should have served as a warning that major rethinking was required. But the Blair administration tragically avoided undertaking the necessary strategic adjustments. Its discomfort was compounded by the failure to anticipate the rise of unilateralism in American foreign policy. The transatlantic bridge fell apart not only because of Iraq. It was also a reflection of Britain's agonising search for a post-imperial role, a preoccupation that seemed anachronistic by the early twenty-first century.

5

Tumultuous Britain
The Iraq crisis unfolds

> Iraq probably has no weapons of mass destruction in the commonly understood sense of the term – namely a credible device capable of being delivered against a strategic city target. Why is it now so urgent that we should take military action to disarm a military capacity that has been there for twenty years, and which we helped to create?
>
> Robin Cook[1]

This chapter will explore the significance of Tony Blair's Iraq policy for the future of British foreign relations and its impact on long-term thinking about UK national strategy. Blair's decision to join the United States and provide political cover for the invasion of Iraq was an apparently rational act, despite strong opposition among the British electorate. The Prime Minister believed that Iraq was concealing weapons of mass destruction, repeatedly reminding the British public of intelligence reports that Saddam Hussein had been within a few months of developing his own nuclear capability.

Since early 2001, Blair had also developed a strong relationship with President George W. Bush. He found the new President easier to work with than Bill Clinton, with whom he clashed repeatedly over Northern Ireland and Kosovo. As President, Bush was straightforward to deal with and tended to do what he promised. The invasion of Iraq also fitted Blair's vision of Britain's world role, while, he believed, encouraging the broader remaking of the Middle East and the establishment of a Palestinian state.

Yet after several hundred thousand lives were lost and no WMD discovered, the invasion of Iraq is now widely viewed as a calamitous decision that destroyed much of Blair's popularity at home and abroad, while tarnishing his reputation for governing competence. The Iraq crisis stretched British foreign policy to breaking point, undermining the global strategy pursued by every British government since 1945, especially New Labour after 1997. It sent shockwaves through the British governing class as Suez had done nearly fifty years previously. The broader significance of Iraq is that it has awakened the trauma of Britain's global role after empire, while highlighting the unresolved choice between Europe and America as one of the central fault-lines in British politics.[2]

The immediate phase of intervention in Iraq ended in the summer of 2003, but the task of reconstruction has continued sporadically amid the wave of violence and instability that has engulfed the country. The long-term implications for Britain, Europe and the United States are still being worked through. But historians will ponder for many years why Blair decided to take such an incalculable risk in supporting what was subsequently derided as the illegal invasion of Iraq.

In fact, the UK's agreement to join the coalition of the willing was far from inevitable. Nor was it the result of intense pressure from Washington. Britain could have avoided military involvement, or instead provided a token military force. In reality, Blair made a conscious decision to give unqualified support to the US campaign.

As Prime Minister, Blair had taken a hawkish approach to Iraq since he came to office in 1997. He had strongly supported all previous military action, including Operation Desert Fox in 1998, as well as the intensive enforcement of no-fly zones in northern Iraq. When the Iraqi government blocked the work of United Nations weapons inspectors in the autumn of 1998, Blair stressed the risks of allowing Saddam to possess WMD and urged the use of air strikes to enforce the UN's will. It was the British who forced the pace of intervention against Iraq rather than Clinton's White House.

It was no surprise that British forces had participated previously in action against Saddam's regime. Blair took a clear moral stand in defending human rights and confronting dictatorships, displaying great determination to defeat Slobodan Milošević during the Kosovo conflict. He also took a firm lead in advocating the use of ground forces to secure victory in the Balkans, despite the opposition of the Clinton administration, after air strikes had failed to break Milošević's resolve.

As other commentators have observed, Blair was to some extent ahead of Bush in accepting the view that intervention by Western democracies in the affairs of sovereign states is sometimes necessary to cope with rogue regimes and terrorists.[3] Blair, like the early twentieth-century US President Theodore Roosevelt, believed that action should be guided by a larger moral purpose in defence of cherished values. Blair's case for humanitarian interventionism was developed well before George W. Bush entered the White House. It is not plausible to suggest that the Prime Minister had simply been captured by neo-conservative ideology.

The British Prime Minister had drawn essentially the same conclusions about the September 11 attacks as Bush and the majority of the American people in insisting that there was a definitive link between terrorism, rogue states and WMD. This was defined as the major post-September 11 strategic issue, and it was believed to demand decisive action by the Western allies who had confronted Saddam over Kuwait in 1991. In November 2002, Blair argued in a key foreign policy speech: 'Terrorism and WMD are linked dangers. States which are failed, which repress their people brutally, in which notions of democracy and the rule of law are alien, share the same absence of rational boundaries to their actions as the terrorist. Iraq has used WMD.'[4]

Within weeks of the 1997 election the Prime Minister reportedly told Lord Ashdown of Norton-sub-Hamdon, the former leader of the Liberal Democrats, that Saddam possessed a deadly arsenal of chemical and bacteriological weapons.[5] The British political commentator Hugo Young revealed Blair's insistence that if the Americans had held back from intervention in Iraq, he would have pushed Bush even further in that direction.[6]

The British government was largely unperturbed by the rhetoric emanating from Washington about the growing threat of military action over the course of 2002. Blair understood, however, that British public opinion and the majority of the Labour Party were opposed to Britain's involvement with the war in Iraq. The Prime Minister was confronted with two particularly hostile audiences. Labour parliamentarians were worried about the general drift of the Bush administration's policies, especially the 'axis of evil' rhetoric and the threat to remove Saddam by force. There had been other disagreements with the US over farm subsidies as well as serious trade disputes that damaged relations still further. The second hostile audience was the British foreign policy establishment, many of whom were sceptical about the evidence of WMD and did not see why the containment policy that had been in place since 1991 should be abandoned.

The Prime Minister believed that the only means of securing support for military action would be the full UN authorisation of force. Sir David Manning, Blair's foreign policy adviser, was dispatched to Washington to reinforce this message to the Bush White House in July 2002. But Blair's unqualified commitment meant that Britain's participation in the war was not conditional on securing a new UN Security Council resolution authorising military intervention. The effort to produce a second UN resolution did lead 10 Downing Street to make serious errors, however, most notably the publication of intelligence dossiers that allegedly distorted the evidence about WMD in Iraq.

The twists and turns of the build-up to the Iraq War have been fully covered elsewhere,[7] but it is worth reflecting on the implications for British foreign policy. The journalist John

Kampfner has argued that the five major wars in which Britain was involved during Blair's premiership would not have been fought had he not been Prime Minister.[8] This observation does not explain the complex motivations that shaped Blair's actions. The more nuanced historical perspective of commentators such as Peter Riddell suggests that Blair's approach fits within a long-established pattern of British support for America in a security crisis, coupled with the desire to be on the inside in Washington.[9]

Another factor that greatly influenced Blair's thinking was his success in previous conflicts after 1997, which inevitably emboldened him over Iraq. The military interventions in Kosovo and Sierra Leone were an enormous risk that could have mired British and American forces in an indefinite quagmire. But neither was to fall prey to mission-creep, and in both cases an adequate exit strategy was achieved.

Inevitably, academic commentary about Blair's actions over Iraq has focused on the debate among international relations experts about why states enter military conflicts on behalf of allies, even in a unipolar world where that ally is the hegemonic power. In one sense, Britain and the US had symmetrical interests: Iraq posed a risk to national security and was a threat to its neighbours and the stability of the wider Middle East. The claim in the government's now infamous 'September dossier' that Iraq could deploy chemical, biological and nuclear weapons within forty-five minutes was believed to justify the use of pre-emptive force. In that sense the perspectives and priorities of Britain and the US in ensuring stability and security in a troubled region were very similar. It was not the special Atlantic relationship that justified Blair's support for the American position on Iraq, but the familiar doctrines of balance-of-power politics and realist diplomacy.

According to the realist doctrine in foreign affairs, states seek continuously to consolidate and enlarge their influence in relation to other countries. The UK, North America and continental Europe are no longer bound together by a collective Cold War threat. Nonetheless, Britain and the US in particular do have an enormous shared interest in sustaining the expectations and commitment inherent in the concept of the strategic alliance. Those countries believe that they will enhance their interests by co-operating closely and working together. In realist terms, Blair was asked to affirm that commitment over Iraq, and he duly obliged.

This interpretation alone is not sufficient to explain why the Blair government chose to act as it did over Iraq, however. It does not consider, for example, why there was such an apparent difference of motive between London and Washington over the Iraq invasion, and how Blair's actions were shaped by his broader philosophical convictions. This was to some extent a matter of presentation: Blair wanted to frame Iraq as part of a global morality tale, as integral to the Third Way philosophy that has shaped New Labour's approach to governing since 1997. The invasion of Iraq was a 'just' war. On the one hand, Blair insisted that the UK would not shrink from involvement in the military battle against terrorism and WMD. On the other, he insisted that this agenda had to be broadened to include the Middle East peace process, action on global poverty, Africa and climate change.

There were also substantive differences in Bush's and Blair's respective philosophical and strategic approaches to Iraq. For Blair, the Iraq War was entirely consistent with the ethical foreign policy doctrine that he expounded in his Chicago speech in 1999. For the Bush administration, the narratives were very different indeed.

The attribution of motives for Iraq on the US side is particularly complex, especially for Europeans, who mistakenly tend to view US administrations as coherent and unified around a single line of authority to the President. It is self-evident that there was no coherent policy stance towards Saddam's Iraq in the period immediately preceding the war itself. There had been little credible foreign policy thinking to inform the incoming administration following Bush's election victory late in 2000. Bush began his term of office in a very uncertain position following the long court battle to capture Florida's electoral college vote. There were also deep divisions over foreign policy in the Bush transition team. There seem to have been several rival intellectual camps vying for supremacy in the early days of the administration, from Paul Wolfowitz's neo-conservative group to Colin Powell's State Department asserting the role of realism in US foreign policy.

Later chapters suggest that the Blair team in London had not done enough preparatory work in understanding the thinking of the key players behind the incoming Bush administration. They assumed too readily that George W. Bush would be motivated by the same cautious internationalism that had guided his father, and there was a strong tendency to underrate his conservatism. New Labour had close links with the defeated Democratic Party candidate, Al Gore, and refused to take Bush's chances seriously until the later summer of 2000.

One of Blair's senior advisers reported in July 2000 that Gore was almost certain to win, though the British embassy in Washington fought to offset the pro-Democrat bias that they accurately perceived in 10 Downing Street. But British diplomats had also failed to appreciate that there would be no revival of the Bush–Baker approach to foreign policy that had characterised the 1989–93 era. George W. Bush's team were consciously reacting against the elder Bush's approach as well as the Clinton presidency, believing in an assertive foreign policy that projected America's national interests, if necessary by unilateral force.

It is important to divert momentarily, however, and to consider the motives that lay behind Washington's policy of regime change in Iraq, before assessing the forces that shaped Blair's approach to the Iraq crisis. David Frum, Bush's speech-writer in his first presidential term, has set the context by speculating that Bush was initially content to allow the State Department and the Pentagon to pursue rival agendas after September 11, and again in the months preceding the invasion of Iraq.[10]

There were several distinct and diverging outlooks that apparently framed Bush's Iraq strategy. The first was the claim of the neo-conservatives that the Iraqi people were desperate to be liberated from the tyranny of Saddam. Richard Perle remarked at a private conference in the spring of 2003 that the US anticipated only low-level resistance in any invasion of Iraq, since the population was desperate to see the removal of Saddam's regime.[11] The United States should use its power to spread freedom and democracy across the world. The overall objective was to expand the circle of development in the Middle East through democratisation, free markets and free trade.

Powell and the State Department did not share Perle's outlook and were extremely cautious about the prospects for military intervention in Iraq. They favoured a strongly internationalist approach and were hostile to instinctive unilateralism, insisting that broader international support for regime change was an absolute prerequisite to military force. Powell was the main voice of caution in the Bush administration, though he swung behind tough and immediate action against Saddam as French intransigence infuriated him.

Such conflicting views had decisive strategic implications. Powell's view was that the United States should call off the war against international terrorism after Afghanistan, entrusting the struggle to international policing and intelligence operations. That would minimise the risk of disrupting the balance of power in the Middle East, satisfying many of the United States' European allies and calming nerves among the Arab nations. But the weakness of Powell's approach according to other Washington policy-makers close to the White House was that it would leave the war on terror unfinished, as the first Gulf War had in 1991.

Donald Rumsfeld and the Pentagon seized the opportunity to advocate a very different strategy, insisting that the US should continue the war on terror until terrorism was entirely uprooted from the Middle East and the Islamic world. If Saddam was overthrown it would create a reliable American ally among the leading Arab states. There was even a possibility that in turn the Iranian people would be encouraged to overthrow their viscerally anti-American dictatorship. The pressure for democratisation in Saudi Arabia and across the Arab world would intensify as Iran and Iraq built moderate and representative regimes.

To understand the significance of the Pentagon's approach, the Bush administration's policies need to be located within a wider historical frame of reference. As the American historian Arthur M. Schlesinger has noted, isolationism was for many decades the key pillar of the American foreign policy tradition.[12] It dominated the thinking of almost all US Presidents until the First World War, and was revived again after 1919. It was during Franklin Roosevelt's presidency, following American involvement in the defeat of Nazi Germany, that an internationalist perspective re-emerged, consolidated in response to the Cold War and the need for collective defence in western Europe.

As President, Roosevelt had been determined to root the US in international institutions such as the UN and NATO, containing the imminent threat posed by the Soviet Union. The US could not pull back unconditionally as the Cold War subsided at the end of the 1980s. But it could insist on doing things unilaterally. This was a new form of isolationism, according to Schlesinger. As such he is highly critical of the shift from containment and deterrence advocated by Roosevelt and Harry Truman to the policy of preventative and pre-emptive war adopted by Bush.

The shadow of Vietnam also did much to underscore American reluctance to become embroiled in foreign wars. The risk of American casualties made US administrations highly cautious in confronting the reality of war and counter-terrorism operations.[13] Blair and Bill Clinton had clashed over the President's reluctance even to consider contingency planning for ground troops in the Balkans. Military force was only considered to be a legitimate option if it involved minuscule American casualties such as the first

Gulf War. Ideally it would require only air power, as Clinton had hoped in Kosovo.

But the Clinton administration was also believed by some on the Republican right to have compounded the image of the United States as too cowardly and constrained to deal ruthlessly with its enemies. Middle East terrorists had struck at US targets in Saudi Arabia, east Africa and Yemen throughout the 1990s during Clinton's presidency. The right argued that the administration had completely failed to retaliate effectively. When missiles were launched against Afghanistan and Sudan in 1998, the attacks were ineffectual. Clinton's policies towards Iraq were criticised for apparently signalling weakness and appeasement.

The Bush administration's decision to adopt the objective of transformation was a bold and risky shift, but for neo-conservatives its significance was enormous. The division between Rumsfeld's Pentagon and Powell's State Department was often described as a split between hawks and doves, a rerun of the bureaucratic struggles of the Cold War. It created an impression of confusion, since Bush's strategy was often to float above these inter-agency conflicts until a final decision had to be taken.

There was, of course, a third strand of thinking at work in the Bush administration: those who viewed Iraq and national security as the means through which an enduring hegemony could be established for the Republican Party in domestic politics. This approach was strongly endorsed by the Vice-President, Dick Cheney, and Bush's chief political strategist, Karl Rove.

In 2002, the *New York Times* authoritatively reported that 'Karl Rove, President Bush's top political adviser, is expanding his White House portfolio by inserting himself into foreign policy matters'. The influential commentator Thomas L. Friedman observed that whenever the Bush administration found itself in trouble, it played the national security card against the Democrats.[14] This worked so effectively in 2004 that in a speech to the Republican National Committee, Rove argued that dividing lines on security should be their campaign theme in all future elections.

Rove's argument was that the United States today faces 'a ruthless enemy'. It needs

> a commander in chief and a Congress who understand the nature of the threat and the gravity of the moment America finds itself in. President Bush and the Republican Party do. Unfortunately, the same cannot be said for many Democrats . . . Republicans have a post-9/11 world-view, and many Democrats have a pre-9/11 world-view. That doesn't make them unpatriotic – not at all. But it does make them wrong – deeply and profoundly and consistently wrong.[15]

Bush himself apparently believed that the September 11 attacks and the prominence of the war on terror would suspend partisan politics in Washington. Subsequent accounts of the build-up to the Iraq War have overwhelmingly focused on the pursuit of grand strategies such as the democratisation of the Middle East and the development of the administration's regime change policy. In reality, however, the Republicans were often divided. Bush lacked a coherent foreign policy doctrine to which he could turn as the crisis unfolded.

Bush's policy on Iraq was seized by Republican hawks who had now assumed influential positions within the foreign policy and military establishment in Washington. The presence of Perle, Wolfowitz, Cheney and Rumsfeld in their respective Pentagon command posts proved to be decisive. They had sought the complete implementation of the regime change policy in Baghdad absent in the first Gulf War, believing that the intellectual rationale would be provided through the doctrine of pre-emptive defence. The group criticised the narrow realism of Bush senior's team, who had been too concerned with stability instead of spreading democracy, and the wishful liberalism of the Clinton era.

In 1998 an open letter was dispatched to Clinton – signed by the quartet mentioned above plus Condoleezza Rice, who was then professor of international relations at Yale – advocating an explicit policy of regime change. They regarded Saddam Hussein as an obstacle to the wider democratisation of the Middle East, including peace and stability in Israel. Without a new Iraqi regime, an end to global terrorism was inconceivable.

This element of the Washington foreign policy establishment believed that modernisation in the Middle East – the introduction of multi-party elections and the embrace of the global economy – should be the primary goal of American foreign policy. David Frum suggests that figures such as Richard Perle and Donald Rumsfeld had been transfixed by the example of Kemal Atatürk, the great early twentieth-century Turkish moderniser who abolished theocracy and introduced Western law. This ensured that Turkey would evolve as the US's most reliable ally in the Islamic world. For half a century, the State Department had been searching for a successor to Atatürk in the Middle East.[16]

The Perle/Wolfowitz/Cheney/Rumsfeld thesis had a decisive influence on the 'axis of evil' doctrine enunciated by Bush in his 2002 State of the Union address. This argued for a shift in the focus of the war on terror from Afghanistan to Iraq. The speech was controversial because observers at the time perceived a deep paradox. If such an axis of evil really existed, Iraq was probably the least developed at manufacturing WMD. North Korea was the most advanced and potentially hostile rogue state. Iran was far more likely to be in a position to manufacture and deploy nuclear weapons. But US foreign policy became almost exclusively focused on removing Saddam's regime from Iraq.

The Bush administration was certainly determined to emit a loud and clear signal that America would not tolerate state-based terrorism. It sought to hit back against its enemies after September 11, and that was a powerful motive for Bush's policy. Opinion polls in the US showed that the majority of Americans believed that Iraq had been complicit in the 9/11 atrocities. Czech intelligence has uncovered a meeting between Mohammed Atta, one of the leading September 11 hijackers, and an Iraqi intelligence officer in Prague during April 2001. This was used to indicate some complicity between Al Qaeda and the Iraqi dictatorship. Saddam was believed to be an extreme secularist, but according to US intelligence sources the Iraqi dictator offered rewards of $25,000 to the families of extremist suicide bombers and members of Hamas.[17]

All of these factors underlined the determination of senior US officials to pursue regime change in Iraq by the spring of 2002. The key fault-line between London and Washington in the build-up to the war remained whether or not to take the UN route. Again the differences of view within the Bush administration are all too apparent. On the one side, State Department officials and veterans of previous Republican administrations warned of the dangers of war in the Middle East. Colin Powell argued passionately that action against Iraq would require an international coalition, reminding the President of the risks involved in unilateralism. On the other side, Cheney and Rumsfeld raised the temperature, casting doubt on the value of a broad coalition to disarm Saddam. Their argument was that the risks of acting without international support were outweighed by the risks of not acting at all.

The differences between London and Washington were exacerbated partly because there were no parallel forces at work in the British government's formulation of its Iraq policy. It is evidently the case that Tony Blair shared Bush's view that the Iraqi regime was a threat to the integrity of the UN and the Security Council, given its flagrant breach of successive UN resolutions. But as this chapter has emphasised, the forces shaping Bush's approach were complex and heterogeneous. Blair himself had also been aware of the threat of Iraqi WMD long before Bush became President. Nonetheless, his outlook and world-view were markedly different to those of the Bush administration.

In part this was because Washington and London faced different domestic pressures. Legal and political constraints prevented Blair from talking explicitly about regime change as an objective of British government policy. Since 1997, Blair had sought to define a humanitarian strategy for reordering the world in which military force would be used to secure and embed liberal progressive values. His 2001 speech to the Labour Party conference immediately after the September 11 attacks affirmed an explicit link between opposition to the Taliban and Al Qaeda and the struggle for social justice and freedom. At the beginning of 2002, Blair's interventionist foreign policy still entailed a clear preference for resolving the Iraqi situation by multilaterally based diplomacy.

The case for war in Iraq assembled by Blair was infused with moral purpose and an ethical doctrine of humanitarian intervention. The British government's explicit support for the invasion of Iraq cannot be explained in terms of upholding the national interest or even the doctrine of pre-emptive defence. Nor does naïve subservience to the Bush administration adequately explain the Blair government's approach to the Iraq crisis.

The accusation that Blair was merely acting as Bush's poodle is inaccurate and misleading. It is necessary, indeed essential, to go beyond superficial and personalised explanations of that kind. The British Prime Minister's and the US President's starting points were very different. Bush's Iraq policy was fundamentally about the unilateral assertion of national interests through global military intervention. Blair's concerns were moralistic, based on the belief in liberal values and human rights. There needs to be a better understanding of why Blair acted as he did over Iraq, inflicting considerable damage on his own domestic political position and thwarting his ambition to be a leading figure in Europe.

First, it should be acknowledged that the Labour Party had taken a consistent view since 1990 that Saddam was a menacing presence in the Middle East and the wider world who needed to be dealt with. As leader of the opposition Neil Kinnock had given unequivocal support to the Major government in 1990–1 during the first Gulf War, and as Foreign Secretary Robin Cook had strongly supported Operation Desert Fox in 1998 following Saddam's persistent breach of UN resolutions. The aim in the late 1990s was clearly containment and internally driven regime change in Iraq.

Second, there were inevitably other factors beyond Blair's leadership that had helped to frame the government's approach. The special Atlantic relationship is an institutionalised habit of security co-operation between two states that no British Prime Minister would easily defy. This was combined with the genuine conviction that Saddam's regime posed a credible threat to national security.[18]

Together with his Foreign Secretary, Jack Straw, Blair persuaded the Bush administration that it must commit to actions that it would not otherwise have done, such as the pursuit of the UN route prior to the Iraq War. Blair's influence also meant that its war aims were couched in terms of an attack on Saddam rather than the Iraqi people. Further, there was a commitment to a concerted drive for Middle East peace through the just resolution of the Israeli–Palestinian conflict as a top foreign policy priority.

Finally, as David Coates and Joel Krieger argue, understanding the Blair government's approach in Iraq requires attention to be focused not only outwards on the pulling force of Washington, but inwards on the governing strategy of New Labour.[19] This is partly because, as Robert Cooper has argued, the domestic and the international are inextricably intertwined in the post-modern world.[20] Foreign policy choices are conditioned and framed by domestic political and electoral imperatives. This helps to explain how, ironically, Blair's liberal internationalism virtually collided with Bush's unilateral militarism as the Iraq crisis unfolded.

In examining New Labour's governing strategy, it is clear that an overriding concern for Blair was domestic electoral politics. He was absolutely determined to sustain Labour's newly acquired reputation for competence on national security. Blair had been convinced that the party's anti-European and anti-American unilateralism in the early 1980s threatened to destroy Labour as a serious contender for power. The dominant electoral constituency in UK politics were middle-class swing voters, who often determined the outcome of general elections. These voters were fiercely pro-American, committed to Britain's conception of the special relationship with the United States as the guarantor of future security. Labour's unilateralism was ruthlessly exploited by the Conservative Party during the 1980s, leaving a lasting imprint on Blair and his modernising ally, Gordon Brown.

For Labour, the risks in breaking with Bush over Iraq were incalculable, exposing the left's traditional knee-jerk anti-Americanism to its political opponents. Had Blair not endorsed Bush's Iraq policy, it is almost certain that New Labour would have lost the support of the Murdoch press. They regarded Iraq as the security issue that was fundamental to preserving peace and stability in the Middle East while preventing the proliferation of international terrorism.

The second related influence on Blair's Iraq strategy was sustaining the conditions for domestic party management. Although anti-Americanism was the dominant force in Labour's ranks during the 1980s, it is something of an aberration in Labour Party history. There is a strong tendency to over-state the radical break between New Labour and previous Labour programmes. There are, in fact, obvious points of continuity that are worth briefly considering.

The Attlee government had played a decisive role in persuading the United States to assume global responsibilities at the end of the Second World War. This was true in relation to security and NATO, in the reconstruction of the world economy through the Marshall plan, and in launching the General Agreement on Tariffs and Trade (GATT) and the World Bank. The strong emphasis on Atlanticism has characterised almost every Labour leadership. It reached a peak during President

Clinton's tenure in the White House, but has since diminished because of antagonism to Bush.

The tensions surrounding New Labour's foreign policy that preceded the Iraq War were also a reflection of long-standing internal conflicts in Labour's conception of international politics and foreign affairs. The Prime Minister's outlook was inevitably shaped by historical tensions and contradictions within the party's ranks that reach back to the era of Ramsay MacDonald in the 1920s.[21]

On the one hand, the special relationship and the Anglo-American alliance were the bedrock of the Labour leadership after 1945 and central to all post-war governments. The Attlee government is now remembered for its domestic achievements – but in affirming the Atlantic alliance it set the terms of Britain's post-war foreign policy. On the other hand, New Labour's approach to foreign affairs was a reflection of the socialist foreign policy tradition and the spirit of left internationalism that had prevailed in the early twentieth century. When the Independent Labour Party was founded in 1883, it had opposed both imperialistic adventures such as the Boer War and conscription immediately before the First World War. This bequeathed a strong spirit of internationalism within the party based on partnership and co-operation. It rekindled the spirit of solidarity and community that was central to Labour's philosophy both domestically and internationally.

This chapter has argued that Blair's actions in Iraq could also be interpreted as a struggle to fuse together apparently disparate ideological traditions.[22] Blair's balancing act was to emphasise strength on national security, but to combine it with an approach to foreign policy infused by ethics and clear moral principles. His actions are explained not only by looking outwards to Washington, but inwards to the dynamics and historical trends of domestic British politics, as Coates and Krieger have themselves suggested.

Blair passionately believed that he could win the support of the Labour Party for regime change in Iraq if the case for war were framed in ethical terms. When Labour returned to power in 1997 it had been quick to unveil an ethical foreign policy under the influence of the new Foreign Secretary, Robin Cook. This concern for ethics reflected long-standing party debates about Britain's role in the world that also embraced the internationalist tradition in British socialism.

The word 'ethical' was quietly abandoned, but Labour continued to insist that its approach to foreign policy must be predicated on multilateralism, in particular through the development of institutions that included the UN, NATO and the EU. Since 1997 Blair had substantially altered the traditional inclinations of the British left towards pacifism and anti-militarism. He insisted that military power could be used as a force for good in the world.

In the event, serious tensions soon erupted over Iraq as Cook and the International Development Secretary, Clare Short, both resigned in March 2003, immediately prior to the outbreak of war. Cook's letter of resignation was a cogent exposition of the case against the invasion of Iraq. He argued: 'In principle I believe it is wrong to embark on military action without broad international support. It is against Britain's interests to create a precedent for unilateral military action. I am dismayed that Britain is once again divided from our major European neighbours.'

The sizeable parliamentary revolt over Iraq was the largest rebellion in Labour's history, presenting a very real threat to the image of Labour as a unified party that had been pivotal to its electoral success. Supporters of the special relationship were now very clearly the minority both within Labour and increasingly – as the Iraq crisis was to demonstrate – in Britain as a whole.

The third influence on New Labour's approach to Iraq was Blair's own philosophical convictions. The Prime Minister was a passionate believer in the partnership between Europe and America, with Britain as the bridge between them. He was equally determined to pursue liberal interventionist policies in the tradition of Gladstone. Blair was convinced that the September 11 attacks would transform the West's calculations of its security interests given the spectre of global terrorism. Together these motives led the UK government to endorse the Bush administration's strategy for Iraq in the early months of 2003.

Of course, other foreign policy concerns also inevitably shaped Blair's actions. The UK government fought to keep the Bush administration as close as possible to the multilateral approach that had prevailed during the first Gulf War. The Americans had to be persuaded to remain within the multilateral framework — hence the massive diplomatic effort to secure the second UN resolution prior to the outbreak of war.

Another motive for Blair's actions was his fundamental concern about the reliability of European allies as the security crisis unfolded in the aftermath of September 11. This concern had first arisen in Kosovo, but was further reinforced by the situation in Sierra Leone, where almost every EU member state had failed to contribute to the international force. In an insecure world it seemed that for all the domestic political turbulence, the United States remained Britain's most dependable and trusted ally.

This period encouraged Blair to draw four distinctive conclusions about British foreign policy.[23] The first was to reinforce his belief in being on the inside, whoever was US President, influencing American decisions. Second, Blair recognised that the United States was now the world's sole superpower, so shaping global events meant working with it. Third, he acknowledged that Europe remained militarily weak. This reinforced the case for military and foreign policy co-operation at the EU level, but not at the expense of the UK's close ties with Washington. Finally, as mentioned above, he saw a special role for Britain as the bridge between Europe and America, seeking mutual understanding on terrorism, trade, missile defence and other foreign policy concerns.

Blair's ultimate goal was not only to preserve the special relationship, as all previous British Prime Ministers had done, while fulfilling his own domestic political priorities. His motives for acting as he did over Iraq are more complex, as this chapter has described. But in confronting the choice between joining with the United States in the unilateral quest to dismantle Saddam Hussein's regime by force, and siding with the Franco-German view of disarmament through multilateral negotiation, Blair went unequivocally with America.

The Iraq crisis serves to demonstrate the potent nature of the special relationship as an ideological force in British politics. As the UK's efforts to keep the Americans to the multilateral route were visibly failing, Britain had to opt either for upholding world order based on the authority of the UN and the legitimacy of global institutions, or for continuing its support for the Bush administration. Blair's choice alienated his western European allies and fatally compromised his liberal humanitarian world-view.

These tensions were exacerbated as the Blair government struggled to demonstrate an unequivocal link between the atrocities of September 11 and the Iraqi regime. The publication of the dossier outlining Iraqi WMD capability in September 2002, based on an outdated doctoral thesis, provoked outrage and a collapse of public trust in the Blair government. The David Kelly affair also transformed perceptions of the Iraq conflict and the war on terror. The word 'Iraq' quickly became shorthand, functioning as a catch-all term denoting spin and sleaze. As the commentator Matthew d'Ancona remarked, Iraq became a dark metaphor for all that voters disliked about the Blair administration, and imperilled Blair's self-image as one of the great British Prime Ministers.[24]

The domestic political costs were incalculable, as the WMD justification for the invasion of Iraq was shown to be false. The attachment of the Labour leadership to an Atlanticist view of security and the British national interest was to provoke the largest parliamentary rebellion in the history of the Labour Party. It had also come close to removing the Prime Minister from office. For many of Blair's critics, his entire period as Prime Minister was tarnished by the Iraq War, since he deliberately misled the public over WMD and recklessly subordinated the British national interest to the whims of George W. Bush.

The decision to go to war in Iraq was also gravely damaging to Britain's standing in Europe. There had been a wider failure to anticipate the emergence of the Franco-German alliance between Jacques Chirac and Gerhard Schroeder, and so a wedge was driven between Britain and its western European allies. This undermined subsequent British attempts to make the argument for institutional reform in the EU. Progress was continually stalled on the reform of the Common Agricultural Policy, world trade, the question of Turkish membership of the EU, market liberalisation, and reform of the European social and economic model.

As David Coates and Joel Krieger suggest, although Blair tried to stand shoulder to shoulder with the United States, there was almost no empathy of values between the White House and Downing Street.[25] Indeed, Bush's wing of the Republican Party was determined to destroy the traditional pillars of American progressive liberalism that had for generations – from Franklin Roosevelt and John F. Kennedy to Bill Clinton – inspired the leadership of the British Labour Party. Unlike Bush, these American politicians acknowledged the social and economic roots of conflict and violence across the world. It was thus an error of Blair's to make the demonstration of personal and political closeness to Washington an object of policy.

Blair's Third Way provided little conceptual or strategic insight in negotiating the run-up to war, and the superficiality of the analysis meant that the Prime Minister struggled to distinguish his stance from Bush's 'war on terror', compounding the divisions in domestic politics. The turbulence in British foreign policy after Iraq was intensified by the decline of support for the United States among British voters and the loss of faith in the special relationship among the British governing class. The new Conservative leader, David Cameron, launched an outspoken attack on the failure of British and US foreign policy, calling for a rebalancing of the special relationship.[26] Cameron argued that being an uncritical ally had become dangerous for Britain: 'We will serve neither our own nor America's nor the world's interests if we are seen as America's unconditional associate in every endeavour.'

The debate about how much influence public opinion exerts on foreign policy has long been a matter of controversy. There are two contradictory verdicts among experts. Political scientists tend to the view that the public will allow the executive to conduct the country's foreign policy relatively unconstrained. This gives Prime Ministers far more latitude on foreign affairs than in domestic politics, partly explaining Blair's passion for foreign matters given the frustration and slow progress involved in reforming the welfare state and public services. Foreign policy is also regarded as an area of specialist technocratic expertise.

On the other hand, former Foreign Secretaries, including Douglas Hurd and Robin Cook, have testified that they do not believe it is possible to conduct a successful foreign policy without the broad support of the domestic electorate. Both claims are valid, however, in the light of the 'tipping point' principle.[27] Until the public's opinion on an important foreign policy issue reaches a certain point on the scale, it does not greatly influence the formulation of policy by the executive. But sufficient momentum over time and the emergence of that tipping point effect begin to exert increasing influence on policy-makers and politicians.

The combination of several factors appears to indicate a tipping point in public opinion. The first is the size of the majority in favour of or against a particular policy. The second is the intensity and urgency of its views. Finally, there is the question of whether that majority believe the government is responsible and could pursue an alternative course of action. Recent studies have revived an interest in how far elected representatives are responsive to shifts in public sentiment. Some experts point to the existence of policy moods. These are powerful tides that surge through the body politic and lead national sentiment in a consistent direction.[28]

Iraq is the issue in British foreign affairs that has most deeply resonated with the public since Vietnam. It raises profound and troubling questions about the nature of US unilateral power and how to deal with it, and Britain's role in the world after empire. This exerts a tipping point effect as the UK's wider strategic relationships with the United States and Europe come under closer scrutiny. US foreign policy appears to have left a deep well of anti-American hostility.[29]

Recent polls have demonstrated that when the British public are offered the choice of maintaining the special relationship with America, building closer links with allies in Europe or following an independent foreign policy, they turn against the United States. Only 15 per cent believe that Britain should continue to align itself with the US, against 46 per cent who believe that the UK should position itself closer to Europe, while 29 per cent support neither option.[30] Seventy-nine per cent of British voters believe that the West is losing the war on terror, and 72 per cent are convinced that Britain's military actions in Afghanistan and Iraq have made the country a greater terrorist target. Seventy-four per cent believe that US policy has made the Middle East more unstable and 58 per cent think that the United States can fairly be described as an 'imperial power – one that wants to dominate the world by one means or another'.[31]

In another survey, 63 per cent responded that the Blair government had tied Britain too closely to the United States.[32] There are other meaningful political differences, however: for example, 77 per cent of Conservative voters are well disposed towards America compared to 58 per cent of Labour voters and only 42 per cent of Liberal Democrat voters.[33] Some 30 per cent of Tories believe that America has made the world a better place compared to only 9 per cent of Liberal Democrats. According to the Pew Global Attitudes poll, 'even though the image of the United States has improved slightly in some parts of the world over the past year, this country's global approval ratings trail well behind those of other leading nations'.[34]

Throughout Europe, even in those countries where governments have traditionally supported the United States, such as Italy, Spain and Portugal, there is further evidence of strong popular opposition to American primacy. The rising tide of anti-Americanism in Britain reached new heights after the Iraq crisis. There have always been strong residues of opposition to US imperialism on the British left. In recent decades this reflected hostility to the ideology of American conservatism and the foreign policy of the United States during the Reagan and Bush years, where proclamations of American supremacy were more strident.

Yet British public opinion showed itself to be avowedly European rather than American in reacting to the security crisis after September 11. A poll commissioned in the summer of 2002 found that more than two-thirds of Britons did not believe that an attack on Saddam Hussein was justified.[35] In February 2003, immediately preceding the outbreak of war, respondents to a UK internet poll voted the United States the country that posed the greatest threat to world peace.[36]

The polling evidence inevitably points to a complex and contradictory mood among British voters. The majority appear to believe that the terror threat is real and likely to continue, and that Britain needs to adopt a tougher foreign policy while giving greater priority to national security. British voters do not take their lead from the French left, choosing America as Europe's defining 'Other'. Yet they also believe that the UK is still too close to the United States.

The British have a generally positive attitude to America itself, but they increasingly oppose the direction of US foreign policy. The overwhelming majority of Europeans, according to Pew Global Attitudes, base their negative view of America on George W. Bush. For instance, 76 per cent of Spanish, 65 per cent of German and 63 per cent of French voters place most blame for anti-Americanism on the US President.

The British electorate have come to perceive the US establishment as increasingly arrogant and materialistic, motivated by oil and money rather than genuine idealism. Three major policy areas – the Kyoto protocol, the Iraq War and the need for an EU constitution – highlight the extent to which anti-American sentiment has been popularised in Europe. Negative perceptions of Bush – where only 16 per cent of UK voters regard him as a satisfactory President – are only part of the picture. The British also see the United States as unequal (72 per cent), divided by class (63 per cent), divided by race (71 per cent), crime ridden (90 per cent), vulgar (65 per cent), uncultured (56 per cent), and dominated by big business (90 per cent).[37] Thirty-six per cent think US culture makes the world a better place, 52 per cent a worse place. Only 8 per cent of the British people trust the United States to protect the environment.[38]

This should be balanced by the recognition that there is a long tradition of deep ambivalence towards America in Europe, especially among European elites that have disdain for the United States. This anti-Americanism is as much to do with the essence of America – and how that identity is constructed by Europeans – as with the United States' actual activities and how it behaves. The growth of resentment towards the US has permeated European discourse since the fall of the Berlin Wall in 1991. It may be largely unrelated to the dislike of Bush and his administration's policies.

Some argue that it is dangerous to extrapolate from current problems to suggest that the relationship between America and Britain will change dramatically now. But the extent of anti-Americanism and its shift from the fringes to the centre of European life cannot be dismissed as a temporary aberration. There is a widespread feeling, as the historian Tony Judt has reflected, that there is something wrong with the kind of place that America is becoming.[39] This allows Europeans – the British included – to identify themselves and their values as everything that this image of America is not.

It is unlikely that any British government will be free to support the US as unequivocally as Tony Blair did over Iraq. In Britain, the majority opposed the Iraq War, as was the case throughout Europe. The foreign policy and intelligence establishment, which has traditionally maintained a strong commitment to Atlanticism, wanted Blair to set far tougher conditions for British involvement. The Bush administration was viewed with increasing scepticism as it sought to abandon and diminish the principles of internationalism and multilateralism in foreign affairs. That led Sir Rodric Braithwaite, the former British ambassador in Moscow and chairman of the Joint Intelligence Committee, to conclude: 'Whatever other casualties the Iraq War produces, whatever difficulties and opportunities appear in the aftermath, one thing is clear. Even in victory the principles on which British foreign policy have been based since Suez are now amongst the walking wounded.'[40]

However, the argument that the special relationship is about to fall apart or that Britain will increasingly distance itself from the United States is greatly exaggerated. It is in any case partly contradicted by the reality of enduring institutional, historical and cultural ties that bind Britain and the United States together. It would be a mistake to ignore the continuing resonance of Anglo-America for significant sections of the governing class in Britain on both right and left. Europe and America are not merely continents and structures of political organisation, but imagined communities defined by their competing identities, values, cultures and models of capitalism.[41] The United States provides an economic model based on enterprise and dynamism that UK policy-makers still find compelling, and the link to America has enabled the governing class to retain the illusion of global influence. That makes the dilemma Britain faces of the choice between Europe and America ever starker.

There are several interpretations of Anglo-America or the 'Anglosphere'[42] that have subsequently emerged stressing the role of values and ideology together with the mutual interests of the governing class in Britain and America. London and Washington are not only natural allies destined to work together because of shared strategic interests. The special relationship reflects the sense of two peoples with a shared destiny. As Andrew Gamble describes it, that relationship is a military alliance, a model of capitalism and a form of government, both a global ideology and a popular culture.[43] It remains a complex set of interlinking narratives and institutions.

The most visible evidence of Anglo-America after the Second World War was the military alliance designed to prevent the expansion of the Soviet Union. The second aspect was the elaboration of a model of capitalism based on globalisation, and the reordering of relations between labour and capital to privilege free markets. A third feature was the advocacy of a model of democracy and government based on individual rights at home and abroad. Finally there was culture itself, the English language, and Protestantism and individualism, giving rise to particular forms of consumerism and community.

In that sense, the Cold War was both a classical great power struggle as well as a battle of ideas about how societies should be organised and the relationship between individuals and states.[44] It is no coincidence that both Thatcherite Conservatism and New Labour as the two dominant projects in contemporary British politics were both powerfully shaped by American ideological influences. The US has long been regarded as the Western society most hospitable to globalisation. Since the triumph of Thatcherism and the implementation of the Conservative programme after 1979, some commentators have argued that Britain increasingly resembles America in its pattern of development.[45] This is inclined to make the special Atlantic relationship even more 'special'.

The implicit claim here is that Britain and America share a cultural and political heritage that marks them off from other advanced capitalist societies. The nature of British national identity and political economy has been shaped by Anglo-America for more than 300 years, just as Britain exerted great influence on the institutions and political culture of the United States. The US and Britain were each other's closest ally in the geo-political conflicts that defined the twentieth century. Britain's commitment to the particular conception of Anglo-America as a global free market economy was also the means of sustaining its influence as a great power in world affairs.

It has also been claimed that Britain became more like the United States after the late 1970s in the role ascribed to the state and the economy, in the character of markets, in the legitimacy of the trade unions and the flexibility of labour markets, in the role of the service sector, and in the organisation of the form and styles of management. Across the members of the Organisation for Economic Co-operation and Development, the share of the labour force engaged in service industries grew from 49.2 per cent in 1970 to 59.9 per cent in 1995. In the US, however, it reached 73.3 per cent and in the UK it was 70.5 per cent by the mid-1990s. Manufacturing industry contracted dramatically over that period in both countries.

These structural changes were the result of contested choices in British politics rather than the working out of predetermined trends.[46] In this respect, the political economy of Britain and America has indeed converged over the last three decades. During the Thatcher period, income tax was reduced dramatically and public spending was brought under tighter control. The state privatised public housing and denationalised almost all of the major industries. By the time Labour returned to power in 1997, these changes had been accepted as an irreversible feature of the political landscape.

The aspiration to emulate American dynamism and to be less influenced by the under-performing economies of Europe was at the heart of the UK model of capitalism. Britain had the opportunity to become the Hong Kong of Europe with a policy regime based on deregulated capital and labour markets, low taxes, global trade and investment, and privatisation.[47] The fastest-growing markets in the world were in east Asia and the priority for British governments was to pursue their traditional open-seas policy rather than becoming embroiled in Europe.

The convergence thesis, however, has to be juxtaposed with evidence of divergence between the UK and the United States. After the Second World War, Britain developed a model welfare state based on universal citizenship and characterised by generous collective provision combined with the maintenance of full employment. The American economic model has in contrast always presumed lower levels of government intervention. There are still strong social democratic elements in the British welfare state based on equal citizenship and universal features such as the National Health Service, which provides treatment to all, free at the point of need.

Britain is still unlike the United States despite the strong appeal of America to the British political class. Many social attitudes on welfare, tax, fairness, inequality, criminal justice, religion, personal morality, public spending and poverty in the UK are broadly in line with those of other European countries and less convergent with those prevalent in the United States.[48] Arguably, British political culture became more European during the Blair era, even if the UK's ambivalence about economic and political union has still not been resolved. The Conservative opposition leader, David Cameron, has been swift to distance his party from American neo-conservatism. He has even embraced socialistic, European-style commitments such as the NHS.

In fact, institutions and ideologies continue to underpin important differences between the United States and Europe. As a whole, government spending in the US is approximately 30 per cent of GDP. In the EU15, government spending has reached 45 per cent. In the UK it is 42 per cent while in the Nordic countries it is more than 50 per cent. Around two-thirds of the difference between Europe and America comes from spending on welfare.

The welfare state in America did not develop on the same lines as in Europe – especially Britain and the Nordic countries – because of the particular character of American political institutions.[49] These features include majoritarianism as opposed to proportional representation, federalism, checks and balances, ethnic heterogeneity, and different beliefs about the nature of poverty in the United States. American institutions are the product of an eighteenth-century constitutional settlement that was deliberately designed to prevent the expropriation of wealth.

Those commentaries that emphasise the dominance of 'Anglo-America' in Britain focus on economic drivers, and take into account only a selected range of social indicators. In fact, Britain and the United States are very different societies with substantial variations in culture. A compelling argument is that America has witnessed the growing atrophy of civil society since the 1960s. Its citizens have been unable to develop the bonds of social trust and stable loyalty that are necessary to participate actively in public life.

That thesis was captured evocatively in Robert Putnam's *Bowling Alone*, which charts the collapse of enduring habits of civic association in contemporary America.[50] In Britain such trends are far less marked: social life is more embedded and the political culture has retained a spirit of allegiance and the sense of a choice between competing ideological alternatives. It seems that the special relationship may have been weakened by the changing socio-demographic composition of the United States, as Chapter 7 will explore.

The extent of the similarity between Britain and the United States therefore appears to be more limited than the convergence thesis suggests. Anglo-America is a set of ideological commitments that runs across and between the two countries. While there may be some evidence of convergence on certain indicators that relate to political economy, the US and Britain are still markedly different. The special relationship is not destined to endure because of structural compatibility and the interlocking nature of economic, social and political institutions between America and Britain.

The ideal of Atlantic community became a potent force in British politics for different reasons. The transatlantic alliance conferred prestige on British Prime Ministers, enabling them to stay on the inside in Washington. There were numerous military, scientific and intelligence interchanges that allowed the UK to project itself and sustain a global role. These were the foundations of the special relationship for the post-war generation. Today that relationship is in a state of flux. Ironically, Britain is no longer suffering from relative social and economic decline. But the UK's image of itself as a pivotal power, echoing Harold Macmillan in the late 1950s, is increasingly delusional. Britain should no longer require the functional and psychological support structures offered by the privileged relationship with Washington. Nevertheless, the familiar balancing act between the United States and Europe still frames the strategic conception of Britain's role in the world, despite the emergence of the new geo-political landscape and the shifting power relationships that previously underpinned classical diplomacy.

The enormous significance of the special relationship was reinforced by the Iraq War. As formulated by the Prime Minister's then foreign policy adviser, David Manning, it meant: 'At the best of times, Britain's influence on the US is limited. But the only way we exercise that influence is by attaching ourselves firmly to them and avoiding public criticism wherever possible.'[51]

Yet new strategic forces have gradually reordered global politics, as later chapters will explore. The centre of gravity has shifted eastwards while globalisation is creating multiple challenges, from cultural conflict between the West and Islam to competition over finite resources and energy supply. The Atlantic alliance after 1945 may have superficially strengthened Britain's influence, but the power it conferred was often illusory. The anachronism of over-reliance on the United States is exacerbated as the balance of geo-political influence shifts to new regions of the world, and the shadowy threat of global terrorism makes the American nuclear shield increasingly irrelevant.

Tony Blair's misinterpretation of George W. Bush's motives on Iraq tied Britain unconditionally to the United States. Ultimately, the British government went to war in Iraq because it calculated that it must keep on the right side of Washington, whatever the implications for Britain's foreign and security policy. Yet the 'war on terror' failed to unify the British public as the Cold War had done after 1945. Britain is a secular and liberal state that has found Bush's unilateralist and Manichean rhetoric increasingly alienating. Blair's avowed commitment to the concept of international community could not be reconciled with the instincts and working methods of the Bush administration. They were determined not to be constrained by international law as they asserted American supremacy in the name of protecting the US homeland against terrorist attacks.

The significance of the Iraq War itself should not be overstated, whatever the enormous human and strategic costs. The war merely illuminated the growing tensions in British policy and the impossibility of squaring the circle of the Anglo-American alliance, European unity and liberal internationalism. At the same time, future US administrations are unlikely to repeat the errors of the Bush White House, while Germany and France appear to have restored closer transatlantic ties. Yet the resulting dilemmas and tensions in Britain's global strategy look set to endure long into the future.

6

Towards a new geo-strategic landscape

> Every nation, in every region, now has a decision to make. Either you are with us, or you are with the terrorists.
>
> George W. Bush[1]

Under Tony Blair's leadership, New Labour sought to explicitly link globalisation with foreign and security policy. As the previous chapter argues, globalisation was believed to have enormous geo-political implications. It created an impulse towards interdependence, necessitating the doctrine of international community outlined by Blair in the now infamous Chicago lecture. This belief in partnership and co-operation to advance self-interest was at the heart of New Labour's governing model, cutting across domestic and foreign policy.[2] The mission was to build community at home and international collaboration abroad. The vehicle was Britain's role as the bridge between Europe and America.

What New Labour's concept of globalisation did not directly address, however, was the major foreign policy challenge that confronts Western states. In the postmodern world, countries will have to deal with an environment where missiles and terrorists apparently ignore borders. The traditional Cold War alliances will no longer guarantee the security of the West. The geo-strategic landscape has been recast by a sweep of structural shocks since the late 1980s, culminating in the end of the Cold War, the rise of new Asian powers including India and China, and the growing threat of Islamic terrorism.

There is no question but that the events of September 11 2001 presented the West with a security threat demanding an entirely new form of defence. The problem is that the invasion of Iraq was an anachronistic response to the strategic risks. Traditional concepts of deterrence no longer have purchase against a 'stateless threat', whereas Iraq appeared to unleash older instincts in British foreign policy based on Atlanticism and the imperialist assertion of British military power.

So far, so familiar: the pattern of Britain's alliances forged in the post-war era by Clement Attlee and Harold Macmillan is increasingly in disarray. The fall of the Iron Curtain meant that the familiar landmarks simply vanished overnight, leaving a major aftershock. As the commentator Philip Stephens reminds us, the threat from Moscow today is higher gas prices rather than nuclear annihilation.[3] US submarines patrol the Pacific rather than the Atlantic. The centre of gravity has shifted to the Balkans, the Caucasus, the Middle East, and central and south-east Asia. In this new landscape, the UK is no longer the pivotal power that it was as the war ended in 1945.

This has major implications for Britain's post-Suez national strategy. Inevitably, the disappearance of communism has had a profound impact on the cohesion of the Western alliance between Europe and the United States, exacerbating the strains in the transatlantic relationship. In reality, it was easier to sustain a continuous consensus when there was a common visible threat focused on continental Europe.

As the former British diplomat Robert Cooper has argued, it will be far more difficult for Americans and Europeans – including the British – to work together in a world where the threats appear to be more shadowy and distant.[4] Even if rogue states such as Iran and Syria assemble a nuclear arsenal, they are unlikely ever to acquire the means to incapacitate a Western country with a first strike, the essence of real war-fighting capability. The traditional doctrine of deterrence, instilling in the mind of a hostile adversary the reality that an act of aggression would be met with a devastating response, is less relevant in a world of 'rogue states' and global terrorist networks. It is simply not credible to frame the debate in Cold War terms any longer.

Indeed, thinking about security often takes place within a particular framework based on the legacy of the nineteenth-century nation-state as the expression of collective power. The military and economic role of the state has been weakened, although governments still have powers and capacities as well as the opportunity to pool sovereignty, guaranteeing security through mutual surveillance. This has meant that a series of fundamental issues are only now emerging as part of the post-Cold War agenda. That includes the decisive role of Asia in the new international order, and the growing threat of nuclear proliferation on the very borders of Europe itself. There is the compelling issue of the relationship between European nations and the Islamic world. The former European Union commissioner Chris Patten has touched on this succinctly: 'The reconciliation of France and Germany was the necessary and admirable accomplishment of the twentieth century. Reconciling the West and the Islamic world, with Europe acting as the hinge between the two, is a big task for the 21st.'[5]

As Prime Minister, Blair was alive to the new realities, highlighting the threat from Islamic terrorism and unconventional weapons of mass destruction. He recognised that some of the most significant policy choices in the next few years will be shaped by the competing impulses of globalisation and national rivalries between existing and emerging powers. Cooper has also acknowledged that while the twentieth century was marked by absolutes such as the imperative of defeating Nazi Germany and containing Soviet communism, Europe now faces a more complex and ambiguous world.

Yet the recent proposals agreed by the British government and the defence establishment in effect tie Britain even more closely to the United States. This follows in the finest tradition of Atlanticist co-operation, as Professor Paul Rogers of the University of Bradford argues.[6] Britain will allow the US base at Menwith Hill in North Yorkshire to become a key component in the new national missile defence system being developed in Washington. The government has also announced its intention to build two new aircraft-carriers for the Royal Navy, giving Britain a global expeditionary capability with American F-35 strike aircraft deployed on the vessels. This will ensure a further extension of the security and intelligence alliance with the United States, but it does not sufficiently address Britain's real security needs, which are increasingly shaped by global environmental, social and economic challenges.

Increasingly, the old solutions to the problem of order that involved balance or hegemony are no longer credible. It is self-evident that the United States cannot control the foreign policies of aggressor states through military means alone. That is beyond the remit of any single state and in any case fosters resentment and hostility that is ultimately self-defeating. Professor Charles Kupchan of Georgetown University argues that the American economy will not be strong enough to sustain the country's role as the globe's strategic guardian.[7]

Since the Cold War, the nature of security in the West has changed profoundly. Relatively little attention has been paid to globalisation as a security issue, to the consequences of the global communications revolution and the ease of mobility across continents. Globalisation, as the policy analyst Iain Kearns argues, means that power is undeniably shifting between states and regions of the world:

- Terrorist groups mount a challenge to Western democracy, using global communications to attack the hypocrisy that they perceive in Western behaviour;
- Organised crime networks, people-traffickers and terrorists are able to organise across state borders with serious consequences for public safety;

- Extended people flows in the global economy increase the risk that disease will spread quickly, with devastating consequences;
- The materials and knowledge to manufacture chemical, biological and nuclear weapons are slipping beyond the control of states;
- As globalisation produces more diverse populations, it has implications for what is a politically viable foreign policy, as Britain has recently discovered over Iraq;
- The world of cheap transportation and global markets make supply chains more complex and vulnerable than ever before. Concerns over energy supply may extend to water, food and other core resources.[8]

The major challenges are therefore likely to be climate change and environmental degradation, demographic pressures, inequalities of wealth and new social divisions. They will be combined with more conventional threats, including global terrorism and the proliferation of WMD. The world changed fundamentally on September 11 2001 as the Pearl Harbor of the twenty-first century dramatically transformed America's sense of its own security. But these changes are structural and the challenges they present will not disappear following withdrawal from Iraq or the defeat of Al Qaeda.

If the UK wishes to develop a credible security doctrine matched by coherent institutional reforms it will have to begin with a cogent assessment of the threat it faces in the world after September 11. There are four key strategic issues at stake: first, how to meet security threats in the post-9/11 world; second, the role of the United Nations Security Council in authorising the use of force; third, when and how to intervene militarily to advance humanitarian ends; and finally, strategies for the preventative use of force that also tackle the root causes of radicalisation and terror.[9]

In an important and influential speech before the outbreak of the Iraq War, Admiral Sir Michael Boyce warned that Britain's legitimate focus on regional as well as global stability would be distorted if it merely followed the United States in the single-minded aim of destroying Osama bin Laden and Al Qaeda's terrorist network.[10] He argued that the UK will need to evolve a more pragmatic approach to the threat of terrorism and WMD. The strategic dilemma posed by the special relationship is that it risks constantly trapping the UK in US-driven 'politico-military' campaigns. The very diffuseness of those campaigns will lead to mission-creep in the absence of an attainable exit strategy. These concerns were recently echoed by General Sir Richard Dannatt as head of the British army. He suggested that the continuing presence in Iraq was jeopardising British security and interests around the world.[11]

Senior figures in the British military establishment argue that the extension of an ill-defined war on terror might have perilous consequences for British national security and British foreign policy. The military impact is inevitably diminished in the absence of coherent strategic thinking about what the UK is able to offer American-led coalitions. This also needs to be accompanied by a consideration of clear 'red lines' and predetermined exit criteria.

At the heart of the debate is the fact that the United States and Europe, including Britain, have different security interests. The two sides of the transatlantic community operate according to a different calculus of risk and reward. In their hearts, Europeans tend to believe that the world should be regulated by international law and the multilateral approach. The US view is that the world's superpower should be free to act without constraint, able to conduct military operations on its own terms unimpeded by wider alliances or coalition partners.

The United States is determined to project power and influence in Asia, Latin America and the Middle East, where it has extensive military obligations. America is a truly global power with significant foreign policy interests. Europe's focus after the end of empire is largely economic. Korea, Japan and Taiwan are not a hard security interest for most Europeans, although North Korea is a common source of concern given its ballistic missile and nuclear programmes.[12] Many EU member states have expressed concern about the inability of the United States to distinguish between its own interests and Israeli priorities in the Middle East. This has greatly complicated American efforts to contain nuclear proliferation and terrorism.

The Bush administration also emphasised a single overriding security threat from terrorists and their sponsoring states, but this raised many questions. For example, is the promise to fight terrorism consistent with the goal of promoting free and open societies? The US had set itself up as a global policeman deciding when and where to intervene, but, as Henry Kissinger has commented, 'it cannot be either the American national interest or the world's interest to develop principles that grant every nation an unfettered right of pre-emption against its own definition of threats to security'.[13] Many of America's allies in the fight against Al Qaeda are not remotely democratic or concerned with human rights. Moreover, critics argue that the strategy of deterrence was working with all three of the 'axis of evil' states identified in President Bush's 2002 State of the Union address. It was not clear why pre-emptive attacks were justified in the American strategy to counter global terrorism.

These philosophical differences are the backdrop to the notable divergence in American and European security interests. The argument here is not about less force in countering rogue states and global terrorism, nor is it an appeal to the innate virtues of European 'soft' power. The Madrid and London terrorist attacks and the discovery of active terrorist cells in France, Germany, Italy and the Netherlands have underlined to Europeans the nature of the contemporary threat, as Boyce has argued.

Other commentators point to the risks posed by security in the postmodern world order beyond the evident threat of global terrorism.[14] One risk of liberal humanitarianism is that states get sucked into conflicts for reasons of ethics and conscience, but have no clear exit strategy and become embroiled in struggles lasting many years. On the other side, there is the danger that the postmodern preoccupation with individual self-fulfilment and materialism undermines the ability of governments to mobilise their societies against common threats, and there is too little willingness to confront 'rogue states' and dictators that pose a collective danger.

What military strategists such as Boyce advocate is a multilateral and multifaceted counter-terrorism strategy. This entails the pragmatic acknowledgement that there is a level of threat the world must live with, and the use of force must be considered in this wider context. The first principle is the primary importance of protection from attack through robust measures to safeguard domestic security. The second is the focused use of force to disarm and disable terrorists rather than pursuing an unspecified war on terror. Finally, preventing future terrorist attacks means resolving the underlying causes of conflict and terrorism. The use of force against terrorist operations has to be finely targeted and differentiated.

This approach also draws on concepts and ideas developed in relation to the values of human security. It means that respect for human rights has to be upheld in counter-terrorism operations. The primary goal is protecting civilians rather than defeating a hostile adversary. Terrorists should be treated as criminals worthy of arrest and detention. All efforts to defeat terrorism depend on upholding legitimate political authority and institutions that have gained the trust of the population. Finally, human security approaches emphasise the importance of multilateralism creating common rules and norms and working within the procedures of international institutions.[15]

For those advocating such an approach to counter terrorism, particularly close collaboration with the present US administration has evident costs.[16] There is the obvious point that conforming to the doctrines, policies and strategic outlook of the United States may not effectively secure the British national interest. The UK's interest is economic and physical security rather than primacy in global geo-politics. There is also the problem of loss of influence within the EU and beyond in the Middle East and Asia. The Iraq War may have set back for decades efforts to forge a coherent and effective foreign and security policy for the EU.

These considerations led a succession of former British Chiefs of the Defence Staff and senior intelligence officials to publicly express their opposition to regime change in Iraq. Sir Stephen Wall, former European adviser to the Prime Minister, recently questioned 'Blair's conviction that he has to hitch the UK to the chariot of the US President'.[17] He argues: '[This government] has too readily lost sight of the fact that Britain's interests and those of the US are not identical.'

Wall's argument is that the special Atlantic relationship does not guarantee Britain's security given the disparate nature of the contemporary terrorist threat. The extent to which the United States and Europe have divergent interests in dealing with the rogue regimes that populate Bush's axis of evil is self-evident. There is a different calculus of risk and reward on either side of the Atlantic. The weakness in Tony Blair's strategy of bridging Europe and America was the failure to anticipate this divergence in security interests, with major implications for the UK as public opinion steadily shifted towards the European view.

The Atlantic alliance can be sustained neither on the basis of strategic interests that were relevant in the immediate aftermath of the Second World War, nor on the assumption that Europe and the United States see the world as one. America is the last remaining global superpower, whereas the UK has assumed the modest position of being one among a number of western European states. As David Coates and Joel Krieger remind us, the US is free to act alone and finds multilateralism constraining. For Britain, multilateralism is fundamental to projecting global power and influence. The UK has an interest in building up the authority of supranational institutions, especially the potency of the EU as a global player. The United States does not.[18]

This will require British governments to break with the imperial mind-set that Britain has a unique world role as the 'sidekick' of the United States. The implication is that British foreign policy should become increasingly European in the future. Europe has a role on the world stage as a peace promoter, extending beyond its own borders the zone of stability that the integration project has achieved since 1945. The EU should develop its own innovative and coherent strategy for global security without aspiring to great-power status. But as further chapters will explore, while the EU provides an attractive space for foreign policy formulation, there are major structural obstacles to stronger British engagement. This goes to the heart of Britain's enduring global strategy dilemma and underlines why the choice between Europe and America appears as stark as ever.

7

American perceptions of Britain and the world
Facing reality?

> Outside its borders, America has become a code word for technological sophistication, meritocracy and opportunity as well as for primitive justice, imperialism and inequality.
> John Micklethwait and Adrian Wooldridge[1]

This study has focused on British perceptions of the special relationship and the implications of the close alliance with the United States for British foreign policy and the future of the European Union. That entails a set of assumptions about the nature of the US as the world's only superpower and leading capitalist democracy. Yet to state the obvious, there is no single monolithic United States. There has been a tidal wave of invective and hostility directed against America, but few outsiders really understand the American nation on its own terms. The difficulty in recent years has been the refusal to distinguish the Bush administration from American society as a whole. The steady and growing resentment of the United States that has permeated European discourse and opinion predates President Bush, having prevailed since the fall of the Berlin Wall in 1991 and the end of the bipolar world that dominated Europe since 1945. Arguably, it has a very long and fertile history and is only marginally related to dislike of George W. Bush and his administration's policies.[2]

The paradox of the United States is that it is at once both the most admired country in the world and the most reviled. Most governments want to emulate and befriend the United States as the sole remaining superpower, yet so often it finds itself alone.

It is equally unhelpful to claim that all disagreements with the US are motivated by anti-Americanism. Of course, ideological debates take place within the Anglosphere itself, dividing opinion within as well as between Britain and America. The neo-conservative philosophy that has influenced US foreign policy is not the sum total of American views about global governance and security.[3]

What is immediately striking about the United States is that there is no single ideology or tradition that defines it. Indeed, there are vigorous debates that reach back to the founding of the colonies in North America, the American Civil War, monopoly capitalism, the rise of immigration, empire, the New Deal and the welfare state, the Cold War and anti-communism, as well as Ronald Reagan's neo-liberalism.[4] These narratives and themes reflect deeper questions about the nature of politics and the role of the state, capturing a rich array of ideas, from citizenship, representative democracy and liberty to equality and justice, republicanism, community and authority.

It is necessary to dispel the powerful and persistent myth that the laissez-faire, market liberal approach to government and the economy has exclusively characterised US politics since the founding of the republic. There is still an unresolved ideological struggle over the kind of political economy that best ensures democracy and growth in modern America. There have been periods of active regulation and intervention, each extending government involvement: the New Deal era in the 1930s, the Great Society project of President Lyndon Johnson in the 1960s and the centrist liberalism of the Clinton presidency in the 1990s. The reforming liberalism of historical figures such as J. K. Galbraith is not dead, though it has been besieged in recent decades as conservatives have openly contested the social changes of the last century.[5] There are signs that progressive liberalism may be ascendant again in the US, calling a truce to the culture wars that have prevailed since Vietnam and on which every presidential campaign since 1968 has been fought.

Yet the almost universal view of European commentators has been that the United States is a divided, unequal and racially polarised society. It appears to have left behind the social unity that characterised the Cold War era. The culture wars between the East Coast and Middle America, the impact of outsourcing on the US jobs market, the wave of illegal immigration from Latin America, misunderstandings with the Islamic world and the war in Iraq have fuelled bitter divisions across American society.

On foreign policy, Americans are sharply divided on partisan lines but, strikingly, that polarisation also tracks the public's religiosity. The more often they attend religious services, the more likely it is that Americans will agree with the current trajectory of US foreign policy.[6] As Daniel Yankelovich explains, the actively religious in America tend to see the world in terms of 'good and evil', hold their own values in high moral esteem, and believe in making sacrifices in the struggle against 'evil'.

What has also become obvious is that the United States is significantly less interested in Britain than it was fifty years ago. The European continent is no longer a significant theatre of operation for the US. Western European countries do not require the Cold War shield and the collective security that it once promised.

After the Second World War, the benefits of the special security partnership were incalculable on both sides of the Atlantic. The US had an unsinkable aircraft-carrier close to Europe: Britain was a reliable and not insignificant military ally. The study of Britain also occupied a prominent position in American universities throughout the post-war period. But the notion of interdependence, as Harold Macmillan described it, became increasingly controversial in British politics, fuelling the accusation that the UK was merely the fifty-first state of America.

The geo-strategic challenges of the twenty-first century, however, are emerging outside Europe – in the Middle East, central and south-eastern Asia, and Latin America. There is some empirical and anecdotal evidence that interest in Europe and Britain among the US political establishment has declined markedly over the last two decades.[7] America's colonial history and the attractions of 'Anglo-America' are less important where the population is increasingly non-European, and flows of immigration are tilting towards Latin America and Asia.

The latest population statistics indicate that the demographic centre of gravity is slowly shifting from the birthplace of the modern United States, in the north-east, to the south and the west.[8] The three fastest-growing states are Nevada, Arizona and Texas. The US is gravitating to a new sun-belt beyond the traditional destinations of California and Florida.

America's ethnic composition is rapidly changing too. In 1970, the new immigrant population of the United States was 5 per cent. Today, it is 12.1 per cent and rising. The largest national immigrant group is now Mexican, and the largest ethnic group Hispanic. According to research by the Brookings Institution, in 2050 the proportion of non-Hispanic whites will have fallen from 69 per cent in the 2000 census to less than 50 per cent.[9] Hispanics will have doubled in number to 24 per cent, Asians to 8 per cent, and African-Americans to 14 per cent as a proportion of the total population of the United States.

Other commentators emphasise how American politics is driven ever more virulently by a fanatical conservative movement, shifting the centre of gravity in political debate ever further to the right.[10] The culture war is being waged against the cosmopolitan liberal elite, just as the tradition of liberal internationalism in foreign affairs has been losing ground. The strength of the neo-conservative right puts the United States even more strongly at odds with Europe. America has produced a far more potent conservative movement than anything observable in other affluent countries, designed to resist the drift towards European-style social democracy. Publications such as the *National Review*, think tanks such as Cato and the Heritage Foundation, gun clubs, evangelical churches and the anti-tax movement all have significant influence in American Republican politics.[11]

The United States is already a far more conservative country than any of its European allies, with a smaller government and a more active religious life. The social scientist Seymour Martin Lipset has referred to the notion of 'American exceptionalism'. Although there is strong evidence of structural convergence among advanced industrialised nations, the United States remains to an astonishing degree 'unique', Lipset concludes.[12] The concept of exceptionalism is intended to account for the absence of working-class radicalism and the lack of a strong labour movement in American society.

American conservatives believe that four factors make their country unique and special, according to John Micklethwait and Adrian Wooldridge.[13] The first is the constitution, with its belief that the only way to prevent people from abusing power is to divide and dilute it. The constitutional framework is based on the population's apparently acquisitive and individualistic instincts, and people's natural desire to enrich themselves. The second feature is geography, and the expanding frontier that enables Americans to aspire to large houses, their own land and an inheritance to pass on to their children. Third, Americans are captivated by the notion of reinvention. The New World is always able to create even newer worlds, hence the continuous movement of people and jobs to the south and the west of the United States. Finally, America is unique according to conservatives because of the deep strain of moralism in its society. G. K. Chesterton famously remarked that the United States was a nation 'with the soul of a church'. This tradition predisposes Americans to see the world in terms of individual virtue rather than the social forces that captivate Europeans, seeking to engage in a Manichean struggle between good and evil. The flourishing of religion in the United States also goes hand in hand with the survival of the work ethic: from 1979 to 1999 the average American's working year rose by fifty hours or 3 per cent, whereas the average German's fell by 12 per cent. The secularisation of Europe has coincided with the steady decline in the work ethic.[14]

The American right exhibits deep hostility to the state and the legitimacy of government itself. The polarisation between America and Europe is reinforced by conflicting conceptions of liberty. In the United States, freedom is equated with the rugged individualism of what Isaiah Berlin has termed 'negative' liberty. It is the freedom to act without restraint: buying, selling, investing and consuming in the market. That makes Americans more tolerant of rising inequalities, while suspicious of apparently benign centralised government programmes such as socialised medicine.

In Europe on the other hand, freedom has traditionally been concerned with the notion of positive liberty. Through the collective power of government every individual should be able to fulfil their potential and obtain security from the misfortunes of sickness, old age and unemployment. The British, like other Europeans, are profoundly committed to the idea of a social contract in which society sustains the institutions that underwrite individual risk. Most Europeans also have a more richly defined conception of the public domain than Americans – from public service broadcasting to the accessibility of scientific research.

The academic study of Britain and its relationship with the United States has steadily declined as American politics, American culture, American institutions and the American economic model are increasingly detached from their roots in British historical experience. The UK and the rest of Europe are expected to defend their own interests as the challenge of containing the Soviet Union no longer dominates America's strategic thinking.

Nonetheless, British history should remain a compelling subject for Americans. Britain was once the dominant power in the world, but its territorial empire proved impossible to sustain. By the end of the twentieth century the remnants of empire had withered away. Historians such as Niall Ferguson have reminded us how British supremacy was replaced by American power.[15] The great flashpoints of Britain's withdrawal from empire over the last century – India, Suez, Kenya, Cyprus, Aden, Rhodesia and Iraq – are all strategically relevant to America's interests in the twenty-first century.

Britain is, of course, not the only country to have felt the strain imposed by the growing rift between America and Europe. The ten new democracies in the EU from eastern and central Europe – Bulgaria, the Czech Republic, Estonia, Hungary, Latvia, Lithuania, Poland, Romania, Slovakia and Slovenia – have been compelled to perform a precarious balancing act between Washington and the major EU capitals, notably in the period immediately before the Iraq War.

Donald Rumsfeld, when US Secretary of Defense, famously divided the EU into 'old' and 'new' Europe. The new countries expressed solidarity with the United States, despite their deep concerns that this would jeopardise successful entry into the EU. The Latvian President, Vaira Vīķe-Freiberga, berated the old/new Europe divisions over the Iraq War: 'I am amazed by the speed with which Europe has forgotten that it was rescued during World War Two when America entered the fight. The contribution of the transatlantic link to European security is something that Europeans have long taken for granted . . . The transatlantic link is intrinsic.'[16] The President of France, Jacques Chirac, had warned that the promise of EU membership might be suspended if these countries did not demonstrate their commitment to Europe. But the accession states were determined to underline their support for Washington, despite never wanting to make a stark choice between Europe and the United States.

To repair the bridge across the Atlantic since Iraq, these countries have fought to enlarge the role and mandate of NATO, viewing it as the glue that binds the transatlantic partnership together. The central and eastern European states are battling not merely to balance European and American interests, but to make these interests complementary, durable and effective. If European integration resumes after the malaise over the failed constitutional treaty, the foreign and security strategy of those member states is likely to converge in Brussels rather than Washington. This partly explains the initial hostility of the Bush administration to the EU, though there are growing signs that it has abated since the Iraq debacle.

Of course, membership of the EU imposes treaty obligations on members and aspirant countries, posing awkward strategic dilemmas and choices. The accession countries were in a conflicted position over the International Criminal Court (ICC), for example. In 2003 the US severed military support to thirty-five countries – including six future EU members – for acceding to the common EU position on the ICC.

Over Iraq, the accession states almost inevitably faced an impossible balancing act. Poland, Hungary and the Czech Republic signed the open 'letter of eight' endorsing the US strategy. Despite the view that finding compromises within and between the EU and the US was vital to their long-term national security interests, these countries struggled to sustain the Atlantic balance.

As far as Washington was concerned, the accession states acted loyally and gave their support when it was most required in Afghanistan and Iraq. The Poles led a contingent of 6,000 soldiers from across eastern Europe. Several allies contributed niche capabilities in demining and chemical, bacteriological and radiological decontamination. Hungary was particularly involved in training Iraqi military and police personnel. This enabled the United States to signal that it was not alone in the pre-emptive strike against Iraq, and that an international coalition had been built.

Poland, like Britain but unlike the smaller eastern European democracies, views its relationship with the United States as both a security guarantee and the means of projecting regional, European and global influence. Warsaw's prominent role in the Iraq War was based on this calculation of interests and the desire to preserve Poland's global stature.

Other tensions have since emerged that underscore the painful dilemmas that EU countries face in balancing the US and Europe. Public support for American foreign policy remains low throughout eastern Europe according to the Pew Global Survey. In Poland, 86 per cent had a positive view of the US in 2000. Three years later this had declined to less than 50 per cent. Nearly half of the respondents blamed their negative view of America on Bush's foreign policy. Younger generations of voters in the eastern and central European states are inclined to identify with the EU on major strategic questions, on everything from climate change to the importance of multilateralism in global governance and security.

8

Europe as a strategic actor in the world
International demands confront domestic restraints

> The use of force alone is but temporary. It may subdue for a moment, but it does not remove the necessity of subduing again: and a nation is not governed which is perpetually to be conquered.
>
> Edmund Burke

The shift in the geo-political landscape described in earlier chapters suggests that the strategic challenges confronting British foreign policy and national strategy will no longer be met through the traditional American nuclear shield – nor will they achieve the security previously guaranteed through NATO. In a world where new forms of collective security are ever more necessary, Europe has the potential to emerge as a pivotal strategic actor. Inevitably, however, it will take time to build up European coherence and credibility. Britain will have to move beyond its troubled role as the bridge between Europe and America.

There is an opportunity, nonetheless, to define a new strategic narrative for Europe based on human security as the European Union seeks to improve its effectiveness and visibility as a global actor. The debate about how Europe engages with the rest of the world is only just emerging, but it reflects the discussion within

Britain about addressing key future security challenges as well as the need to recast foreign policy to avoid the errors of Iraq. This includes how to meet the security threats in the post-9/11 world, the role of multilateral institutions in authorising the use of force, when and where to intervene militarily to advance humanitarian ends, and strategies for the preventative use of force. Deeper consideration is also being given to providing an enduring organising framework for security that addresses the plethora of risks Britain faces, long and short term, direct and indirect, individual and collective.

The future of the EU will inevitably be shaped by what occurs beyond its own borders. That embraces a host of geo-strategic threats, but it is also shaped by the insecurities that have led to popular alienation from the European project itself: from unemployment and strains on the welfare state to immigration and fears over cultural cohesion. Globalisation and the geo-political upheavals that have arisen in the last two decades inevitably demand partnership between nations. The case for a strong EU has never been more compelling, but it needs to be properly understood and explained.[1]

The development of the EU alludes to the existence of an alternative space for the formulation of contemporary British foreign policy. The Blair government, like all previous Labour administrations, sought to demonstrate that it would robustly defend the British state and the British nation from external threats. It resolutely refused to go 'soft' in the maintenance of Britain's defences, nor to cut the UK adrift from its closest allies. In the recent debate over the renewal of Trident, some commentators complained that the Labour Party should no longer espouse defensive power politics in order to affirm its governing competence.

A decade on from Labour coming to power, Britain is now a country confident in its embrace of the world. Yet it is still searching for a coherent conception of its global role, and the unresolved choice between Europe and America looms large.

Globalisation has brought the era of post-imperial decline to an end, and is carving out new alignments between classes and countries that will recast the parameters of political debate. For the pro-European constituency in the British governing class, Labour has a historic opportunity to transform the terms of Britain's post-war security and foreign policy, looking increasingly to Europe rather than across the Atlantic.

But for this strategy to be viable, the EU needs to reorder the three pillars of integration established by the Maastricht treaty in 1991, as Robin Niblett has recently argued.[2] Although trade, industrial policy and economic convergence drove the process of European integration after the birth of the European Economic Community in 1957, economic reform is likely to become a national preoccupation in the future. The search for a common foreign policy and closer co-operation on domestic security will be the primary drivers of European integration in the next decade and beyond.

The pressure on the EU to devise a common foreign policy is set to grow. New dynamics and forces have come into play in the last two decades that will deepen European integration in defence and security. Europe will be compelled to invest increasing quantities of time and resources in promoting modernisation and stability on its eastern and southern periphery: north Africa, the Balkans and the Black Sea region. The EU's borders run up against some of the world's most unstable territories and conflict zones, exposing member states to the threat of human- and drug-trafficking, crime, illegal immigration, weapons proliferation, and other trans-national movements of materials and people.

In perpetrating their attacks, international terrorists can take advantage of Europe's relatively porous borders, exploiting the lack of co-ordination among intelligence and law enforcement agencies. The EU now faces a very different challenge from two decades ago. It needs to project stability onto those countries at its border without always being able to hold out the powerful prospect of eventual EU membership.

North Africa, the eastern Mediterranean and the states of the former Soviet Union have all emerged as worrying zones of political volatility. EU governments should seek a positive impact in these regions of the world. That alone creates a stronger imperative for common EU policies alongside the co-ordination of diplomacy and resources. But if Europe is really to extend its influence, the EU will also need to expand its borders to the south and the east.

There is still great uncertainty about Turkey's prospects of joining the EU, and it remains an unresolved issue among Europe's capitals. Turkey first applied to join the EEC in 1963, and it has since made more than 700 legislative changes to its constitutional laws, demonstrating an avowed commitment to reform. But Turkish membership has been blocked repeatedly, given its record on human rights and the persecution of minorities, and over fears about the rise of Islamic fundamentalism. There have also been concerns that despite the secular nature of Turkey's government, incorporating an Islamic state would stretch multi-culturalist values too far, fomenting economic and cultural unrest throughout the rest of Europe.

The opposition to Turkey in member states including France and Germany has increased as political leaders seek to exploit the issue of membership to gain domestic advantage. But it is unlikely that Turkey's desire to join the EU will be suppressed indefinitely. The United States regards Turkey as a bridge between 'East and West'. Many commentators argue that the EU will weaken itself and the internal security of the European continent if it cannot hold out the reasonable prospect of inclusion to neighbouring countries. It is precisely the prospective advantages of membership that often persuade countries to enter into the perilous process of internal democratic reform and modernisation. This is vital for European defence and security, as it projects stability towards Europe's southern and eastern periphery.

The second driver of an active and cohesive European defence and security policy is the recognition that Europe is becoming a global, not merely a regional, player. States such as Russia, China and India increasingly look to the EU as a potential partner in shaping their national and international priorities and enlarging their share of the global economy. The EU's strategic partnership with China is indeed emblematic of an enlarged global role.

The EU–China partnership is being driven by that flourishing economic relationship. The EU is China's leading trade partner, and China is becoming increasingly pivotal to European interests, as unprecedented levels of EU investment flow into the country. Since the early 1980s, China has witnessed average growth rates of more than 10 per cent per annum. In 2004, its industrial output exceeded $1.5 trillion.

These relationships have been strengthened because the EU has the ability to engage successfully with rising powers. The EU works through an incremental, consensus-orientated approach based on internal negotiating processes between member states. For many in Europe, however, the practical benefits of EU negotiation and engagement with China, from advancing human rights to relations with Taiwan, are as yet unproven.

The third driver of European integration in foreign and security policy arises from the transformation in popular perception of America's role in the world. The philosopher Jürgen Habermas argues: 'The normative authority of the United States of America lies in ruins.'[3] The emphasis in George W. Bush's first administration on rolling back multilateralism and tackling terrorism by spreading democracy and 'freedom' through military force has made some of its closest allies – including sections of the British political class – increasingly nervous and circumspect about the role of US power. The fear is that American actions will have unpredictable consequences for regional and global stability.

It is believed that the emphasis in Europe on diplomatic means and multilateral consultation, the primary role of democratic institutions, and the importance of negotiated agreements starkly contrasts with the US approach. The EU also has global economic leverage, making it an increasingly attractive partner for other global players.

It is often forgotten that for fifty years the major driver of European integration was the United States itself, encouraging the emergence of a unified Europe as a bulwark against the Soviet threat. In the 1950s, President Harry Truman complained bitterly about British reticence over participation in the EEC as European integration gathered momentum. Later, shortly before Bush's first election victory, Condoleezza Rice argued: 'The United States has an interest in shaping European defence identity,' with the caveat of 'welcoming a greater European military capability as long as it is in the context of NATO'.[4] Today, it is clear that since the Iraq conflict and the apparent drift towards unilateralism in American foreign policy, the strongest force for European co-operation will be the desire for a relationship of greater equality with the United States.

There have been several major developments in the light of this strategic shift. Since the late 1990s, the EU has sought to develop common security approaches. At the Anglo-French summit at St Malo in December 1998, Tony Blair and Jacques Chirac reached agreement on a new European defence initiative. This was a limited proposal allowing EU countries to intervene in regional problems as peace-keepers when the United States did not wish to get involved. It also meant further action in creating joint European capacities for intelligence-gathering and strategic planning. In 1999, the EU15 had committed themselves to providing a collective peace-keeping and humanitarian force, deployable in non-EU territories within sixty days. This initiative was joined by a proposal in 2004 to set up a series of battle-groups capable of rapid and sustained deployment of up to 1,500 troops around the world.

Eurosceptics in Britain condemned the St Malo agreement since it was perceived to tip the balance away from NATO, enabling the EU to act with capacity for autonomous action backed by credible military force. They argued that Blair had undermined the Anglo-American special relationship, allying Britain with the country – France – that had done most to damage NATO and US influence in Europe since the end of the Second World War.[5]

But the St Malo initiative was defined in such a way that it would not threaten existing treaty obligations within NATO, being intended to contribute towards the modernisation of the Atlantic alliance. In 2003, however, the EU Council agreed the European Security Strategy (ESS), which advocated preventative engagement and effective multilateralism. This was later augmented by *A Human Security Doctrine for Europe*,[6] taking forward the implementation of the ESS and diverging significantly from the security doctrine forged by the Bush administration in Washington. The idea of civilian crisis management was also given prominence during the 2006 Finnish presidency and was intended to establish effective mechanisms of rapid military co-ordination and deployment.

The ESS report insisted that Europe required the capability to make a more active contribution to global security with military forces configured in new ways. The analysis focused on regional conflicts and failed states as the source of global threats that included terrorism, the proliferation of weapons of mass destruction and organised crime. It acknowledged that simply leaving it to the United States and NATO as the authoritative 'hard' power was no longer a tenable basis for Europe's security and defence strategy. One notable innovation was to put the doctrine of human security at the heart of the European approach. The concept of human security has the potential to advance EU policy co-ordination, bringing together civilian and military capabilities. The doctrine is based on a notion of human security as 'freedom for individuals from basic insecurities caused by gross human rights violations'[7] and proposed a new Human Security Response Force led by the EU.

There are several arguments as to why the EU should incorporate human security in addition to conventional defence and foreign policy as the fourth pillar of European integration.[8] The first is the moral claim that human beings have the right to live with dignity and security, owing a moral obligation to one another when their security is breached. There are universal human norms rather than distinctively or uniquely European values that should be upheld, where necessary through force. Indeed, humanitarian intervention in Kosovo, East Timor and Sierra Leone occurred precisely because of popular pressure from Europe's citizens.

The second argument involves legal obligations. Institutions such as the EU have a duty in international law to concern themselves with human security throughout the world. Articles 55 and 56 of the United Nations Charter encourage states to promote universal respect for human rights. In the draft EU constitution, this obligation was explicitly acknowledged: 'The Union shall uphold and promote the protection of human rights and in particular children's rights.' Europe should recognise that it has human security commitments beyond its own borders.

Another argument is that it is in Europe's enlightened self-interest to embrace a human-security approach to foreign policy. This new outlook is more realistic than the traditional national-security approach, and is the only viable strategy given the plethora of insecurities that human beings will face in the twenty-first century. Intelligence and security measures within Europe's borders have some impact, but will not resolve the underlying causes of global terrorism and global conflict. In failing states and conflict zones, the criminal economy expands and gets exported: the drug trade, human-trafficking and the easy availability of small arms are not contained within the conflict area, but spill out into the European continent itself.

This perspective on global security emphasises that Europe should evolve as a capable strategic actor. It will require newly configured military forces that help to prevent and contain violence across different parts of the world, rather different from classical defence and war-fighting. Instead of short campaigns using overwhelming firepower followed by brief occupations and then rapid pull-outs, there would be a more considered strategy based on the reconstruction of failed states.

The German government recently announced plans for the radical restructuring of its military, turning the Bundeswehr into an international intervention force as part of a defence review launched by Chancellor Angela Merkel after she won office in November 2005.[9] This will see Germany's armed forces abandoning their primary post-war task of defending the country's borders, but expanding the capacity to allow for the deployment of a total of 14,000 troops to five international missions simultaneously. The most likely tasks will involve crisis prevention and peace-keeping, intervention in conflict zones and the fight against international terrorism.

It has been noted elsewhere that while the West spends far greater sums on military technology than developing countries, it fails to gain advantages anywhere near as great. The sophisticated use of air power and new weapons systems may be hugely destructive against governments and 'rogue states'. It is clear, however, that advanced technology does not help military forces to impose order, or to protect civilians against suicide bombers and the threat of ethnic cleansing, as has been so painfully obvious in Iraq since the 2003 invasion.

At present, Europe still evidently lacks the capability to undertake a different approach to security. There are approximately 1.8 million soldiers under arms in the EU, yet only a fraction could actually be deployed in a crisis situation. The EU has more soldiers than the United States, but it still lags seriously behind in technological capability. The Kosovo conflict revealed Europe's weakness in precision strike, mobility and intelligence.[10] The American senator Jesse Helms caustically remarked at the time that the EU could not fight its way out of a wet paper bag. If Europe wishes to embrace a new approach to security, the EU will also need to commit the resources to more police, human rights monitors, aid specialists and civilian experts, as the ESS report has recommended.

The traditional doctrines of security emphasised only the defence of borders and the containment of threats in Europe's near-abroad. At times, they even required support for authoritarian regimes to maintain military bases and other war-fighting capabilities; they reflected a very narrow definition of self-interest. The European human security perspective insists that such short-termism is entirely counter-productive in a world of porous borders where cultural and religious networks are a new and potent force in global politics. It also merges national security, as traditionally understood, with personal security, ensuring that counter-terrorism strategies, through investment in long-term prevention both at home and abroad, enable people to go about their lives freely and with confidence.

For the pro-Europeans in Britain, this is a critical moment in the development of the EU as a strategic actor in the security field. The EU has recently expanded to include twelve new member states, and it has finally agreed on the new reform treaty. Those who favour a stronger Europe insist that in the aftermath of September 11 and the war in Iraq, the EU has the historic opportunity of contributing to a safer, more humane world. In the past, Europeans have railed against American unilateralism while refusing to address festering security crises on their own doorsteps, in the Caucasus, north Africa and the Middle East.

Many of the architects of the EU, including Jean Monnet, initially regarded Europe as essentially a peace project. After the Second World War the 'founding fathers' had sought to prevent the outbreak of any further conflicts on European soil. At the end of the Cold War, the EU was considered to be a vital instrument in overcoming East–West divisions. A recent poll for the German Marshall Fund revealed that 65 per cent of respondents in six countries (91 per cent in France) thought that the EU should seek to 'become a superpower like the US'. There is now a heightened concern about global security and the ability of the EU to protect its citizens and to assert their values.[11]

In principle, Europe now has firmer foundations for pursuing a multilateral foreign policy.[12] The EU Council Secretariat under Javier Solana has a multinational planning unit and military staff. EU monitors are managing the Rafah crossing point between Israel and the Gaza strip. In spite of disagreements over Iraq, British, French and German foreign ministers have together undertaken negotiations over nuclear issues with Iran, despite opposition in parts of the Washington defence establishment.

The European reform treaty will ensure an enhanced capacity for the EU to act on the world stage. At present, EU representation is divided between the high representative for the Common Foreign and Security Policy, the European Commissioner for External Relations and Neighbourhood Policy and the foreign affairs minister of the member state that holds the rotating presidency. The new treaty brings together the roles of council representative and commissioner, ensuring a consistent voice for the EU. Henry Kissinger's famous request for a phone number to call will now have an answer.[13] The new European External Action Service is intended to pool the diplomatic resources of the Commission, the Council Secretariat and officials drawn from the foreign services of member states. But the vast bulk of the assets used in foreign policy-making, from diplomatic representation to military power, will remain in the hands of the member states.

There are others who object that greater optimism about Europe's role should be tempered by the reality of events since the 1990s. It is one thing to have a common voice; it is another thing to use it. They insist that Europe failed to offer a coherent policy towards the former Yugoslavia in the early 1990s. It has vacillated despite growing instability in the Middle East and the breakdown of the Palestinian Authority. In the Iraq crisis, there were bitter divisions between 'old' and 'new' Europe, as depicted by Donald

Rumsfeld. In the recent dispute over Israel, Syria and the Lebanon, no coherent European view emerged.

On the other hand, the perception of Europe's innate strength partly reflects an idealistic narrative of the post-war continent, as Tony Judt argues in *Postwar*.[14] This has conventionally fallen into four stages. First, there is reconstruction and the emergence of the Cold War landscape immediately after the Second World War. The West then experiences the 'Age of Affluence', rupturing after the oil crisis in 1973–4. The next stage is the revolutionary sequence that led to the collapse of communism in 1989–91 and the reunification of the European continent. Finally, the EU triumphantly undertakes enlargement to twenty-seven member states at the beginning of the twenty-first century.

This 'Whig' interpretation of contemporary history suggests inexorable progress while hinting at Europe's moral superiority over the United States, but it distorts the present, obscuring counter-trends, events and processes. This is not a simple story of Europe becoming ever more united. Mark Mazower's phrase 'dark continent' is particularly apposite.[15] The history of Europe in the twentieth century is one of discontinuities and regressions as well as advances.

Indeed, the constraints on effective EU action are formidable. It is inherently difficult to build up a coherent strategic focus among twenty-seven member states. Some, such as Poland, will seek to remain closer to America. Others will pursue bipolarity or at least greater differentiation, as France has. Intergovernmental foreign and security policy-making can also have paralysing effects, such as the unwillingness to use economic sanctions if it would put the commercial interests of member states at risk.

There have been real problems in generating the commitment to build joint capabilities. The EU has failed to reach the Helsinki goal of having 60,000 troops that can be deployed within sixty days and sustained for at least a year in peace-keeping and related tasks. The emphasis on nation-building is perfectly legitimate, but there have to be forces to keep the peace while reconstruction is going on. If European states want to be in a position to influence the global agenda, they must be willing to contribute towards hard security capabilities, as well as the deployment of 'soft' power.

These tensions were echoed strongly in the British diplomat Robert Cooper's conception of security in the postmodern world:

> Within the shelter of NATO and the European Union the state itself may weaken or fragment – if devolution turns to disintegration. A medieval patchwork of states may be too diverse to organise and too diverse to allow the decisiveness required in security matters. The next decades will show whether a union of states can be as effective in dealing with external threats as it has been in eliminating internal conflicts.[16]

In reality, there are few countries in the EU other than the UK and France that have hard security interests in foreign policy beyond Europe's periphery combined with the genuine desire to play a global role. Both Britain and France aspire to a major role in global security; historically they have chosen very different means. After Suez, as was highlighted in Chapter 2, the French were determined to sustain their independent role and status as a great power. From the late 1950s, Charles de Gaulle saw an opportunity for European co-operation to displace the US and embrace a vision of Europe as a distinct security entity. The British governing class did not agree, however, believing that the UK had to choose the United States over Europe if it wanted to play a significant role in global affairs.

France's opposition to the invasion of Iraq in 2003 was an attempt to lead a coalition in counter-balancing America, after half a century in which the French had fought against a bipolar world and the emergence of the United States as the sole remaining superpower after the collapse of the Soviet Union. With these differences in mind, some critics have questioned whether the EU will ever be in a position to act coherently and strategically outside its own borders given the paralysing divisions among key players in Europe.

Optimists insist that it will take time to build up European coherence and credibility. The EU has a track-record on which it can build. It has already undertaken several autonomous missions in the Balkans and Africa, involving military, peace and civilian personnel. The EU mission that took over the NATO-led SFOR forces in Bosnia and Herzegovina at the end of 2004 involved both military and civilian capabilities.

After September 11, the bombings in Madrid in March 2004 and the July 2005 attacks on London – as well as the war in Afghanistan and Iraq – it was inevitable that fundamental rethinking should occur on the nature of the security threat in Europe. This is an urgent concern for the whole of the European continent since it is unlikely that the old nuclear umbrella and the security afforded by NATO will provide much respite from the new global threats.

Meanwhile, pro-European voices in Britain insist that the crisis in Europe will eventually be overcome. EU institutions might at times be frustrating, opaque and bureaucratic. Yet far from being broken, the EU has shown in the last decade that it can function effectively. The successful launch of euro notes and coins is one notable example. But the EU is also forging a defence identity, shifting steadily towards common standards of justice and home affairs. The pace of enlargement is unifying Europe in a manner that would have seemed unthinkable thirty or so years ago.

Those opposed to Britain's participation in Europe have also failed to appreciate how the special security partnership with the United States has repeatedly circumscribed the strategic choices available to Britain. Many leading members of the British foreign policy and defence establishment now argue that the special relationship has undermined British interests in the UN and NATO, weakening Britain's relationship with the Islamic world. It has inflicted real damage on Britain's relationship with its main

EU partners.[17] Atlanticism meant a shield against Soviet communism, as well as offering an immediate solution to wartime crisis and post-war economic decline – but the era of relative decline in Britain is now over, and 'declinism' no longer offers a compelling rationale for British national strategy.

These concerns have been compounded by the issue of how far Britain is realistically able to influence American policy. The Prime Minister was unable to change President Bush's view after September 11 that the West was engaged in a global 'war against Islam'. Even if the UK is able to exercise some leverage in Washington – as Tony Blair did in guiding Bush towards the UN route with regard to Iraq in late 2002 – its impact there is likely to be less decisive than on policy formulation in Europe, where it is dealing with states of equivalent size and weight. If Britain strengthened its commitment to the EU, this would increase its ability to influence European approaches to security.

Those anti-Europeans in Britain who attack the failings of the EU also refuse to acknowledge the relative decline of the United States as a military and economic power, its decline in influence after the failures of Iraq, and the erosion of American 'soft' power. The global strategic balance increasingly appears to be tilting away from the United States. It is the richest country with the most sophisticated high-tech military power in the world, spending more on defence in real terms than at any point since the Second World War.[18] Yet the US has been exhausted by the combination of the insurgency in Iraq and the jihadist militants in Afghanistan. America's generals failed to prepare the US Army to deal with the counter-insurgency, confused between protecting civilians and destroying the war aims of its enemy. Strategists speculate that America might now be on the path to imperial decline. There is also a substantial and influential body of opinion in the US – not exclusively in the Democratic Party – that does not share the unilateralist conception of America's role in the world.

There is evidently a growing appetite among the British public and in sections of the British governing class for Europe to determine its own global security role, with Britain engaged as a full and active participant. The terms on which the British are likely to be persuaded are an EU with a foreign policy and defence identity that complement national priorities. For some commentators, that provides a stronger starting point for the realisation of British national interests than relying on the Anglo-American special relationship. They are surely correct that the parameters of British policy cannot remain fixed forever.

Today's world is defined by new threats, as previous chapters have explored. The myriad challenges of globalisation will need to be tackled. They include everything from competition for finite energy resources to cultural conflicts between the West and Islam. There are new foreign policy actors, even the crowd on the street protesting against the publication of cartoon images. It is a world of infinitely porous national borders. The UK should act within Europe rather than merely relying on the US to meet the strategic priorities that should now serve as the compass for British foreign policy.

The doctrine of human security requires Europe to develop a greater capacity for civilian and military intervention. In the aftermath of the Iraq crisis, anti-Europeans queried the EU's capability for collective action. But the recent European record demonstrates that capacities to intervene are gaining strength. The division that occurred between old and new Europe reflected the exceptional circumstances of the post-September 11 climate. It is far from inevitable that EU member states will continue to differ so in viewing global challenges.

In Europe's approach to Iran, China, Afghanistan and the Middle East – including the Israeli–Palestinian peace process – there is a large measure of agreement rather than division over strategy. In the Balkans, there is now coherence and full acceptance of responsibility where there was chaos in Europe's approach a decade ago. Other areas of visible agreement include combating climate change and promoting development in Africa, both areas highlighted by the UK's presidency of the EU in 2005.

Europe has witnessed successful military intervention in central Africa, involving British and French troops, which averted the risk of 'Rwanda-style' genocide. Much of the practical support given to the Palestinian authority has come from Europe. The priority must be to build up the EU's intervention capacities in a realistic and credible fashion, as well as investing in strategic instruments for long-term prevention abroad – tackling, for example, the roots of radicalisation in the societies to which Muslim populations are closely connected.

As the centre of geo-strategic activity shifts eastwards, some of the biggest policy choices in the coming years will be shaped by the competing impulses of globalisation and national rivalries between existing and emerging powers. It remains to be seen whether China, India and other rising powers can be peacefully accommodated into the new international order, and how Iran's quest for nuclear capabilities is likely to destabilise relations in the Middle East. The growing influence of China in Africa has exposed the need for greater co-ordination of development efforts between EU member states.

In certain areas, American and European instincts and interests are still likely to diverge. Washington wants to constrain China and limit its freedom of manoeuvre, acting as the sole remaining superpower. Most Europeans would prefer to bind emerging powers into a new multilateral order. This raises the issue of what precisely is the relationship of interests between the UK and the United States.[19] During the Clinton presidency it was implied that British and American interests overlapped in a 'Third Way' fashion, as both leaders embraced the interdependence that was seen as complementary to globalisation. Even then, however, Britain and America still had very distinct strategic interests.

Today, the relationship is not just a reflection of different political philosophies in London and Washington. It also reinforces the fact that the two countries have a different global position and standing. The US is the world's last remaining superpower, while the UK has a modest position among the leading western European states. The fundamental difference, as David Coates and Joel Krieger remind us, is that America has the freedom to act alone, and often regards multilateralism as an unnecessary constraint. This does not mean that coalition-building is not still important in foreign affairs, as the Bush administration has found to its detriment. But for the UK, multilateralism is fundamentally enabling and empowering rather than constraining. Britain has an interest in the effectiveness of supranational institutions and the potency of the EU as a global player.

EU decision-making will still require a constructive relationship with the United States. Any credible reflection on global security has to begin with the acknowledgement that the American projection of power dominates the foreign policy horizon from the Middle East to west Africa and the Korean peninsula. The EU has a finite capacity to intervene with real effect. Greater balance is still required, however, not least because the US will increasingly expect Europe to resolve more of the problems that occur in its own near-abroad.

There are several ways in which Europe can create the military strength that is required for a more balanced partnership. The first and for many the most unlikely scenario is for EU member states to increase their defence spending as a proportion of national income, which currently stands at just 60 per cent of the US defence budget. Europe should consider restructuring its military capability, reducing territorial defences, abandoning conscription, cutting manpower levels and building up volunteer forces to operate at greater distances. Europe should organise as a single entity within NATO, with a combined command structure and a centralised authority for planning, programming and budgeting.

Although the EU will not realistically close the defence spending gap with America in the foreseeable future, member states could maximise the impact of limited resources by creating rapidly deployable multinational forces, such as EU battle-groups and an EU constabulary for conflict avoidance and post-conflict stabilisation. Another challenge for Europe in its quest to become a global actor will be the successful restructuring and consolidation of the defence and aerospace industries, narrowing the technological gap between Europe and the US.

The UK would bring much to the next phase of European construction. On institution-building, Britain will continue to push the realistic, hard-headed alternative to the false choice between 'intergovernmentalism' and 'supranationalism'. This stance rests on the assumption that the EU is not ready to behave like a country, nor should it be. Its strength comes from synthesising the national and regional capabilities that exist around Europe, not from seeking to replace them altogether.

The EU needs to develop on the basis of national identity and democratic legitimacy, not at the expense of either. As Jean Monnet argued in the late 1950s, the EU is not a potential federal state, but a unique political form based on power-sharing between representatives of nations, peoples and the common European interest. Britain's role might be to emphasise that which citizens want above all from the EU: the tangible benefits of membership. The real source of discontent in Europe is not the 'democratic deficit'. It is the ineffectiveness of EU action, from tackling security to promoting sustainability in the European social and economic model, securing jobs, pensions and welfare for future generations throughout Europe.

These insights also have clear institutional implications, even for pro-Europeans in the UK. As mentioned above, the divided responsibility between the chair of the Council of Foreign Ministers and the European Commissioner for Foreign Affairs will cease with the creation of a single line of authority on foreign policy housed within the Commission, the post-holder reporting regularly to national foreign ministers.

The full participation of Britain in the development of a European doctrine of human security has vital implications for the wider transatlantic project. Irrespective of the Anglo-American special relationship, European countries will need to continue to work closely with the United States to disrupt and where necessary destroy networks dedicated to the use of terror for political ends. That still requires intelligence-sharing, judicial co-operation and joint military activity in global conflict zones. The EU can also use its political and economic muscle to help construct networks that build engagement, whether based on trade, mediation or aid.

Of course, the persistent structural constraints that have impaired the EU's capacity to forge a coherent European foreign and security doctrine will not disappear overnight. But the extent to which a multitude of external pressures are forcing European governments to co-ordinate their foreign policies is self-evident.

The EU represents a quarter of world GDP, and gives nearly a third of all foreign assistance, with growing diplomatic and security reach beyond its borders. The EU itself has a population of 380 million people, and a gross regional product of €10 trillion. It has the potential to develop powerful instruments of collective action that can meet the complex challenges of human security in an unstable world.

This does not mean reviving the grand project for the development of a European 'superstate'. It requires the necessary revision of existing structures and institutions within the EU. Instead of complaining about the quality of US leadership, European governments have to combine to provide leadership themselves. The most urgent priority is to define a shared European approach to the Middle East.

The expansion of the EU's role in the wider world requires it to address what has been described in the past as Euro-hypocrisy.[20] It is not credible to hide behind American military power and global hegemony while repeatedly castigating the failings of American leadership in global affairs. Belief in the supremacy of European values is less compatible with honest reflection on the legacy of European colonialism in Africa, Asia and the Middle East. While the EU may want to be in the forefront of aid to the developing world, the persistence of agricultural protectionism and the Common Agricultural Policy sends a rather different message.

The key argument of this chapter is that acts of terrorism and threats to global security must be countered through strong and effective multilateral institutions rather than military force alone. Of course, simply decrying the use of force by the United States – or insisting on a reading of international law that makes an effective response impossible – is untenable. But the erosion of international legal authority and the diminution of the UN since September 11 have been deeply troubling, since collective defence has to be underpinned by upholding the authority of supranational institutions. Such a premise must be at the core of Britain's global strategy.

That puts the interests of the UK fundamentally closer to Europe rather than the United States. The unconditionality of Tony Blair's commitment to the United States was misplaced, and both Britain and Europe need to develop a more nuanced understanding of how to deal with America. Yet too many policy-makers apparently believe that if only Britain could extract itself from Iraq, energise the Middle East peace process and contain Al Qaeda, it would be possible to return to normal business. That is a dangerous and misguided view in the post–Cold War world. The strategic landscape is unrecognisable compared to two or three decades ago.

This will also mean that inevitably the drivers of European integration in the field of foreign and security policy will intensify in the coming years. That sets up new conflicts and dilemmas for the British political class and British public opinion in the next generation, as the following chapter will explore. It requires Britain to extend the transatlantic bridge onto the continent, working with European allies to develop a common position as the basis for renewed co-operation with Washington. That in turn needs Britain to eschew the grand role of bridging continents, in favour of the more prosaic task of building partnerships in Europe on the basis of a renewed commitment to liberal internationalism.

9

The future of Britain and Europe
The awkward partner no longer?

A cordial and good understanding between France and England is essential to the peace and welfare of Europe.

Robert Peel[1]

Britain is a great and ancient citadel behind whose walls the peoples of these islands have sheltered for almost four centuries. Within these walls, liberty, justice and human progress have flourished in a manner unsurpassed anywhere else in the world.

Margaret Thatcher[2]

The reason why the issue of Europe has been so persistent and so divisive is that there is a lot at stake. For the future of British politics there is no more important issue, involving as it does a reassessment of British identity, security and political economy, and a judgement about the relative priority to be given to Europe as opposed to other relationships, particularly those with America. Such choices occur rather rarely but when they do they often trigger political realignments which can constitute major turning points in the life of parties and states.

Andrew Gamble[3]

If British foreign policy is to become more definitively European in the future, the UK can no longer cling tenaciously to the ambivalent semi-detached position it has adopted for much of the post-war period.[4] In certain respects the unanticipated success of Britain's global strategy in fashioning a world role after Suez has delayed the British political class and the British electorate from acknowledging that the UK's future lies as much in Europe as in the special security partnership with the United States. As long as the UK sees its role as maintaining the bridge between Europe and America, it will continue to accord primacy to the transatlantic alliance as opposed to other strategic alliances and relationships.

The dominant narratives in British politics have tended to depict Britain as a people and a state apart from Europe. This builds on Britain's early abstention from the European Economic Community and subsequent reputation as an awkward partner member state.[5] The mood of alienation was not helped by the failure of successive governments in the 1960s and 1970s to promote the advantages of integration, stymieing a more sophisticated debate about the merits of European Union membership. Britain's relationship with the EU has been one of the most divisive issues in British politics over the last fifty years. Europe divides political parties, fusing together sovereignty and identity in powerful ways. It was the protagonist of two electoral collapses in British politics – first Labour in 1983 and then the Conservatives in 1997.[6]

The causes of Britain's ambivalence towards Europe have recently been traced in great detail by the historian Peter Hennessy. That reluctance ensured that France and Germany were able to assume the leadership of the EEC after 1957.[7] The permanence of the Anglo-American alliance distorted British attitudes to the inexorable wave of European economic and political integration, perpetuating the myth that Britain could still act alone as a global power. The abiding belief that Britain is uniquely influential in shaping American policy has in turn created a dysfunctional relationship with other western European powers.

An influential group of commentators have also claimed that such ambivalence has weakened Britain economically, preventing it from taking full advantage of the European market while distancing it from the defence of western Europe and the maintenance of British influence on the continent.[8] The British political class since 1945 has sought to devise strategies that will effectively manage the relative decline of Britain as a pivotal power. As Ernest Bevin put it in the late 1940s,

> His Majesty's Government does not accept the view . . . that we have ceased to be a great power, or the contention that we have ceased to play that role. We regard ourselves as one of the powers most vital to the peace of the world, and we still have an historic role to play.[9]

Too often, a stark choice was presented between remaining a world power and being nothing at all. The Anglo-American special relationship was interpreted as a British diplomatic strategy to gain strength from American power and influence that dated back to the early nineteenth century. But that view relies on a strongly functionalist explanation of the Atlantic alliance, focused explicitly on the pursuit of British national interests.

The subtlety of British decline since the nineteenth century has often been misinterpreted, as has the inability of British policy-makers to adapt to change. The weakness, indecision and vacillation of the British governing elite is now receiving greater attention in contemporary historiography. These are crucial arguments because they serve to explain Britain's ambiguous and hesitant relationship with the European project.

The British experienced the realities of decline as the loss of absolute and relative power. In the 1870s, Britain had more battleships than the rest of the world put together. It controlled more than one-fifth of the world's land surface. Indeed, Britain was the world's largest economy, producing a quarter of all industrial output. As industrialisation advanced it enabled Britain to consolidate the empire. The world's first great industrial nation – the workshop of the world – was to become the first of the great powers.

Yet within 100 years, Britain had lost nearly all its overseas territory. The manufacturing base was perishing in the face of intense international competition. The UK had retained the trappings of a great power such as an independent nuclear deterrent, well-equipped armed forces and a permanent seat on the UN Security Council. But the British state was increasingly circumscribed by the new realities of globalisation and interdependence. Inevitably, post-industrial Britain was rapidly to become post-imperial Britain. An exhaustive search commenced among the governing class for the underlying causes of British decline. The problems had accumulated rapidly over the past century. Britain suffered a gradual descent in which the political class had attempted to buy time, stave off challenges from international competitors, and delay structural adjustments.[10] The effort to sustain a world role also imposed exceptionally heavy burdens on the British economy.

Alongside the United States, it was obvious that the UK was continuing to bear a substantially higher proportion of the costs incurred in sustaining the liberal world economy than it could afford. It no longer had the industrial base to support such a world role. In the period between 1945 and 1974, for example, Britain's military expenditure was higher than any other European state's despite its relatively weak economic performance. For many commentators, the British governing class had become excessively concerned with the precipitate decline in the UK's status as an independent global power – of which Suez had been the most painful reminder – focusing too little on the more prosaic tasks of economic reconstruction and renewal.

But Britain's past greatness was also gravely misunderstood. It is clear that power itself is a rather more complex entity than the possession of armies, navies or vast empires. Instead, it was the actual character of British power that changed during the nineteenth and twentieth centuries.

The power of the state is inevitably a relationship rather than a possession. The UK's economic and military status was objectively weaker in 1980 than in the mid-nineteenth century. But power is a relative commodity: it is important to appreciate that just as Britain changed, the world around it changed too. The UK's power depended on its relationship with other states, and also on its ability to derive influence in a world of greater openness and global interdependence.

Much of the debate about the causes of British decline has been problematic since it assumes that Britain lost a position it arguably never really held.[11] The British economy was never as strong in comparison to its industrial rivals as some historians have claimed. Britain in the so-called glory days of the mid-nineteenth century was under-industrialised, heavily dependent on foreign trade and increasingly uncompetitive in export markets. The perspective of steady decline from glorious victor in the Second World War to delusions of grandeur in the late 1950s exaggerates Britain's nineteenth-century strengths and over-emphasises the twentieth-century weaknesses. It also negates the powerful argument that Britain's failure to respond and adapt effectively to change led to relative industrial, economic and military decline after 1945.

The case advanced increasingly in the 1960s was that Britain pursued grandeur at the expense of growth: it was too slow in coming to terms with its altered status in the post-war world. UK governments were accused of giving priority to restoring Britain's imperial and cultural supremacy instead of strengthening the domestic industrial base. Indeed, economists such as Andrew Shonfield attributed British decline to a policy choice that gave greater weight to foreign economic priorities.[12] Too much emphasis had been given to higher overseas military spending and measures to defend sterling as an international currency.

These policies were not sustainable, imposing an enormous handicap on British economic performance. According to this line of argument, British national strategy has struggled to adapt ever since. Historians have been prompted to ask whether Britain should have accepted what was inevitable after the Second World War, reducing its defence spending and abandoning any explicit role in world affairs.

This option was remote for reasons that were all too clear at the time, since there was already an identifiable threat to European security. Despite the partitioning of Germany, there was no permanent peace settlement. However pronounced Britain's weaknesses appeared, the UK was by far the strongest European power at the end of the Second World War. In 1948 for example, British military expenditure exceeded that of all other European powers combined.

The prestige of the armed forces in Britain had never been higher. The British public and large sections of the political class, including the newly elected Attlee government, anticipated that the UK would remain a great power. The historian A. J. P. Taylor has observed that the Battle of Britain may have been the last truly great moment in English history, but the British people have lived off its memory for decades.[13] After the war, the public sentiment was that Britain had made too many sacrifices to be reduced to 'a cold and unimportant little island, where we should all have to work very hard and live mainly on herrings and potatoes', as the novelist George Orwell decried it.[14]

The British seemed more than prepared to endure the indignity of protracted decline. But the extent of Britain's relative decline in the twentieth century was also consistently exaggerated. The British economy had been contracting severely even since the 'glorious days' of industrial and military supremacy in the mid-nineteenth century. That point is crucial in helping to explain how the Anglo-American special relationship was framed after 1945, as Chapter 2 has explored.

As Britain felt that economic and military power was disappearing, it turned increasingly to the United States. After the Second World War, the priority of the British political class was to re-establish the familiar model of British capitalism based on the trading and financial links of Britain's territorial and commercial empires built up over the previous three centuries.[15] But sustaining the liberal and global character of British capital now required the assistance of the United States.

The need to come to terms with the changing balance of power in the world, the prospect of fuller engagement with Europe and the demand for withdrawal from empire were further confused by the problems of making and implementing policy in the British political context. These difficulties isolated Britain from the process of European integration.

All larger powers inevitably confront sporadic crises of national adaptation and co-ordination. Almost all twentieth-century democratic societies have had to accommodate the conflicting demands of national security with the need to develop universal welfare states based on equal citizenship. But Britain's case is unusual since it has experienced European integration since the late 1950s to be so contentious and divisive. No enduring settlement was to emerge that favoured Europe within the governing class.

Despite the reputation of England as a liberal trading economy, British political institutions tended to reinforce national barriers, rather than encouraging greater interdependence and pooling of sovereignty. The political system had not been shaken by revolution as occurred elsewhere in Europe in 1789, 1848 and 1917. The 1688 settlement remained substantially intact until the recent constitutional reforms of the Blair governments. The British institutional culture was based on political parties ruling alone rather than forging consensus, in contrast to the culture of bipartisan negotiation that prevailed in most of Europe.

As Vernon Bogdanor, professor of government at the University of Oxford, suggests, the 'Glorious Revolution' that occurred in seventeenth-century Britain emphasised the undivided sovereignty of Parliament.[16] But the very notion of the European Community implies that Parliament will not remain sovereign. The primacy of European law was asserted by the European Court of Justice in a landmark case in 1964, nine years before Britain joined the EEC.

The principle of the separation of powers governing the European institutions is also alien to the British constitutional tradition. The role of the European Parliament, for example, is to sustain a dialogue with other community institutions, primarily the European Commission and the Council of Ministers. In contrast, the House of Commons is a debating chamber dominated by the binary dialogue between government and opposition.

Britain's strong attachment to the principle of national sovereignty was itself the consequence of the Second World War. Only in later generations did commentators begin to reflect that the UK had ended the war as a warrior satellite of the United States, dependent on American subsidies. Britain's collective psychology was brilliantly captured by Jean Monnet in 1978: 'Britain had not been conquered or invaded; she felt no need to exorcise history.'[17]

This tradition of thinking in terms of undivided sovereignty often inhibited more constructive approaches to European engagement. It assumed that there must be a supreme political authority, either the national parliaments or the European Parliament, and that membership of the EEC involved obliterating national identity, as implied by the former Labour leader Hugh Gaitskell's notion of 1,000 years of history. It has been difficult for the British to conceive of a third alternative to Europe – the division and sharing of powers between the EU and member states where the identity of the component units is not compromised – and where each undertakes the tasks it is best equipped to do.

Despite UK entry into the EEC in 1973, deep divisions have remained within the British political class and the country as a whole about Britain's place in Europe. Europe was held to be fundamentally distinct from Britain. The notion that Europe was itself a complex amalgam of national identities was not widely understood, and it was believed impossible to be both 'British' and 'European'. Europe has often been the 'other' against which the particular qualities of Britishness are defined. One of the 'metric martyrs' – small shopkeepers fined in 2001 for refusing to introduce metric weights in their shops – declared after the court hearing: 'I am British; I am *not* European.'[18] The belief that Britishness and Europeanness should be mutually exclusive still animates political debate.

Britain's relationship with Europe has been described as a persistent pattern of missed opportunities, given its refusal to seize wholeheartedly the benefits of EU membership, despite the increasing influence of European institutions on British national life. The first was Britain's failure to participate in the foundation of the European Coal and Steel Community in the early 1950s. The commentator Hugo Young has claimed that this rejection cost Britain the moral leadership of Europe which it unquestionably held after the war. The second missed opportunity was Britain's decision to withdraw from negotiations at Messina on the creation of the EEC, to which it had been invited on the same basis as the members of the Coal and Steel Community.

That refusal to join the EEC at the outset meant that Britain was eventually compelled to enter on less favourable terms. Further missed opportunities included the failure to join the European Exchange Rate Mechanism (ERM) until 1990, when the UK might have joined at a more favourable rate in the mid-1980s, and the decision in 1991 to opt out of the development of the single currency enshrined in the Maastricht treaty.

Although it finally ratified membership of the European club in 1975, the British political class struggled to manage Britain's relations with Europe effectively, and to negotiate within its decision-making institutions. Britain's ambivalent relationship with the process of European integration is one of the dominant themes in post-war British politics. In the late 1940s, Britain had stood at the peak of prestige in Europe as a result of war, far above defeated Germany and humiliated France. At the beginning of the twenty-first century, Britain stands more often on the fringes of Europe, which has been dominated since the 1950s by the Franco-German alliance.

Other forces have since consolidated this historical pattern of British marginalisation from the European project. Sceptics argue that the disintegration of the Soviet Union has paved the way for a new era of the unified global economy that may fragment rather than consolidate the single European market. The UK Treasury fought hard to preserve its monetary sovereignty and independence over economic policy-making. Whitehall tended to be internally consensual, while most senior posts in the civil service are held by permanent officials. No major transition of personnel ever occurred, as it does in the French and American systems of government.

The weaknesses in the architecture of British policy-making have been keenly felt. The resistance to peacetime conscription within the senior civil service prior to both wars in the twentieth century weakened British land power and made the nation more vulnerable to military invasion. As many commentators have argued, British economic policy and the Treasury were biased towards the protection of sterling rather than the promotion of full employment and growth. The interests of financial capital and the City of London often prevailed over the needs of the industrial economy.[19] If Britain was to compete effectively after 1945, it needed a major reconstruction of the social and economic base of its economy – but such a strategy was never forthcoming.

The paradox alluded to by many critics of Britain's close relationship with America is that the continuity of post-war British policy – underscored by the intensity of the Anglo-American special relationship – has made Britain less open to other centres of power and influence. It became too difficult for Britain to take radical decisions about empire or Europe, so adjustment to relative decline became more problematic.

Addressing the contentious relationship between Britain and Europe since the Second World War provides the parallel against which to assess the Anglo-American special relationship. Europe has never been a constant and unchanging policy challenge for the UK.

Britain's self-perception as closer to the imagined community of Anglo-America was also a reflection of the Hobbesian tradition that prevailed in British political culture for more than 300 years. This saw British sovereignty as undivided and indivisible, with membership of Europe as a threat to its very essence. It is the Whig imperialism of Burke, Churchill and Trevelyan embodied in the hegemonic conception of British identity.

In the 1940s, the very concept of 'Europe' had still not been clearly defined. Britain was separated from continental Europe by force of experience since most European countries had suffered military defeat and foreign occupation. Britain's leaders on both left and right were determined that the UK should retain its great-power status, instead of naturally consolidating its role as a regional power within Europe.

Meanwhile, the war appeared to undermine further Britain's incipient Europeanism. It affirmed the innate suspicion that Britain's fate was to be separate from the continent, remaining a great power with reach and influence far beyond Europe's borders. For those enthusiastic about Europe, Britain's delay in deciding to join the EEC meant that the UK played almost no part in devising the rules of the club. Ominously, protracted disputes over the European budget dominated the first decade of British membership.

There has also been an enduring suspicion of the foreigner in British culture that encouraged a semi-detached relationship with other European countries. British leaders would play the European card ruthlessly for domestic political advantage. Hugh

Gaitskell in 1962 claimed that 1,000 years of British history were at risk. Harold Wilson in 1974 denounced the terms of membership negotiated by Edward Heath. In the late 1980s, Margaret Thatcher protested over the budget, as did John Major over the 'beef wars' with France.

Most British politicians have been reluctant to express sympathy for British membership of the EU, fearful of antagonising those elements of the governing class such as the Murdoch press that remain bitterly opposed to Europe. In the 1997 general election campaign, even the avowedly pro-European Tony Blair wrote an article for the *Sun* newspaper entitled 'Why I love the pound'. British politicians have constantly struggled to convey deeper idealism about the European project, unlike the founding fathers such as Adenauer and Schuman, and later figures such as Mitterrand and Kohl.

While most of the British political class came to support British membership of the EU and full participation in its activities, that was largely to do with pragmatic acceptance of reality rather than any passionate or principled commitment to the European ideal. For example, Europe never commanded the emotional and ideological pull among the Conservatives that empire had. Others have suggested that Britain's ties have always been closer to the United States because of a common language and shared models of free market capitalism. The Anglo-American relationship will inevitably be stronger than relations with Europe.

Another factor is the lack of consensus over Europe, which runs within as much as between the major political parties in Britain. The Conservatives approached the question of Europe in the twentieth century as the party of empire. After 1945, the element of the party in the one-nation tradition of Chamberlain and Disraeli argued that it was a strategic necessity for Britain to join a political and economic entity broader than the British Isles. Membership of the EEC came to be seen as essential for Britain's future economic prosperity. At the same time European models of capitalism were widely studied and discussed in Britain.[20] Europe implied a pooling of sovereignty in which Britain would be a leading if not dominant player. This was also preferable to the Anglo-American alliance, which was compelling the UK to disengage from its colonial possessions and was painfully unequal on the British side.

By the early 1990s, that strategy had been imperilled by the explosion of anti-European sentiment in the Conservative Party, fomented by its former leader Margaret Thatcher. The strategic choice facing Britain tended to be posed more starkly as a choice between Europe and America, where priority should be given to the latter. In the last fifteen years the US economic model had gained in attractiveness as the performance of the other models from France, Germany, Sweden and Japan faltered.[21] This was also the most viable means of preserving an open liberal economy, while national sovereignty should take precedence over economic integration. For Thatcherism, Europe represented a fundamental threat to the British state and British national identity.

The British Labour Party was also deeply ambivalent about Europe.[22] The two world wars, the Spanish Civil War, the student movements of 1968 and the long, complicated process of European integration had all had a major influence on the party. Indeed, sixty years ago, the Attlee administration explicitly refused to involve Britain in European integration with the emergence of the Schuman plan. There was the persistent belief in Britain as a great power, the suspicion of European unreliability, the dislike of abstract integrationist rhetoric and the abiding faith in the Commonwealth as a force for good in global affairs. There was also a highly sceptical view of the capacity of Europe's nations to work together and a deep commitment to the uniqueness of British socialism.

British political parties tend to be insular, and Labour has been like so many others. There is also a strong patriotic or chauvinist streak that dislikes European regimes and prefers the exceptionalism of what Andrew Gamble terms the English model.[23] Neither does 'New Labour' have a single view on the EU. Some Labour modernisers are enthusiastic advocates for greater European integration, but there are also sceptics who argue that important areas such as monetary policy, taxation, border controls and foreign and defence policy should remain under national control.

As Gamble has remarked, the British labour movement and its traditions have long been distinct from the rest of Europe.[24] The nature of trade union collective bargaining differs from continental Europe, and the British working class has had a major impact in shaping British political culture since 1945. The unions were treated as a corporate interest outside the state with special legal privileges. This gave the labour movement a degree of power and prestige in British politics that no other labour movement in Europe could match.

The iconic British social democrat of his generation, Anthony Crosland, concluded in the late 1970s:

> If I list all the things that I have fought and written and argued for over more than 20 years – greater equality, the relief of poverty, more public spending, educational reform, housing policy, the improvement of the environment – I do not find that any of these will be decisively affected one way or the other by the Common Market.[25]

In the late 1980s, Labour began to overcome its instinctive suspicion of the European project as a means of countering the free market hegemony encouraged by the Thatcher governments. It did so, however, only after it was clear that the alternatives – such as moral leadership of the Commonwealth and 'socialism in one country' – were no longer viable. Some have argued that the most promising future governing strategy for Labour would be to embrace Europe as a model, participating fully in the deepening integration of the EU and joining the euro.[26] Yet the proportion of the party that is deeply committed to the European project remains small.

These are some of the underlying reasons why Britain has found adjustment to membership of the EU so problematic. The special relationship with the United States became the preferred strategic choice after 1945. During the Thatcher government and in the Blair era, the transatlantic security partnership took on renewed importance as a major force in British politics. Initially for Blair, this was an affirmation of Labour's commitment to the moderate Third Way and the ascendancy of progressive liberalism. But after Bill Clinton's departure it posed numerous domestic political management problems, conflicting viscerally with Blair's desire to commit Britain fully to the European project. As a result, Blair pulled Labour away from the unconditional pro-Europeanism of the early 1990s. The firm commitment to the ERM, for example, was replaced by a conditional commitment to the euro. The Labour Party agreed to sign the European Social Chapter, but did not want to reverse the employment rights legislation introduced by the Thatcher governments in the 1980s.

The UK's privileged relationship with Washington inhibited it from undertaking vital adjustments to British global strategy. Since the end of the Cold War it had to come to terms with changing geo-political realities and the advent of globalisation — yet the American alliance continued to undermine the necessary recasting of British foreign policy. Margaret Thatcher had clung to the United States and NATO as Britain's primary international partnership, but the basis for that position was already shifting by the end of the 1980s. In the US, George Bush Sr's administration was more interested in developing a special security partnership with Germany than Britain, largely because the UK was seen as being on the sidelines of European developments.[27] American priorities were shifting, but British leaders had been perilously slow to realise the new context.

Of necessity, British foreign policy will need to become more European in the future. American and British strategic interests significantly diverge: Britain needs to uphold the authority of international institutions. It benefits from the very multilateralism that the United States finds constraining. But that requires a major change in Britain's long-standing attitude to the process of European integration. This presents conflicts and dilemmas for the British political class, though there is some evidence that British public opinion would accept greater European co-operation in areas such as security and defence.[28]

It is not simply the case that the EU is evolving in a direction more compatible with British interests and preferences. New Labour's ideas have become increasingly attractive to other EU member states shifting from an Anglo-American model of capitalism under Thatcher to an Anglo-social model of capitalism under Blair and Gordon Brown.[29] It is striking that Britain's voice continues to be heard in debates about Europe's economic future despite remaining outside the euro zone. While many on the continent have been critical of the British model, the Blair government remained at the centre of discussions about the future direction of Europe's political economy and the European social model.

It is also clear that the British view of Europe as a loosely organised group of nations with continuing ties to the United States rather than a federal superstate is attractive, especially among the new member states in eastern Europe. Britain now has to decide what kind of European actor it wants to be: an awkward partner, a pragmatic player or at the heart of Europe?

Some commentators have argued that Europe should be presented as integral to the emergence of 'progressive' Britain, a society that has moved decisively beyond the era of relative decline.[30] Blair's effort to engineer a fundamental shift in popular opinion on Europe coincided with the strong revival of the British economy. The sluggish performance of the euro zone economies compared with Britain's undermined support for the pro-European argument.

In the twentieth century and especially during the 1960s, 1970s and 1980s, British politics was dominated by the theme of decline.

The British economy had been among the weakest with high rates of unemployment and inflation, and a large number of days lost through strikes. 'UK plc' was regarded as unstable and crisis prone. This period of protracted decline appeared to end in the 1990s, when the UK emerged as one of the strongest performers among the industrialised economies. Euro-land appeared to be in the doldrums. This was certainly a novel experience.

This also transformed the terms of political argument about Europe in British politics. It was no longer plausible to make the claim that Europe offered a way out of British decline, as Harold Macmillan and Edward Heath had in the 1960s and 1970s respectively. As the former City minister Ed Balls noted in a recent pamphlet, 'the idea that Britain is in inevitable decline and needs Europe as its salvation now looks absurd'.[31] The City of London, for example, has emerged as one of the world's leading financial centres despite the UK's decision not to join the euro.

But as New Labour came to power, the economic landscape was already in flux. It was the European economies that were now suffering insufficient growth and higher unemployment. Germany entered five years of stagnation. Italy fell into recession. French growth was a little better, but still declined. Europe and east Asia were roundly criticised as sclerotic and inflexible, unwilling to restructure themselves to face the challenges of the global economy. The political class increasingly saw Britain's proximity to America as the source of their country's renewed success, concluding that absorption into Europe would imperil that new-found prosperity. British politicians on both left and right became evangelists for the superiority of the American model.

Today, as Europe appears to have turned the corner after a decade of stagnation, the terms of debate about economic policy in Britain should be rebalanced. In the last ten years, competence has been restored to economic management, symbolised by Gordon Brown's historic decision to give operational independence to the Bank of England. The UK economy has enjoyed steady and consistent growth, with higher living standards, full employment and record levels of investment in public infrastructure and public services.

But there has been no miracle in British performance. The UK economy is still characterised by a low-wage, low-skill, low-productivity syndrome. A recent report noted that Britain still faces real challenges including lack of affordable housing, skills shortages and high rates of economic inactivity. Productivity still lags behind the United States.[32] Britain has not been able to generate a high rate of economic growth on the basis of sustained private investment in UK-based manufacturing.

Those who favour stronger links with Europe have to show how the EU enhances the growth potential of the British economy. Britain should learn from those in Europe that have adapted to meet the imperatives of the global economy, but within a different tradition of market capitalism and social democracy. That requires pro-Europeans to challenge both the myth that the UK substantially outperforms Europe and the received wisdom that greater association with the EU undermines British success.

If the EU can no longer be sold as providing an alternative focus for economic management, the case for Europe in Britain is that it helps to embed the conditions for long-term stability and growth irrespective of any eventual decision on the euro. The UK growth rate has been broadly similar to the EU's over the last five years. Only Germany and Italy have fallen significantly behind. Spain and Sweden have performed more strongly.

In so far as the Anglo-Saxon economies have outperformed others in western Europe, much of the explanation is to be found in the permissive policies pursued by the US Federal Reserve and the Bank of England's Monetary Policy Committee. In the meantime, Germany has had to absorb the twin shocks of unification and the adoption of the single currency at an over-valued exchange rate.

The choice for the UK is not between a flexible Anglo-Saxon model and a rigid continental model. Some member states have achieved more flexible labour markets without the rising wage and income inequalities witnessed by the UK since the late 1970s. The Nordic countries invest heavily in childcare and support for working parents. In the Netherlands, a statutory framework of employment rights to promote security within a flexible labour market has massively expanded part-time work among women.

A recent study for the Lisbon Council think tank, *European Growth and Jobs Monitor*, illustrates how different European economies have adapted.[33] One notable trend is the leap in labour productivity, with some evidence of structural improvements. Likewise, more than ten million jobs have been created in the EU15 since 2000, and employment rates are rising. This is due largely to moderation in labour costs and greater flexibility in the job market.

There is also far stronger recognition that Europe must evolve into a vibrant knowledge economy if it is to head off international competition. To avoid any trade-off between productivity gains and employment growth, policy-makers regard technical progress and more innovation as essential. The positive trends in innovation potential include the steady increase in the proportion of the workforce with tertiary-level qualifications. The sustainability of public finances within the EU15 is also improving: the 2006 budget surplus as a percentage of GDP has slightly increased, while the debt ratio is steadily shrinking.

It is of course right to be cautious about the EU's growth prospects given intense competition in product, capital and labour markets, and the rapid shifts in competitive advantage wrought by globalisation. But the view of European stagnation is misplaced. For the UK, there are enormous potential gains to be found in Europe. A recent study found that the extension of the single market into services alone would add 0.6 per cent to European GDP, while the creation of a single capital market would add 1.1 per cent.[34]

Member states, including the UK, will need to push hard for a further wave of reforms. The European Commission should crack down severely on dominant companies that abuse their market position. The completion of the World Trade Organization's Doha round of talks must remove global barriers to trade. There should be full liberalisation in industries from energy to telecoms, as well as public procurement. Another priority is the modernisation of the European budget, focusing on investment in new sources of long-term growth including research and development, human capital and public infrastructure.

In a recent study Professor John Sutton of the London School of Economics and Political Science warns that it is not higher levels of social provision that damage western European economies.[35] It is the weight of market-unfriendly policies combined with inappropriate regulation that slows the growth in real incomes necessary to finance public investment over the long term.

This transformation in the terms of debate about Europe in Britain should be matched by an acknowledgement that the American model has limitations. The US system is under greater protectionist pressure because the population includes a significant proportion of losers from globalisation, and because of the weakness of safety nets including access to basic healthcare. Average incomes in the US are now lower than they were seven years ago in real terms, while wages and salaries make up the smallest share of GDP since records began in 1947.[36]

There is a widespread perception that the majority of the American workforce has not been gaining from recent growth. This makes a protectionist backlash more likely, eroding support for globalisation. That alone should prompt a fundamental debate about the nature of modern capitalism and the policy frameworks required for adaptation to the global economy.

In a paper for the *Cambridge Journal of Economics*, Mića Panić shows, against the conventional orthodoxy, that the best-performing industrial economies are those that have least in common with neo-liberalism.[37] His analysis takes into account a range of variables from GDP per head to measures of inequality, life expectancy and social trust. Within Britain, there needs to be greater acknowledgement of Europe's virtues, notably the competitive advantages of the European social and economic model. There is also compelling evidence that models of capitalism that encourage investment in well-being, solidarity and trust improve economic as well as social welfare. Britain should not ignore the virtues of the economic and social institutions that prevail elsewhere in Europe.

Europe is not a last resort, a final resting place for a nation on an inexorable downward spiral, nor is European Monetary Union a way for the Labour Party to be trusted to run the economy competently. The credibility of an independent Bank of England has grown while the case for adopting the euro has rapidly diminished. Instead, engagement with the EU should be framed as the means of fulfilling enduring progressive ideals in British politics.

The first argument for deepening Britain's attachment to Europe is that if the UK does not play its full role in consolidating the single market, it will lose out from the growth dividend that is crucial to future investment in Britain's public services. Outside the EU Britain's ability to sustain its high-investment, high-quality public services is significantly diminished. Second, outside Europe Britain will lose its ties to the progressive model of capitalism embodied in the European social market: a framework of rules incorporating principles of social justice and environmental sustainability. The opportunity to shape global capitalism, producing a fairer distribution of the costs and benefits between winners and losers, would also be lost. Finally, outside the EU, Britain will lose influence in a world where China, India and Brazil are rapidly emerging as the great economic powers. China's GDP now surpasses that of Britain or France. Indeed, China will overtake the United States around 2027 as the world's largest economy. The UK alone cannot shape globalisation or act as an effective force for good in the world. Britain would fall prey to the post-war disease of exaggerating its power at the centre of Churchill's three intersecting circles of influence.

The British debate about Europe also has to acknowledge that the essence of European governance is the balance between supranationalism and intergovernmentalism. Yet it is the potential for supranational action – through the Commission's right of initiative, the European Court's supremacy over national law, the directly elected Parliament and qualified majority voting in the Council of Ministers – that makes the EU effective and legitimate. British governments need to confront Eurosceptics with the incontrovertible evidence both about the EU's strengths and about the real nature of European institutions.

The EU also represents a new model of governance tailored to the information age, neither a union of nation states nor an embryonic superstate.[38] It works through bargaining and arbitration, where everyone has an interest in making the system work for the good of each. Common policies are not desirable per se: they need to be justified concretely and then politically legitimised. There is, of course, also a strong case for a leaner EU with a clearer set of priorities.[39] But these subtleties have rarely been captured in the British debate about the future of Europe.

The point is that the EU is a work in progress rather than a set of stable arrangements that are apparently settled. Europe is the product of pushing and pulling between member states with often uncertain and ambiguous agendas, rather than a project under the strategic direction of any particular dominant group. Its principles, laws and institutions are therefore contested and sometimes fragile.[40] The process of European integration is neither irresistible nor irreversible, but the result of political choices and decisions made by national governments in response to changing economic and political conditions. At the same time there are inevitably tensions involved in reconciling democracy with growing international interdependence. This issue goes well beyond the boundaries of the EU; it is one of the key debates about the very nature of globalisation itself.[41]

It is also important for Britain to look closely at policies in other European countries that could be implemented in the UK.[42] For example, the Scandinavian countries have outperformed Britain in their rates of growth over the past ten years, but they also have far lower rates of inequality. It is vital to learn from successes – not all of which are due to higher taxation – as well as weaknesses in the Nordic model and other European capitalisms.

The British now have an opportunity to actively contribute to shaping the next phase of Europe's development. But that will mean confronting the biggest question about the future of Europe: the apparently contradictory tendencies of deepening integration and the widening of the EU through enlargement. Reaching decisions in an EU of twenty-seven states will be a very challenging endeavour even if the new reform treaty is agreed. The EU has appeared divided on major security and foreign policy questions, especially over Iraq in 2003. Even the most passionate British pro-Europeans cannot ignore the reality that significant obstacles to a unified and cohesive EU still remain.

Conclusion
Changing perspectives on Europe and America

> The empires of the future will be empires of the mind.
> Winston Churchill[1]

The central theme of this book is how Britain should balance Europe and America. The argument is that the traditional conception of the transatlantic bridge that shaped British foreign policy since the 1950s no longer provides a coherent strategic view of Britain's place in the world. The divergence of interests and conceptions of global power – rather than endemic failure in Iraq alone – are set to transform the terms of the Atlantic alliance. If Britain can resolve its deep-seated historical antagonism towards the project of a unified Europe, it should adopt a national strategy in the next decade that operates the bridge *within* the European Union as the precursor to sustainable transatlantic cooperation.

Europe requires an effective architecture of collective security given the threat of Islamist terrorism and the disorder wrought by globalisation. Britain and France will be vital strategic actors in any security and defence settlement. Six decades after the end of the Second World War, the Atlantic alliance between Europe and the United States is in disarray. This was predictable at the end of the Cold War, but September 11 has also put NATO under unprecedented strain.

This study has sought to highlight that there was a constant danger of over-emphasising the novelty of this approach during the Blair era and the likelihood of a major rupture now. We are still unlikely to witness any immediate and substantive shift in British national strategy. The UK will continue to exhibit the cautious pro-Europeanism of the Blair era, while remaining deeply attached to the special security partnership with the United States. Of course, as Walter Russell Mead has argued, the special relationship results not so much from policy decisions made by Britain or the US as from the similar choices the two countries so frequently and coincidentally make. The chief 'Anglo-Saxon' powers often reach identical conclusions about what needs to be done.[2]

The bridge between Europe and the United States will remain Britain's conception of its role in the world, but the circumstances that sustained that bridge strategy have changed. The end of the Cold War and the appearance in Washington of an administration that disregarded the collective voice of Europe left Tony Blair stranded in the middle. The common EU approach was also undermined by Jacques Chirac and Gerhard Schroeder, who at times acted recklessly. Their respective successors, Nicolas Sarkozy and Angela Merkel, have rejected the strategy of multipolarity, building up Europe as a superpower that competes with the United States.

It is clear that British public opinion towards the Anglo-American special relationship and the inclinations of the governing class have also been transformed. The UK is unable to act as the unconditional ally of the United States, although this is not an entirely novel situation: history is littered with examples of the disjuncture between the aspirations of the American foreign policy establishment and the instincts of British voters. Another factor underlying the shift in preferences is that the context of Britain's national strategy and British politics has been transformed since the Second World War. Fifty-three per cent of British voters now believe that western Europe should take a more independent approach to security and diplomatic affairs than it has done in the past.³

There are three leading views about the special relationship between the United States and Britain, and the UK's role in the world. And they are all wrong, or at least misguided. The pro-Europeans argue that since the UK is no longer a global power in its own right, it should deepen and widen its alliances at the heart of Europe. That would require the British to reconcile themselves to a fundamentally European future. This is a plausible national strategy, but there is no clear evidence that the British are yet ready to embrace it. Many of the setbacks since 1997 occurred in European policy and Blair largely failed in his repeated aim of ending decades of British distance and hesitation about Europe: Britain remains the perpetual awkward partner.⁴

Anglo-Americans insist that Britain must embrace the comfort-blanket of the special relationship. The United States remains the most reliable and trusted ally of the UK, as well as sharing an economic model based on the commitment to neo-liberal globalisation. Maintaining the special relationship is Britain's best chance to exercise more influence than might be expected from a country with 1 per cent of the world's population and roughly 3 per cent of its GDP. Yet the Anglo-American special relationship is imperilled as never before, as the United States government has never been more distrusted among the British electorate.

The third option is British multilateralism, where the UK attempts to avoid the dilemma of Europe and America altogether. Britain would become a third force, as some urged it to do after the Second World War between the Atlantic alliance and Soviet communism. The perception that London is merely Washington's lapdog actually reduces Britain's international prestige. Britain has long been thought of as an exceptional place with its own path of economic and political development that distances it from American and European influences, each of which has been seen as the enemy and a threat. The homogeneity of Britain and British identity is one of the bulwarks of the British state. Its role in the world has been shaped by the legacy of empire and the links between the UK and the Commonwealth countries. Given this sphere of influence Britain should act on the basis of its Enlightenment values.

Yet there are significant tensions between the notion of multilateralism in foreign policy and the ethos of 'Britishness'.[5] The inclination towards independence and the focus on the primacy of British national interests rest uneasily with the desire to co-operate alongside other partners and allies. The view of Britain as an independent and great power tempers any effort to engage in extensive co-operation on foreign policy issues and crises within Europe and elsewhere.

Inevitably, any fundamental change of course will also arouse vociferous opposition from sections of the British media and the governing class. The combination of economic reforms since 1979 and the constitutional changes of the last decade have ended the period of British fixation with national decline and transformed the terms of debate about Britain's world role in an era of globalisation. Britain no longer needs America to define a post-imperial purpose.

Logically, the United Kingdom should no longer aspire to great-power status. It is a medium-sized economic and military power, and an increasingly engaged partner in European integration. It does not need the Atlantic alliance to fuel pretensions of a great-power role or imperial rule, though empire still casts a long shadow over British politics and British national life. It recognises that while there is not a fundamental choice of alignment between Europe and America, there is a question of priority to be resolved.

The argument of this book is that although the era of empire has strongly influenced the construction of British identity, it was an aberration in the long history of the nations of the UK. For much of history, the fates of Britain and the European continent have been deeply intertwined. Britain's imperial experience was a deviation: there is no fundamental reason why, post-empire, Britain should remain separate from Europe.

These assumptions are increasingly, albeit reluctantly, accepted within the British electorate and the political class. The change in attitude towards the special relationship reflects fundamental historical and structural trends and the divergence in strategic interests across the Atlantic – although the Iraq War has deepened its resonance in public opinion. It is no longer tenable to argue that full public support for the Bush administration can be combined with the construction of effective multilateral institutions and rules-based regimes. The neo-conservative view that President Bush himself has embraced is that the national security mission should determine the coalition. But this is fundamentally at odds with the effort to foster greater multilateralism.[6]

Some commentators ascribe the divisions across the Atlantic to fundamental differences in philosophical outlook.[7] Taking up the essential theme highlighted by Robert Cooper, the world is divided into modern states, which pursue their national interests in the classic nineteenth-century sense, and 'postmodern states', which reject power politics in favour of integration and systems of mutual interference.

Britain and Europe clearly belong in the postmodern age. They have made progress towards political and economic integration, while they are prepared to solve wider global problems through sovereignty-pooling. In contrast, America stands out as the archetypal modern state, determined to preserve its own freedom of movement and rejecting multilateralism from the International Criminal Court to Kyoto.

The American commentator Robert Kagan reinforces this approach, contrasting the power of the US with the weakness of the EU.[8] He argues that America possesses force and is not afraid to use it to pursue its ends. In contrast, Europe attempts to enforce its will through persuasion and consent. There are few alternatives between these competing conceptions of international order. Americans and

Europeans are drifting apart. This makes co-operation increasingly difficult, even impossible. The EU is held to be militarily weaker by choice, preferring comfortable prosperity to foreign adventures. If Europe and America are no longer strategically compatible, any effort to rebuild the Atlantic alliance is unlikely to succeed. As a consequence, the transatlantic bridge as the fundamental component of British foreign policy is set to collapse.

Yet this perspective draws too stark a distinction between modern and postmodern states. Kagan draws a simplistic connection between the philosophical traditions of Kant and Hobbes on the one hand, and national policies and mentalities on the other.[9] It is not the case that Europe's nations have abandoned all claims to advancing their own national interests, as demonstrated by recent British and French disagreements over the Middle East, for example. There is also the constant danger of caricaturing America's position: the shift towards neo-conservatism in US foreign policy is neither uncontested nor likely to be permanent.

The debate about global governance and security takes place within the Anglosphere itself. The neo-conservative view that has exerted influence in Washington since September 11 2001 is not the sum total of American opinion. There are many credible security and foreign policy analysts in the US who disagree profoundly with the Bush administration. American politics is dynamic and cyclical. There has already been a significant shift in the outlook of the Bush presidency towards the EU, the Middle East and the engagement of Syria and Iran. The American deputy assistant secretary for European affairs, Kurt Volker, recently argued: 'Our strategic relationship with our European partners and allies is just as fundamental to addressing these challenges today as it has been to addressing the challenges of the past.'[10]

Neither do opinion surveys demonstrate such a sharp difference in outlook between Americans and Europeans. Kagan defines power in its narrowest sense, but it could be argued that the primacy of international law or collaboration to limit the effects of climate change is a form of power that both Europeans and Americans have willingly embraced.[11] Violence through military force in the absence of negotiation is a last resort since it fails to deliver stability.

The crisis across the Atlantic over Iraq was also fuelled by dysfunctional policy-making, strategic blunders and inept diplomacy. It seems implausible that Europe and America should suddenly become strategically incompatible. Many of the problems may be due less to the fundamental philosophical divide, more to the refusal to reorient the alliance towards an increasingly interdependent and globalised world.

The traditional Anglo-American special relationship has nonetheless markedly weakened since its apotheosis in the age of Reagan, Thatcher, Clinton and Blair. This is due to underlying structural forces in British politics that compel both the public and the governing class to consider a new set of choices in national strategy, as reflected in recent voter surveys. There is also a profound reassessment of Britain's national interests underway.

This has major implications for the future of British politics, the future of the British economy and the future of the British state. The Iraq War only served to demonstrate how fundamentally the global security context has changed. The consequences have also been dramatic for the United States and American foreign policy. In the decades after the Second World War, it was widely believed that the special relationship was an impregnable feature of the geopolitical landscape.

The reliability of the UK as a dependable ally of the United States is no longer taken for granted, while Britain might emerge as a far more influential actor in Europe. Some voices in the US fear this development, arguing that America's closest ally in the war on terrorism would be unable to operate its own foreign policy and stand alongside America when and where it chose to do so: 'A neutralised Britain would be forced to remain on the sidelines while America confronted rogue states such as Iran, North Korea, and Syria.'[12]

Another scenario is that Britain disengages from foreign affairs, resorting to an independent British policy based on British identity and values. There is an increasingly potent isolationist tendency emerging where the temptation has been to eschew foreign policy activism, giving priority to domestic politics. The complex choice between Europe and America and the strategic dilemmas that it creates for Britain's domestic and foreign policy may revive a more isolationist stance as a major force in British politics.

The temptation to stand apart has been heightened by the withering of familiar Cold War certainties. During that era states knew almost exactly where they stood as a reflection of history and geographical realities. Today, there is no all-encompassing struggle in which every nation-state is engaged. But however painful the choices, divorcing Britain from its strategic partnerships with Europe would have perilous consequences. Detaching it from the international community would also damage British national interests.

The case for British engagement today is stronger than ever. The world of the twentieth century was defined by the power of the state. The world of the twenty-first century is one in which nation-states are fast losing their monopoly of power to a new set of global actors, as well as the awakening of a once passive citizenry. It is an age where, as Jeremy Rifkin argues, 'geographic boundaries of all kinds are loosening or disappearing altogether'.[13] A new strategic and security landscape is emerging as a consequence of the global communications revolution and the ease of mobility across borders.

These circumstances are propelling nations including Britain to seek answers to questions that are increasingly global in scope. What worries most European countries today is not the threat of invasion from their neighbours. It is the spread of nuclear weapons, missiles, and biological and chemical weapons. AIDS and avian flu can flow rapidly between continents, crime operates within global networks, and terrorist activity, like religious fundamentalism, is increasingly trans-national.

In reality there is, of course, a single global superpower in the contemporary international system: the United States. There are emerging powers such as China and India, and also those who because of population and position are likely to join them, including Brazil, South Africa, Nigeria, Indonesia, Egypt and Saudi Arabia. It is clear that gaining influence in the new international order will require regional alliances: NAFTA in North America, Mercosur in South America, the ASEAN pact and, of course, the EU. The emergence of the EU as the global rule-maker in the international economy, 'the regulatory capital of the world', has recently been highlighted.[14]

The other set of changes concerns the future of Europe itself. The preservation of peace in Europe since 1945 has been an astonishing historical accomplishment. Every European country now has a stake in regional and global stability. They want to see a process of orderly change rather than chaos. Nevertheless, the EU has suffered from a deep and intractable malaise. Poor economic performance within the euro zone has made much of Europe deeply resistant to change.[15] The rejection of the constitutional treaty left a cloud of uncertainty hanging in the air about the future of European institutions. The legitimacy of the EU has appreciably diminished among large sections of the European electorate. The European Commission is weaker, and few national leaders appear to care very much about the future of Europe itself.

The weaknesses have been compounded because too many European citizens see the EU as the source of insecurity, rather than a tool to cushion their societies from the destabilising impact of globalisation. These challenges and the mood of anxiety they unleash have been brilliantly encapsulated by the historian Paul Kennedy: 'Today's global society, even before its predecessor sixty years ago, confronts the task of reconciling technological change and economic integration with traditional political structures, national consciousness, social needs, institutional arrangements, and habitual ways of doing things.'[16]

Instead of hesitating nervously about Europe's emerging stake in global stability, the British should be in the vanguard of the argument for Europe as a force for good in managing globalisation and the physical and economic insecurity that it engenders. Sir Stephen Wall, former adviser to the Prime Minister on European affairs, has argued that Europe 'is massively in Britain's interest in a dangerous world where democracy is sometimes under attack and where we need economic strength that comes from working with a group of powerful democracies'.[17] This approach should be combined with a more mature understanding of how Britain's relationship with the United States must evolve.

An influential section of British public opinion and the political class will, of course, never accept that argument. They insist that the movement towards European political union compromises the values of democracy and freedom that are at the heart of the Atlantic alliance.[18] Britain trades with the rest of Europe, but its values and the commitment to collective security are guaranteed by looking across the Atlantic.

This constituency of opinion refuses to accept that the institutionalised defence and intelligence partnership between the UK and the US that has endured for so long needs to be modified and adapted. There is more than a hint of anachronistic thinking here: the perceived threat of WMD proliferation is markedly different in Britain and America, endangering the reinvigoration of the NATO alliance. The technological impact of American military transformation will make the special security partnership considerably less special in the future. British and US interests are inevitably set to diverge: the transatlantic relationship will evolve in a different frame to the post-war fixation with relative national decline.

The old outlook is rooted in the era when the commitment to the Atlantic alliance was a sufficient explanation of the national interest. It fails to acknowledge that new geo-political contours are remaking the context for British foreign policy. The UK cannot remain a pivotal power, to echo Harold Macmillan fifty years ago, simply by preserving the Anglo-American special relationship. This also highlights the tough choices that Britain now faces about its role in the world. As Andrew Gamble has expressed it, 'although Britain will always be part of both Europe and of Anglo-America, there remains a question of priority between the two which was posed ever more insistently by the circumstances leading up to the second Iraq War in 2003'.[19] The Blair government's foreign policy at times exposed the huge contradictions between Europe and America. The opposition of leading European powers to the Bush administration's Iraq policy reflected much wider hostility to increasing American unilateralism and the more profound distaste towards the conservatism of American culture and politics. As Gamble reminds us, the choice between Europe and America for the UK will never be exclusive, but there is a question of priority for the future.

The Cold War may have ended, but the new threats to European security are not figments of the imagination. The emergence of 'home-grown' terrorism is distressingly real. The Middle East is on Europe's doorstep. Europe is at risk from the illegal flow of people, drugs, terrorism and weapons of mass destruction, far more so than the United States, as globalisation continues to erode national borders. Without further consolidation of joint EU capabilities, Europe will merely be a colony of the US and not an equal partner. Yet the Americans will expect Europe to resolve more of its own problems, from relations with Turkey to the growing dependence on Russian gas.

Equally, America's ability to fulfil its top foreign policy priorities, including the defence of the US homeland and winning the war against global terrorism, requires a strong, outward-looking Europe. In fact the United States has a fundamental interest in the enhanced effectiveness of the EU as a global actor. But that requires total British commitment to Europe, not half-hearted acquiescence: the UK must take its place at the heart of a cohesive, unified EU. The time has also come for Europe to revisit its foreign policy priorities such as Russia and the Middle East, as well as reassessing European military capabilities. It should take the next steps such as a new deal between Britain and France that builds on the 1998 St Malo declaration.[20]

Inevitably, the United States relies heavily on peace and stability in Europe. The very fact that Europe is no longer a site of geopolitical competition and conflict is an outstanding historical achievement. It is also clear that Washington needs the influence of the EU to radiate beyond its borders into more fragile democracies such as Turkey, Ukraine, Georgia and the southern Caucasus, the wider Black Sea region and the Middle East. Europe can assist in locking in the transformation towards full democracy. The challenges of the twenty-first century are very different to those of the twentieth. Collaboration on homeland security may be as important today as the Western alliance was in the past for constraining the Soviet empire.

Britain's traditional conception of its role as a pivotal power in the world is incompatible with full participation in Europe. The establishment of a common position with insiders in the EU has to take precedence over bilateral relationships with outsiders. Whether or not the United States is Britain's most important ally, Britain is fundamentally part of Europe. The UK has accepted such obligations over many areas of policy, but not in defence, foreign policy or monetary affairs.

Only by harnessing Europe as an alternative strategic space will Britain begin to resolve the dilemmas of foreign policy and national strategy. Recalibrating Britain's role in the context of changing geo-political forces will be one of the most insistent themes of contemporary British politics in the next generation. The UK may be less dependent on the US, and America perhaps less concerned about Britain. The UK should act as one of the pivots of the new transatlantic partnership within Europe – as the centre of the world's geo-strategic activity shifts towards Asia and the southern hemisphere.

The terms of debate about Britain's defence and security policy have changed irrevocably. Soviet long-range nuclear missiles are no longer targeted at the British Isles. What is of concern to all Western governments is the danger of nuclear proliferation, and the reality that 'rogue states' such as North Korea or Iran might acquire nuclear forces in the future. These are the great challenges for the next decade.

As previous chapters have argued, Britain's post-imperial destiny is to be part of a regional bloc informed by a European rather than an 'Anglo-American' vision of how the global economy and the international system should be organised. Britain's future is centred around the changing shape of the new world economy, the balance between regionalisation and globalisation that is evident in debates about the role of the EU, migration, sovereignty, national identity and climate change. The UK's self-perception of a uniquely global role is incompatible with full participation in the EU.

Britain should make a radical break with the special-relationship illusions that are a hangover from the second half of the twentieth century. In future, British governments will be required to build bridges within the EU as their first priority rather than across the Atlantic. The new transatlanticism must involve a more equal partnership between an effective and united EU and an internationalist United States. This poses multiple challenges – to the traditional German reluctance to contemplate the use of force, to French illusions of a multipolar world and to the Anglo-American pretensions of the post-war age. Britain's world role must shift from one of transatlantic bridging to one of European partnership.

Neither France nor Britain, as the engines of security and foreign policy in Europe over the last four decades, should be enslaved to traditional post-Suez assumptions. Tony Blair discovered that the precarious balancing act between Europe and America is not sustainable. France has acknowledged that it is impossible to unite a Europe of twenty-seven member states against the United States. While in reality Britain is fundamentally attached to Europe, equally, Europe cannot be organised in opposition to the US. The EU needs a coherent approach to foreign policy, but such an approach will be credible only if Britain and France — as the two actors with significant hard power capability and a United Nations Security Council presence — can reach agreement about how to organise Europe in the international system.

This is also a moment of great opportunity for Europe. Globalisation does not inevitably drive individuals back to national governments and the familiar certainties of national identity. Instead, it makes regional organisations such as the EU ever more vital to the stability and security of the world. The historian Niall Ferguson has argued that the EU is an entity on the brink of decline and perhaps ultimately even of destruction. It is certainly the case that the collapse of the Berlin Wall in 1989, 'Europe's 9/11' according to Thomas Friedman,[21] has entirely changed the nature of the EU. It has fuelled numerous national identity problems that remain unresolved, reflected in the rejection of the 2004 draft constitutional treaty in France and the Netherlands. The EU has also been represented as a threat to the living standards and way of life of the hard-working majority.[22]

Of course, all countries and institutions have to cope with destabilising trends, not only the EU. The acceleration of globalisation, the emergence of the world-wide information order and the rise of new forms of individualism and consumer power are inescapable. But the underlying strength of Europe's social model is that equity and solidarity are the major sources of comparative advantage in the global economy, providing the long-term conditions for high-value international competitiveness.

Inevitably, of course, a significant section of the British political class will remain attached to the traditional idea of Britain as a pivotal power bridging Europe and America. The major question in political debate for fifty years has been how the UK should remain a player of global importance when its relative strength is declining. The historical roots of Britain's ambiguous attitude to the EU lie in the conception of Britain as a global trading network centred on London. Britain is still the fifth or sixth largest economy in the world, a major player in the world's financial markets, a permanent member of the UN Security Council and an independent nuclear power. It has key positions in the International Monetary Fund and the World Bank.

Blair's foreign policy, like that of so many previous British Prime Ministers, was to punch above his country's weight – as well as seeking to embrace an ethically progressive vision of Britain's role in the world. In some respects this approach was eminently successful. The UK has an excellent record in pushing other countries towards agreements on debt relief and climate change. Blair led the case for intervention in Kosovo, without which Slobodan Milošević would have pursued ethnic cleansing even further.

Nonetheless, the task of squaring the circle between internationalism, European unity and the Anglo-American relationship was more feasible during the Clinton presidency, when the emphasis was on collaboration, multilateralism and the view of globalisation as a force that harmonised states' interests. There was a shared Third Way vision of the link between economic globalisation and political democratisation, as well as an abiding faith in the unique importance of international institutions. But it also disguised many underlying tensions and dilemmas for British policy that were badly exposed during the Bush presidency.

Britain has just 1 per cent of the world's population and a declining share of production and trade in the global economy. As rising powers such as Brazil, India and China grow in influence, Britain's capacity to shape world events – unless it is in concert with other powers – will continue to diminish. For Britain to contribute to global developments such as combating climate change or alleviating poverty in the developing world, it must punch its weight in Europe. The UK has taken on many burdens which its forces struggle to bear. The most senior British general in Afghanistan has warned that the country is close to anarchy and that Western forces are running out of time.[23] The perils of the mission itself have been vastly under-estimated.

Every British leader since the Second World War has calculated that staying close to America will make Britain a more influential player. Yet as the central premise of Britain's strategic approach to the world this model looks increasingly outdated. It is neither appropriate to the UK's world role post-empire nor valid in the light of recent evidence about the challenges and threats born of rapid globalisation. In the recent Middle East crisis over Lebanon, Britain's almost total acquiescence to US policy prevented it from voicing its own position and projecting influence.

The evidence also suggests that Britain's ambivalent status in Europe has significantly reduced its ability to influence the next stage of European integration and the next phase of the European agenda: consolidating the enlargement of the EU to the east, fashioning the new institutional framework for Europe, developing new regulatory capacities to counter global inequality and contributing to the development of a multipolar world. The greatest danger is that in failing to resolve the complex choice between Europe and America, Britain becomes semi-detached, gravely weakening its economic and military influence in a globalised world.

Indeed, the world is moving, albeit slowly and erratically and despite the unipolarity of the United States, towards a more balanced and complex international system, reflecting the shift of wealth and population away from North America and western Europe. The very supremacy of the West is under direct challenge. Meanwhile, British and other European leaders have to break out of the Cold War mind-set that still awaits Washington's lead in security matters.

In a complex geo-strategic environment Britain cannot resort to simply embracing the best of both worlds: a constructive relationship with the White House that involves no political cost in being close to the US President, and stronger ties to Germany and France that do not require deeper European integration.[24] That is not a credible global strategy and it will prove unsustainable in the longer term. The danger for the UK now is an ambivalent role in Europe combined with lack of influence in Washington.

The alternative to Blair's strategy after Iraq is not for Britain to define itself against Washington, as the French have done since Suez. The philosopher Jürgen Habermas urges Europe to 'offer at least a political counterweight to hegemonic unilateralism',[25] but this divisive stance has little potential as a strategy for global governance. Britain must work with its European allies to set out a common position through which the EU can influence the United States, of course where necessary constraining the misguided unilateralism of American power. The debate should not be about how to refurbish the transatlantic alliance on old Cold War terms, but how to recast the relationship as the global environment changes. This world is likely to produce a landscape in which alliances and allegiances shift constantly, requiring a new kind of international order founded on values of human rights, democracy and justice. We face a future based on what Richard Haass terms 'selective co-operation',[26] where countries are neither automatically predictable adversaries nor allies, placing a premium on consultation and coalition-building to manage the threats inherent in globalisation.

The purpose of *Shifting Alliances* has been to understand the substance of Britain's global strategy and the conception of its world role after empire. There is not a fundamental choice of alignment between Europe and America, but there is a question of priority for Britain to resolve. The challenge is then to forge an ethically progressive notion of foreign policy, acknowledging that basic security is the first priority but relying on coherent principles of justice: a 'moral but muscular' approach, as Amitai Etzioni defines it.[27] It also means thinking expansively about how national interests are defined in an interdependent world, acknowledging that 'our' security and prosperity is likely to be predicated on achieving security and prosperity for others. Too often in the past British governments have over-estimated what they can change in the short term and under-estimated what they can change in the long term.

This new British model of liberal internationalism rooted in the commitment to Europe must intelligently integrate domestic and foreign concerns, bridging the gap between the perpetual demands for humanitarian intervention and our finite capacity to intervene with real effect. It must encourage the development of a global civil society that embeds progressive values and norms to deal with three particular challenges, alluded to in this volume: civic disengagement, loss of accountability through the nation-state, and increasing complexity. An influential British commentator recently remarked that in the last century Britain's leaders saw their job as being to manage decline. Blair saw his as managing ambiguity. For that, he was a natural.[28]

But that ambiguity is not inevitable. Instead of transforming Britain's foreign policy, the Blair government became the unwitting victim of its contradictions.[29] The challenge instead is to fashion a set of subtle but credible assumptions about Britain's role in the world – where the question of priority between Europe and America is at long last resolved, enabling Britain to assume a new kind of global role as an innovator in science, culture, finance and technology: a hub whose language, public sphere and reputation for scientific excellence provide a solid platform for European engagement. Britain would no longer be trapped between two unsatisfactory options; to echo Dean Acheson, she would have lost an empire but at long last found a role.

Notes

Preface

1. *The Prince*.
2. See Andrew Gamble, *Between Europe and America: The Future of British Politics* (Basingstoke: Palgrave Macmillan, 2003). Gamble defines the choice between Europe and America as the defining question for British politics in the early twenty-first century, arguing that the UK increasingly faces a fundamental choice of alignment. I have drawn substantially on Gamble's insights in framing my own arguments about the future of British politics.
3. Ivo H. Daalder and James M. Lindsay, *America Unbound: The Bush Revolution in Foreign Policy* (Washington, DC: Brookings Institution, 2003).
4. See Peter Riddell, *Hug Them Close: Blair, Clinton, Bush and the 'Special Relationship'* (London: Politico's, 2003).
5. Amitai Etzioni, *Security First: For a Muscular, Moral Foreign Policy* (New Haven, CT: Yale University Press, 2007).
6. See for example Philip Stephens, *Tony Blair: The Making of a World Leader* (New York: Viking, 2004); Roger Liddle, *The New Case for Europe: The Crisis in British Pro-Europeanism and How to Overcome It* (London: Fabian Society, 2005).
7. See Alan Milward, 'Approaching Reality: Euro-Money and the Left', *New Left Review* (1996), vol. I/216, pp. 55–65.
8. See Benedict Anderson, *Imagined Communities: Reflections on the Origin and Spread of Nationalism* (London: Verso, 1983).

Introduction

1. Cited in Vernon Bogdanor, 'Footfalls Echoing in the Memory: Britain and Europe in the Twentieth Century – A Historical Perspective', unpublished paper, University of Oxford, 2005.

2. This notion is developed by the British political commentator Peter Riddell in *Hug Them Close: Blair, Clinton, Bush and the 'Special Relationship'* (London: Politico's, 2003).
3. Chris Giles, 'Ties that bind: Bush, Brown and a different relationship', *Financial Times*, 27 July 2007.
4. See Julian Glover and Ewan MacAskill, 'Stand up to US, voters tell Blair', *Guardian*, 25 July 2006.
5. See Polly Toynbee, 'In Europe, not America', *Guardian*, 17 June 2005.
6. See Peter Clarke, *A Question of Leadership: Gladstone to Thatcher* (London: Hamish Hamilton, 1991).
7. See Robert Kagan, *Paradise and Power: America and Europe in the New World Order* (London: Atlantic, 2003).
8. Hugo Young, *This Blessed Plot: Britain and Europe from Churchill to Blair* (London: Macmillan, 1998).
9. See Peter Riddell, *The Unfulfilled Prime Minister: Tony Blair's Quest for a Legacy* (London: Politico's, 2005).
10. The phrase 'warrior satellite' was invented by the British historian Correlli Barnett in *The Verdict of Peace: Britain between Her Yesterday and the Future* (London: Macmillan, 2001).
11. John Callaghan, *The Labour Party and Foreign Policy: A History* (London: Routledge, 2007).
12. Philip Stephens, 'A political awakening that recasts the global landscape', *Financial Times*, 13 July 2007.
13. Jeremy Rifkin, *The European Dream: How Europe's Vision of the Future Is Quietly Eclipsing the American Dream* (Cambridge: Polity, 2004).
14. Peter Unwin, *Hearts, Minds and Interests: Britain's Place in the World* (London: Profile, 1998).
15. Jürgen Habermas, 'Euroskepticism, Market Europe, or a Europe of (World) Citizens?', in *Time of Transitions* (Cambridge: Polity, 2006).

Chapter 1: Bridging the divide?

1. Quoted in J. A. Hobson, *Imperialism*, 3rd ed. (London: George Allen & Unwin, 1938).
2. Cited in Andrew Roberts, *A History of the English-Speaking Peoples since 1900* (London: Weidenfeld & Nicolson, 2006).
3. Quoted in N. J. Ashton, 'A Rear Guard Action: Harold Macmillan and the Making of British Foreign Policy 1957–63', in T. G. Otte

(ed.), *The Makers of British Foreign Policy: From Pitt to Thatcher* (Basingstoke: Palgrave Macmillan, 2001).
4. Quoted in David Dimbleby and David Reynolds, *An Ocean Apart: The Relationship between Britain and America in the Twentieth Century* (London: Hodder & Stoughton, 1988).
5. Paul Addison, *The Road to 1945: British Politics and the Second World War* (London: Jonathan Cape, 1975).
6. See David Reynolds, *From World War to Cold War: Churchill, Roosevelt and the International History of the 1940s* (Oxford: Oxford University Press, 2007).
7. Cited in Peter Hennessy, *Never Again: Britain 1945–51* (London: Jonathan Cape, 1992).
8. See Philip Stephens, 'Capital E', *E!Sharp*, September–October 2006.
9. See Alan S. Milward, *The Rise and Fall of a National Strategy 1945–63* (London: Whitehall History Publishing, 2002).
10. Quoted in Andrew Gamble, *Between Europe and America: The Future of British Politics* (Basingstoke: Palgrave Macmillan, 2003).
11. See John Dumbrell, 'The US–UK Special Relationship after September 11', lecture at the University of Westminster, 14 March 2006.
12. Quoted in Alex Danchev, 'Tony Blair's Vietnam: The Iraq War and the "Special Relationship" in Historical Perspective', *Review of International Studies* (2007), vol. 33, pp. 189–203.
13. See Gamble, *Between Europe and America*.
14. See William Hopkinson, *The Atlantic Crises: Britain, Europe, and Parting from the United States* (Newport, RI: Naval War College Press, 2005).
15. Peter Clarke, *The Last Thousand Days of the British Empire* (London: Allen Lane, 2007).
16. Dimbleby and Reynolds, *An Ocean Apart*.
17. Ronald Hyam, *Britain's Declining Empire: The Road to Decolonisation 1918–1968* (Cambridge: Cambridge University Press, 2007).
18. See Andrew Gamble, *Britain in Decline: Economic Policy, Political Strategy and the British State*, 2nd ed. (London: Macmillan, 1985).
19. See Linda Colley, *Britons: Forging the Nation 1707–1837*, 2nd ed. (London: Yale University Press, 2005).
20. J. D. Chambers, *The Workshop of the World: British Economic History from 1820 to 1880*, 2nd ed. (Oxford: Oxford University Press, 1968).
21. Roberts, *A History of the English-Speaking Peoples since 1900*.

Chapter 2: The Anglo-American alliance and British global strategy since 1945

1. Quoted in Stephen Haseler, *Sidekick: Bulldog to Lapdog – British Global Strategy from Churchill to Blair* (London: Forumpress, 2007).
2. Quoted in Andrew Gamble, 'Hegemony and Empire: British Exceptionalism and the Myth of Anglo-America', paper presented at the Political Studies Association conference, University of Bath, 11–13 April 2007.
3. David Reynolds, *From World War to Cold War: Churchill, Roosevelt and the International History of the 1940s* (Oxford: Oxford University Press, 2007).
4. See Christopher Coker, *The Future of War: The Re-enchantment of War in the Twenty-First Century* (Oxford: Blackwell, 2004).
5. Tony Judt, *Postwar: A History of Europe since 1945* (London: William Heinemann, 2005).
6. Quoted in Christopher Coker, 'Foreign and Defence Policy', unpublished paper, London School of Economics and Political Science, 2005.
7. Quoted in N. J. Ashton, 'A Rear Guard Action: Harold Macmillan and the Making of British Foreign Policy 1957–63', in T. G. Otte (ed.), *The Makers of British Foreign Policy: From Pitt to Thatcher* (Basingstoke: Palgrave Macmillan, 2001).
8. Quoted in David Dimbleby and David Reynolds, *An Ocean Apart: The Relationship between Britain and America in the Twentieth Century* (London: Hodder & Stoughton, 1988).
9. See Andrew Gamble, *Between Europe and America: The Future of British Politics* (Basingstoke: Palgrave Macmillan, 2003).
10. See Rhiannon Vickers, *The Labour Party and the World, vol. 1: The Evolution of Labour's Foreign Policy 1900–51* (Manchester: Manchester University Press, 2004).
11. Quoted in Dimbleby and Reynolds, *An Ocean Apart*.
12. See Alan S. Milward, *The Rise and Fall of a National Strategy 1945–63* (London: Whitehall History Publishing, 2002).
13. See Philip Ziegler, *Wilson: The Authorized Life of Lord Wilson of Rievaulx* (London: Weidenfeld & Nicolson, 1993).
14. See Constantine A. Pagedas, *Anglo-American Strategic Relations and the French Problem 1960–1963: A Troubled Partnership* (London: Frank Cass, 2000).
15. Quoted in Ben Pimlott, *Harold Wilson* (London: HarperCollins, 1992).

16. Rhiannon Vickers, 'Harold Wilson, the Labour Party and the War in Vietnam', paper presented to the British International Studies Association annual conference, Cork, 18–20 December 2006.
17. Quoted in Ziegler, *Harold Wilson*.
18. Quoted in Dimbleby and Reynolds, *An Ocean Apart*.
19. Gamble, *Between Europe and America*.
20. See James E. Cronin, 'Britain and America beyond Empire: Neo-Liberalism, the "Special Relationship", and the Search for Global Order', paper presented to the Conference of Europeanists, Chicago, 1 April 2006.
21. Quoted in Ashton, 'A Rear Guard Action'.
22. Andrew Gamble, *The Free Economy and the Strong State* (Basingstoke: Macmillan, 1988).
23. See Ashton, 'A Rear Guard Action'.
24. See Lee Edwards, *Ronald Reagan: A Political Biography*, rev. ed. (Houston: Nordland, 1981).
25. See Dimbleby and Reynolds, *An Ocean Apart*.
26. Gamble, *The Free Economy and the Strong State*.
27. Quoted in Ashton, 'A Rear Guard Action'.
28. Cited in John Dumbrell, *A Special Relationship?: Anglo-American Relations in the Cold War and After* (Basingstoke: Macmillan, 2001).

Chapter 3: British global strategy in the Blair era

1. Speech at the Foreign and Commonwealth Office leadership conference, 7 January 2004.
2. See Christopher Hill, 'Putting the World to Rights: Tony Blair's Foreign Policy Mission', in Anthony Seldon and Dennis Kavanagh (eds), *The Blair Effect 2001–5* (Cambridge: Cambridge University Press, 2005).
3. Cited in Jason Ralph, *Tony Blair's 'New Doctrine of International Community' and the UK Decision to Invade Iraq* (Leeds: University of Leeds School of Politics and International Studies, 2005).
4. Ibid.
5. Tony Blair, speech at the Bush Presidential Library, College Station, TX, 7 April 2002.
6. Luke Martell, *Globalizations* (Cambridge: Polity, forthcoming).
7. See Andrew Gamble, *Between Europe and America: The Future of British Politics* (Basingstoke: Palgrave Macmillan, 2003).
8. See Colin Hay, *The Political Economy of New Labour: Labouring under False Pretences?* (Manchester: Manchester University Press, 1999).

9. See Steven Philip Kramer, 'Blair's Britain after Iraq', *Foreign Affairs*, July–August 2003.
10. Philip Stephens, 'Capital E', *E!Sharp*, September–October 2006.
11. Joseph S. Nye Jr, 'U.S. Power and Strategy after Iraq', *Foreign Affairs*, July–August 2003.
12. See Peter Riddell, *Hug Them Close: Blair, Clinton, Bush and the 'Special Relationship'* (London: Politico's, 2003).
13. Gamble, *Between Europe and America*.

Chapter 4: Is Britain back?

1. Speech to the British-American Chamber of Commerce, New York, 1997.
2. See Christopher Coker, 'Foreign and Defence Policy', unpublished paper, London School of Economics and Political Science, 2005.
3. See Philip Stephens, 'Time for Britain to look at the world afresh', *Financial Times*, 21 February 2006.
4. See Robert Cooper, *The Breaking of Nations: Order and Chaos in the Twenty-First Century* (London: Atlantic, 2003).
5. See Andrew Gamble, *Between Europe and America: The Future of British Politics* (Basingstoke: Palgrave Macmillan, 2003).

Chapter 5: Tumultuous Britain

1. Hansard, HC Deb, vol. 401, cols 727–8, 17 March 2003.
2. See Andrew Gamble, *Between Europe and America: The Future of British Politics* (Basingstoke: Palgrave Macmillan, 2003).
3. See Irwin Stelzer (ed.), *Neo-Conservatism* (London: Atlantic, 2004).
4. Tony Blair, speech at the Lord Mayor's Banquet, London, 11 November 2002.
5. See Paddy Ashdown, *The Ashdown Diaries, vol. 2: 1997–99* (London: Allen Lane, 2001).
6. Quoted in Peter Riddell, *The Unfulfilled Prime Minister: Tony Blair's Quest for a Legacy* (London: Politico's, 2005).
7. See Philip H. Gordon and Jeremy Shapiro, *Allies at War: America, Europe, and the Crisis over Iraq* (New York: McGraw-Hill, 2004).
8. See John Kampfner, *Blair's Wars* (London: Free Press, 2003).
9. See Riddell, *The Unfulfilled Prime Minister*.
10. See David Frum, *The Right Man: The Surprise Presidency of George W. Bush* (New York: Random House, 2003).

11. Confidential interview with the special adviser to the UK Prime Minister, London, 23 May 2005.
12. Arthur M. Schlesinger, *War and the American Presidency* (New York: W. W. Norton, 2004).
13. See Philip Jenkins, *A History of the United States*, 2nd ed. (Basingstoke: Palgrave Macmillan, 2002).
14. See Thomas L. Friedman, 'War of the worlds', *New York Times*, 24 February 2006.
15. Quoted ibid.
16. See Frum, *The Right Man*.
17. Quoted selectively ibid.
18. See James K. Wither, 'British Bulldog or Bush's Poodle?: Anglo-American Relations and the Iraq War', *Parameters*, Winter 2003–4.
19. See David Coates and Joel Krieger, *Blair's War* (Cambridge: Polity, 2004).
20. See Robert Cooper, *The Breaking of Nations: Order and Chaos in the Twenty-First Century* (London: Atlantic, 2003).
21. See Paul D. Williams, *British Foreign Policy under New Labour 1997–2005* (Basingstoke: Palgrave Macmillan, 2005).
22. Ibid.
23. For further exploration of these arguments see Peter Riddell, *Hug Them Close: Blair, Clinton, Bush and the 'Special Relationship'* (London: Politico's, 2003), p. 118.
24. Matthew d'Ancona, 'Confessions of a Hawkish Hack: the Media and the War on Terror', Philip Geddes Memorial Lecture, University of Oxford, 27 October 2006.
25. Coates and Krieger, *Blair's War*.
26. See Miranda Green, 'Cameron seeks "rebalancing" of alliance', *Financial Times*, 12 September 2006.
27. See Daniel Yankelovich, 'Poll Positions: What Americans Really Think about US Foreign Policy', *Foreign Affairs*, September–October 2005.
28. See Pippa Norris and Joni Lovenduski, 'Why Parties Fail to Learn: Electoral Defeat, Selective Perception, and British Party Politics', *Party Politics* (2004), vol. 10, pp. 83–102.
29. Anthony Wells, 'What Britain thinks of the USA', UK Polling Report website, 4 July 2006.
30. *Spectator*/YouGov poll, 14–15 August 2006.
31. Wells, 'What Britain thinks of the USA'.
32. *Guardian*/ICM poll, 21–23 July 2006.

33. Wells, 'What Britain thinks of the USA'.
34. *American Character Gets Mixed Reviews: US Image Up Slightly, but Still Negative* (Washington, DC: Pew Global Attitudes Project, 2005).
35. See Benedict Brogan and Anthony King, 'Attack on Iraq rejected by 2 in 3 voters', *Daily Telegraph*, 12 August 2002. The poll also found that 68 per cent had 'not much confidence' or 'no confidence at all' in Bush's ability to manage the Iraq crisis.
36. Cited in James K. Wither, 'British Bulldog or Bush's Poodle? Anglo-American Relations and the Iraq War', *Parameters*, Winter 2003–4.
37. See Wells, 'What Britain thinks of the USA'.
38. See *American Character Gets Mixed Reviews*.
39. See Tony Judt, *Postwar: A History of Europe since 1945* (London: William Heinemann, 2005).
40. Rodric Braithwaite, 'The end of the affair', *Prospect*, May 2003.
41. Benedict Anderson, *Imagined Communities: Reflections on the Origins and Spread of Nationalism*, rev. ed. (London: Verso, 1991).
42. The 'Anglosphere' is defined by the British historian Andrew Roberts as 'the union of the English-speaking peoples' embracing the United States, Britain, Canada, Australia, New Zealand, the British West Indies, and more often than not the Republic of Ireland.
43. See Gamble, *Between Europe and America*.
44. See Lawrence Freedman, 'The Transatlantic Agenda: Vision and Counter-Vision', *Survival* (2005), vol. 47, no. 4, pp. 19–38.
45. See James E. Cronin, 'Convergence by Conviction: Politics and Economics in the Emergence of the "Anglo-American Model"', *Journal of Social History* (2000), vol. 33, pp. 781–804.
46. Ibid.
47. See Michael Spicer, *A Treaty Too Far: A New Policy for Europe* (London: Fourth Estate, 1992).
48. See Tom Sefton, *A Fair Share of Welfare: Public Spending on Children in England* (London: Centre for Analysis of Social Exclusion, 2004).
49. See Alberto Alesina and Edward L. Glaeser, *Fighting Poverty in the US and Europe: A World of Difference* (Oxford: Oxford University Press, 2004).
50. See Robert Putnam, *Bowling Alone: The Collapse and Revival of American Community* (New York: Simon & Schuster, 2000).
51. Quoted in John Kampfner, *Blair's Wars* (London: Free Press, 2003).

Chapter 6: Towards a new geo-strategic landscape

1. Address to Joint Session of Congress, 20 September 2001.
2. See David Coates and Joel Krieger, *Blair's War* (Cambridge: Polity, 2004).
3. Philip Stephens, 'The debate about Europe is haunted by shared delusions', *Financial Times*, 22 June 2007.
4. See Robert Cooper, *The Breaking of Nations: Order and Chaos in the Twenty-First Century* (London: Atlantic, 2003).
5. Chris Patten, *Not Quite the Diplomat: Home Truths about World Affairs* (London: Allen Lane, 2005).
6. See Paul Rogers, 'Gordon Brown's white elephants', OpenDemocracy website, 26 July 2007.
7. See Charles Kupchan, *The End of the American Era: U.S. Foreign Policy and the Geopolitics of the 21st Century* (New York: Alfred A. Knopf, 2002).
8. Ian Kearns, 'From crisis to strategy: new thinking on national security', OpenDemocracy website, 1 June 2007.
9. See Coates and Krieger, *Blair's War*.
10. Admiral Sir Michael Boyce, 'Achieving Effect', Annual Chief of Defence Staff Lecture, Royal United Services Institute, 18 December 2002.
11. See Richard Norton-Taylor and Tania Branigan, 'Army chief: British troops must pull out of Iraq soon', *Guardian*, 13 October 2006.
12. For this point, see William Hopkinson, *The Atlantic Crises: Britain, Europe, and Parting from the United States* (Newport, RI: Naval War College Press, 2005).
13. Cited in Peter Riddell, *Hug Them Close: Blair, Clinton, Bush and the 'Special Relationship'*, rev. ed. (London: Politico's, 2004).
14. See Robert Cooper, *The Post-Modern State and the World Order* (London: Demos, 1996).
15. See Mary Kaldor, Mary Martin and Sabine Selchow, 'Human Security: A New Strategic Narrative for Europe', *International Affairs* (2007), vol. 83, pp. 273–88.
16. See Hopkinson, *The Atlantic Crises*.
17. See Stephen Wall, 'In hock to George Bush', *Guardian*, 28 July 2006.
18. See Coates and Krieger, *Blair's War*.

Chapter 7: American perceptions of Britain and the world

1. *The Right Nation: Why America Is Different* (London: Penguin, 2004).
2. See Andrei Markovits, *European Anti-Americanism (and Anti-Semitism): Ever Present Though Always Denied* (Ann Arbor: University of Michigan Centre for European Studies, 2003).
3. Ian Kearns, 'Cameron throws down foreign policy challenge', Progress website, 16 October 2006.
4. See Andrew Gamble, *Between Europe and America: The Future of British Politics* (Basingstoke: Palgrave Macmillan, 2003).
5. See Conrad P. Waligorski, *John Kenneth Galbraith: The Economist as Political Theorist* (Lanham, MD: Rowman & Littlefield, 2006).
6. See Daniel Yankelovich, 'Poll Positions: What Americans Really Think about US Foreign Policy', *Foreign Affairs*, September–October 2005.
7. See Micklethwait and Wooldridge, *The Right Nation*.
8. See Ed Pilkington, '300 million and counting...: US reaches population milestone', *Guardian*, 13 October 2006.
9. See Micklethwait and Wooldridge, *The Right Nation*.
10. Ibid.
11. John Micklethwait, 'The Bush Re-Election and Foreign Policy after Bush', *International Politics* (2005), vol. 42, pp. 499–510.
12. Seymour Martin Lipset, *American Exceptionalism: A Double-Edged Sword* (New York: W. W. Norton, 1996).
13. See Micklethwait and Wooldridge, *The Right Nation*.
14. Ibid.
15. See Niall Ferguson, *Empire: How Britain Made the Modern World* (London: Penguin, 2004).
16. 'The sound of dissent', *Daily Telegraph*, 29 January 2006.

Chapter 8: Europe as a strategic actor in the world

1. See Philip Stephens, 'Europe cannot afford to retreat from the world', *Financial Times*, 12 July 2005.
2. See Robin Niblett, 'Europe Inside Out', *Washington Quarterly*, Winter 2005–06.
3. Jürgen Habermas, *The Divided West*, tr. Ciaran Cronin (Cambridge: Polity, 2006).

4. Condoleezza Rice, 'Campaign 2000: Promoting the National Interest', *Foreign Affairs*, January–February 2000.
5. See Bill Cash, 'United States Policy on European Integration: An Understandable but Strategic Error since 1990', *European Journal*, March–April 2006.
6. Ulrich Albrecht, Christine Chinkin, Kemal Dervis, Renata Dwan, Anthony Giddens, Nicole Gnesotto, Mary Kaldor, Sonja Licht, Jan Pronk, Klaus Reinhardt, Geneviève Schméder, Pavel Seifter and Narcís Serra, *A Human Security Doctrine for Europe: The Barcelona Report of the Study Group on Europe's Security Capabilities* (2004).
7. See ibid.
8. See Mary Kaldor, *New and Old Wars: Organized Violence in a Global Era* (Palo Alto, CA: Stanford University Press, 1999).
9. See Hugh Williamson, 'Germany's military to take on global role', *Financial Times*, 25 October 2006.
10. See Hans-Christian Hagman, *European Crisis Management and Defence: The Search for Capabilities* (Oxford: Oxford University Press, 2002).
11. The six were France, Germany, Italy, the Netherlands, Poland and the UK. The poll was conducted by the German Marshall Fund of the United States and the Chicago Council for Foreign Relations in June–July 2002. Press release, 4 September 2002.
12. See William Wallace, 'Europe should fill the global leadership gap', *Financial Times*, 27 September 2006.
13. Richard Laming, 'A treaty for foreign policy', EUobserver website, 28 June 2007.
14. See Tony Judt, *Postwar: A History of Europe since 1945* (London: William Heinemann, 2005).
15. See Mark Mazower, *Dark Continent: Europe's Twentieth Century* (London: Allen Lane, 1998).
16. Robert Cooper, *The Breaking of Nations: Order and Chaos in the Twenty-First Century* (London: Atlantic, 2003).
17. See Rodric Braithwaite, 'The end of the affair', *Prospect*, May 2003.
18. See 'The hobbled hegemon: American power', *Economist*, 30 June 2007.
19. See David Coates and Joel Krieger, *Blair's War* (Cambridge: Polity, 2004).
20. See Anthony Giddens, *Europe in the Global Age* (Cambridge: Polity, 2006).

Chapter 9: The future of Britain and Europe

1. Quoted in Andrew Gamble, *Between Europe and America: The Future of British Politics* (Basingstoke: Palgrave Macmillan, 2003).
2. Quoted in P. Sharp, 'British Foreign Policy under Margaret Thatcher', in T. G. Otte (ed.), *The Makers of British Foreign Policy* (Basingstoke: Palgrave Macmillan, 2001).
3. Quoted in Ian Bache and Andrew Jordan, 'Britain in Europe and Europe in Britain', in Ian Bache and Andrew Jordan (eds), *The Europeanization of British Politics* (Basingstoke: Palgrave Macmillan, 2006).
4. See David Marquand, *The Unprincipled Society* (London: Jonathan Cape, 1988).
5. The concept of Britain as the 'awkward partner' is developed in Stephen George, *The Awkward Partner: Britain in the European Community*, 3rd ed. (Oxford: Oxford University Press, 1998).
6. See Gamble, *Between Europe and America*.
7. See Peter Hennessy, *Having It So Good: Britain in the Fifties* (London: Allen Lane, 2006).
8. See Roger Liddle, *The New Case for Europe: The Crisis in British Pro-Europeanism and How to Overcome It* (London: Fabian Society, 2005).
9. Speech in the House of Commons, 16 May 1947.
10. See Andrew Gamble, *Britain in Decline: Economic Policy, Political Strategy and the British State* (London: Macmillan, 1981).
11. See David Dimbleby and David Reynolds, *An Ocean Apart: The Relationship between Britain and America in the Twentieth Century* (London: Hodder & Stoughton, 1988).
12. See Andrew Shonfield, *Modern Capitalism: The Changing Balance of Public and Private Power*, 2nd ed. (Oxford: Oxford University Press, 1969).
13. A. J. P. Taylor, *English History 1914–1945*, rev. ed. (Harmondsworth: Penguin, 1975).
14. George Orwell, *The Road to Wigan Pier* (London: Victor Gollancz, 1937).
15. See Andrew Gamble, 'A British Miracle?: The UK Model of Capitalism', paper presented at the Political Studies Association conference, University of Lincoln, April 2004.
16. See Vernon Bogdanor, 'Footfalls Echoing in the Memory: Britain and Europe in the Twentieth Century – A Historical Perspective', unpublished paper, University of Oxford, 2005.

17. Jean Monnet, *Memoirs*, tr. Richard Mayne (London: Collins, 1978).
18. Quoted in Gamble, *Between Europe and America*.
19. See Andrew Gamble, *Britain in Decline: Economic Policy, Political Strategy and the British State*, 4th ed. (Basingstoke: Macmillan, 1994).
20. See Gamble, 'A British Miracle?'.
21. Ibid.
22. See Rhiannon Vickers, *The Labour Party and the World, vol. 1: The Evolution of Labour's Foreign Policy 1900–51* (Manchester: Manchester University Press, 2004).
23. See Gamble, *Between Europe and America*.
24. See Gamble, *Britain in Decline*.
25. Cited in Kevin Jefferys, *Anthony Crosland* (London: Richard Cohen, 1999).
26. See Liddle, *The New Case for Europe*.
27. See Stephen George and Matthew Sowemimo, 'Conservative Foreign Policy towards the European Union', in Steve Ludlam and Martin J. Smith (eds), *Contemporary British Conservatism* (Basingstoke: Macmillan, 1996).
28. YouGov/*Spectator* poll, 23 August 2006.
29. See Bache and Jordan, 'Britain in Europe and Europe in Britain'.
30. See Liddle, *The New Case for Europe*.
31. Ed Balls, *Britain and Europe: A City Minister's Perspective* (London: Centre for European Reform, 2007).
32. See Nick Pearce and Julia Margo (eds), *Politics for a New Generation: The Progressive Moment* (Basingstoke: Palgrave Macmillan, 2007).
33. *European Growth and Jobs Monitor* (Frankfurt: Allianz Dresdner Economic Research / Brussels: Lisbon Council), 2007.
34. *Economic Assessment of the Barriers to the Internal Market for Services* (Copenhagen: Copenhagen Economics, 2004).
35. See Anthony Giddens, Patrick Diamond and Roger Liddle (eds), *Global Europe, Social Europe* (Cambridge: Polity, 2006).
36. See Gene Sperling, *The Pro-Growth Progressive: An Economic Strategy for Shared Prosperity* (New York: Simon & Schuster, 2005).
37. Mića Panić, 'Does Europe Need Neoliberal Reforms?', *Cambridge Journal of Economics* (2007), vol. 31, pp. 145–69.
38. See Geoff Mulgan, *Connexity: How to Live in a Connected World* (London: Chatto & Windus, 1997).
39. Loukas Tsoukalis, *What Kind of Europe?* (Oxford: Oxford University Press, 2003).
40. Sharp, 'British Foreign Policy under Margaret Thatcher'.

41. Tsoukalis, *What Kind of Europe?*.
42. See Giddens et. al, *Global Europe, Social Europe*.

Conclusion

1. Speech at Harvard University, March 1943.
2. Walter Russell Mead, *God and Gold: Britain, America and the Making of the Modern World* (London: Atlantic, 2007).
3. See *American Character Gets Mixed Reviews: US Image Up Slightly, but Still Negative* (Washington, DC: Pew Global Attitudes Project, 2005).
4. See Peter Riddell, *The Unfulfilled Prime Minister: Tony Blair's Quest for a Legacy* (London: Politico's, 2005).
5. See Clara Marina O'Donnell and Richard G. Whitman, 'European Policy under Gordon Brown: Perspectives on a Future Prime Minister', *International Affairs* (2007), vol. 83, pp. 253–72.
6. Ian Kearns, 'Cameron throws down foreign policy challenge', Progress website, 16 October 2006.
7. See David Clark, 'Britain's bridge across the Atlantic is fated to collapse', *Guardian*, 14 May 2002; Mark Leonard, *Network Europe: The New Case for Europe* (London: Foreign Policy Centre, 1999).
8. See Robert Kagan, 'Power and Weakness', *Policy Review*, June–July 2002.
9. See Jürgen Habermas, *The Divided West*, tr. Ciaran Cronin (Cambridge: Polity, 2006).
10. Kurt Volker, 'The United States and the European Union: A Renewed Partnership Delivering Results', remarks at the New Instruments of International Governance: Transatlantic and Global Perspectives conference, Good Governance Consortium, Vienna, 11 May 2006.
11. See Anthony Giddens, *Europe in the Global Age* (Cambridge: Polity, 2006).
12. See Nile Gardiner and John Hulsman, 'Britain is the key to Bush project of flexible Europe', *Business*, 20 February 2005.
13. Jeremy Rifkin, *The European Dream: How Europe's Vision of the Future Is Quietly Eclipsing the American Dream* (Cambridge: Polity, 2004).
14. Tobias Buck, 'Standard bearer: how the European Union exports its laws', *Financial Times*, 10 July 2007.
15. See Charles Grant, *Europe's Blurred Boundaries: Rethinking Enlargement and Neighbourhood Policy* (London: Centre for European Reform, 2006).

16. Paul Kennedy, *Preparing for the Twenty-First Century* (New York: Vintage, 1994).
17. Interview on *Today*, BBC Radio 4, 28 September 2004.
18. See Bill Cash, 'United States Policy on European Integration: An Understandable but Strategic Error since 1990', *European Journal*, March–April 2006.
19. Andrew Gamble, *Between Europe and America: The Future of British Politics* (Basingstoke: Palgrave Macmillan, 2003).
20. See Philip Stephens, 'Capital E', *E!Sharp*, September–October 2006.
21. See Thomas Friedman, *The World Is Flat: A Brief History of the Twenty-First Century* (New York: Farrar, Straus & Giroux, 2005).
22. See Rene Cuperus, 'The Vulnerability of the European Project', in Anthony Giddens, Patrick Diamond and Roger Liddle (eds), *Global Europe, Social Europe* (Cambridge: Polity, 2006).
23. See Andrew Rawnsley, 'It wasn't the "Yo" that was humiliating, it was the "No"', *Observer*, 23 July 2006.
24. Chris Giles, 'Ties that bind: Bush, Brown and a different relationship', *Financial Times*, 27 July 2007.
25. Habermas, *The Divided West*.
26. Richard N. Haass, 'The Palmerstonian Moment', *National Interest* (2008), no. 93.
27. Amitai Etzioni, *Security First: For a Muscular, Moral Foreign Policy* (New Haven, CT: Yale University Press, 2007).
28. John Rentoul, 'His policy on Europe is a failure. But can you really blame the man?', *Independent on Sunday*, 20 June 2004.
29. Riddell, *The Unfulfilled Prime Minister*.

Bibliography

Paul Addison, *The Road to 1945: British Politics and the Second World War* (London: Jonathan Cape, 1975).

Ulrich Albrecht, Christine Chinkin, Kemal Dervis, Renata Dwan, Anthony Giddens, Nicole Gnesotto, Mary Kaldor, Sonja Licht, Jan Pronk, Klaus Reinhardt, Geneviève Schméder, Pavel Seifter and Narcís Serra, *A Human Security Doctrine for Europe: The Barcelona Report of the Study Group on Europe's Security Capabilities* (2004).

Alberto Alesina and Edward L. Glaeser, *Fighting Poverty in the US and Europe: A World of Difference* (Oxford: Oxford University Press, 2004).

American Character Gets Mixed Reviews: US Image Up Slightly, but Still Negative (Washington, DC: Pew Global Attitudes Project, 2005).

Matthew d'Ancona, 'Confessions of a Hawkish Hack: the Media and the War on Terror', Philip Geddes Memorial Lecture, University of Oxford, 27 October 2006.

Benedict Anderson, *Imagined Communities: Reflections on the Origin and Spread of Nationalism* (London: Verso, 1983).

Benedict Anderson, *Imagined Communities: Reflections on the Origins and Spread of Nationalism*, rev. ed. (London: Verso, 1991).

Paddy Ashdown, *The Ashdown Diaries, vol. 2: 1997–99* (London: Allen Lane, 2001).

N. J. Ashton, 'A Rear Guard Action: Harold Macmillan and the Making of British Foreign Policy 1957–63', in T. G. Otte (ed.), *The Makers of British Foreign Policy: From Pitt to Thatcher* (Basingstoke: Palgrave Macmillan, 2001).

Ian Bache and Andrew Jordan, 'Britain in Europe and Europe in Britain', in Ian Bache and Andrew Jordan (eds), *The Europeanization of British Politics* (Basingstoke: Palgrave Macmillan, 2006).

Ed Balls, *Britain and Europe: A City Minister's Perspective* (London: Centre for European Reform, 2007).

Correlli Barnett, *The Verdict of Peace: Britain between Her Yesterday and the Future* (London: Macmillan, 2001).

Vernon Bogdanor, 'Footfalls Echoing in the Memory: Britain and Europe in the Twentieth Century – A Historical Perspective', unpublished paper, University of Oxford, 2005.

Admiral Sir Michael Boyce, 'Achieving Effect', Annual Chief of Defence Staff Lecture, Royal United Services Institute, 18 December 2002.

Rodric Braithwaite, 'The end of the affair', *Prospect*, May 2003.

Benedict Brogan and Anthony King, 'Attack on Iraq rejected by 2 in 3 voters', *Daily Telegraph*, 12 August 2002.

Tobias Buck, 'Standard bearer: how the European Union exports its laws', *Financial Times*, 10 July 2007.

Edmund Burke, *Select Works*, ed. E. J. Payne (Clark, NJ: Lawbook Exchange, [1881] 2005).

John Callaghan, *The Labour Party and Foreign Policy: A History* (London: Routledge, 2007).

Bill Cash, 'United States Policy on European Integration: An Understandable but Strategic Error since 1990', *European Journal*, March–April 2006.

J. D. Chambers, *The Workshop of the World: British Economic History from 1820 to 1880*, 2nd ed. (Oxford: Oxford University Press, 1968).

David Clark, 'Britain's bridge across the Atlantic is fated to collapse', *Guardian*, 14 May 2002.

Peter Clarke, *The Last Thousand Days of the British Empire* (London: Allen Lane, 2007).

Peter Clarke, *A Question of Leadership: Gladstone to Thatcher* (London: Hamish Hamilton, 1991).

David Coates and Joel Krieger, *Blair's War* (Cambridge: Polity, 2004).

Christopher Coker, 'Foreign and Defence Policy', unpublished paper, London School of Economics and Political Science, 2005.

Christopher Coker, *The Future of War: The Re-enchantment of War in the Twenty-First Century* (Oxford: Blackwell, 2004).

Linda Colley, *Britons: Forging the Nation 1707–1837*, 2nd ed. (London: Yale University Press, 2005).

Robert Cooper, *The Breaking of Nations: Order and Chaos in the Twenty-First Century* (London: Atlantic, 2003).

Robert Cooper, *The Post-Modern State and the World Order* (London: Demos, 1996).

James E. Cronin, 'Britain and America beyond Empire: Neo-Liberalism, the "Special Relationship", and the Search for Global Order', paper presented to the Conference of Europeanists, Chicago, 1 April 2006.

James E. Cronin, 'Convergence by Conviction: Politics and Economics in the Emergence of the "Anglo-American Model"', *Journal of Social History* (2000), vol. 33, pp. 781–804.

Rene Cuperus, 'The Vulnerability of the European Project', in Anthony Giddens, Patrick Diamond and Roger Liddle (eds), *Global Europe, Social Europe* (Cambridge: Polity, 2006).

Ivo H. Daalder and James M. Lindsay, *America Unbound: The Bush Revolution in Foreign Policy* (Washington, DC: Brookings Institution, 2003).

Alex Danchev, 'Tony Blair's Vietnam: The Iraq War and the "Special Relationship" in Historical Perspective', *Review of International Studies* (2007), vol. 33, pp. 189–203.

David Dimbleby and David Reynolds, *An Ocean Apart: The Relationship between Britain and America in the Twentieth Century* (London: Hodder & Stoughton, 1988).

John Dumbrell, *A Special Relationship?: Anglo-American Relations in the Cold War and After* (Basingstoke: Macmillan, 2001).

John Dumbrell, 'The US–UK Special Relationship after September 11', lecture at the University of Westminster, 14 March 2006.

Economic Assessment of the Barriers to the Internal Market for Services (Copenhagen: Copenhagen Economics, 2004).

Lee Edwards, *Ronald Reagan: A Political Biography*, rev. ed. (Houston: Nordland, 1981).

Amitai Etzioni, *Security First: For a Muscular, Moral Foreign Policy* (New Haven, CT: Yale University Press, 2007).

Euro-barometer survey, European Commission, May 2006.

European Growth and Jobs Monitor (Frankfurt: Allianz Dresdner Economic Research / Brussels: Lisbon Council), 2007.

Niall Ferguson, *Empire: How Britain Made the Modern World* (London: Penguin, 2004).

Lawrence Freedman, 'The Transatlantic Agenda: Vision and Counter-Vision', *Survival* (2005), vol. 47, no. 4, pp. 19–38.

Thomas L. Friedman, 'War of the worlds', *New York Times*, 24 February 2006.

Thomas Friedman, *The World Is Flat: A Brief History of the Twenty-First Century* (New York: Farrar, Straus & Giroux, 2005).

David Frum, *The Right Man: The Surprise Presidency of George W. Bush* (New York: Random House, 2003).

Andrew Gamble, *Between Europe and America: The Future of British Politics* (Basingstoke: Palgrave Macmillan, 2003).

Andrew Gamble, *Britain in Decline: Economic Policy, Political Strategy and the British State* (London: Macmillan, 1981).

Andrew Gamble, 'A British Miracle? The UK Model of Capitalism', paper presented at the Political Studies Association conference, University of Lincoln, April 2004.

Andrew Gamble, *The Free Economy and the Strong State* (Basingstoke: Macmillan, 1984).

Andrew Gamble, 'Hegemony and Empire: British Exceptionalism and the Myth of Anglo-America', paper presented at the Political Studies Association conference, University of Bath, 11–13 April 2007.

Nile Gardiner and John Hulsman, 'Britain is the key to Bush project of flexible Europe', *Business*, 20 February 2005.

Stephen George, *The Awkward Partner: Britain in the European Community*, 3rd ed. (Oxford: Oxford University Press, 1998).

Stephen George and Matthew Sowemimo, 'Conservative Foreign Policy towards the European Union', in Steve Ludlam and Martin J. Smith (eds), *Contemporary British Conservatism* (Basingstoke: Macmillan, 1996).

Anthony Giddens, *The Nation-State and Violence* (Cambridge: Polity, 1985).

Anthony Giddens, Patrick Diamond and Roger Liddle (eds), *Global Europe, Social Europe* (Cambridge: Polity, 2006).

Chris Giles, 'Ties that bind: Bush, Brown and a different relationship', *Financial Times*, 27 July 2007.

Julian Glover and Ewan MacAskill, 'Stand up to US, voters tell Blair', *Guardian*, 25 July 2006.

Philip H. Gordon and Jeremy Shapiro, *Allies at War: America, Europe, and the Crisis over Iraq* (New York: McGraw-Hill, 2004).

Charles Grant, *Europe's Blurred Boundaries: Rethinking Enlargement and Neighbourhood Policy* (London: Centre for European Reform, 2006).

Miranda Green, 'Cameron seeks "rebalancing" of alliance', *Financial Times*, 12 September 2006.

Richard N. Haass, 'The Palmerstonian Moment', *National Interest* (2008), no. 93.

Jürgen Habermas, *The Divided West*, tr. Ciaran Cronin (Cambridge: Polity, 2006).

Jürgen Habermas, *Time of Transitions* (Cambridge: Polity, 2006).

Hans-Christian Hagman, *European Crisis Management and Defence: The Search for Capabilities* (Oxford: Oxford University Press, 2002).

Stephen Haseler, *Sidekick: Bulldog to Lapdog – British Global Strategy from Churchill to Blair* (London: Forumpress, 2007).

Colin Hay, *The Political Economy of New Labour: Labouring under False Pretences?* (Manchester: Manchester University Press, 1999).

David Held and Anthony McGrew (eds), *The Global Transformations Reader: An Introduction to the Globalization Debate*, 2nd ed. (Cambridge: Polity, 2003).

Peter Hennessy, *Having It So Good: Britain in the Fifties* (London: Allen Lane, 2006).

Peter Hennessy, *Never Again: Britain 1945–51* (London: Jonathan Cape, 1992).

Christopher Hill, 'Putting the World to Rights: Tony Blair's Foreign Policy Mission', in Anthony Seldon and Dennis Kavanagh (eds), *The Blair Effect 2001–5* (Cambridge: Cambridge University Press, 2005).

'The hobbled hegemon: American power', *Economist*, 30 June 2007.

J. A. Hobson, *Imperialism*, 3rd ed. (London: George Allen & Unwin, 1938).

William Hopkinson, *The Atlantic Crises: Britain, Europe, and Parting from the United States* (Newport, RI: Naval War College Press, 2005).

Ronald Hyam, *Britain's Declining Empire: The Road to Decolonisation 1918–1968* (Cambridge: Cambridge University Press, 2007).

Kevin Jefferys, *Anthony Crosland* (London: Richard Cohen, 1999).

Philip Jenkins, *A History of the United States*, 2nd ed. (Basingstoke: Palgrave Macmillan, 2002).

Tony Judt, *Postwar: A History of Europe since 1945* (London: William Heinemann, 2005).

Robert Kagan, *Paradise and Power: America and Europe in the New World Order* (London: Atlantic, 2003).

Robert Kagan, 'Power and Weakness', *Policy Review*, June–July 2002.

Mary Kaldor, *New and Old Wars: Organized Violence in a Global Era* (Palo Alto, CA: Stanford University Press, 1999).

Mary Kaldor, Mary Martin and Sabine Selchow, 'Human Security: A New Strategic Narrative for Europe', *International Affairs* (2007), vol. 83, pp. 273–88.

John Kampfner, *Blair's Wars* (London: Free Press, 2003).

Ian Kearns, 'Cameron throws down foreign policy challenge', Progress website, 16 October 2006.

Ian Kearns, 'From crisis to strategy: new thinking on national security', OpenDemocracy website, 1 June 2007.

Paul Kennedy, *Preparing for the Twenty-First Century* (New York: Vintage, 1994).

Steven Philip Kramer, 'Blair's Britain after Iraq', *Foreign Affairs*, July–August 2003.

Charles Kupchan, *The End of the American Era: U.S. Foreign Policy and the Geopolitics of the 21st Century* (New York: Alfred A. Knopf, 2002).

Richard Laming, 'A treaty for foreign policy', EUobserver website, 28 June 2007.

Mark Leonard, *Network Europe: The New Case for Europe* (London: Foreign Policy Centre, 1999).

Roger Liddle, *The New Case for Europe: The Crisis in British Pro-Europeanism and How to Overcome It* (London: Fabian Society, 2005).

Seymour Martin Lipset, *American Exceptionalism: A Double-Edged Sword* (New York: W. W. Norton, 1996).

Niccolò Machiavelli, *The Prince*, tr. George Bull, rev. ed. (London: Penguin, 1999).

Andrei Markovits, *European Anti-Americanism (and Anti-Semitism): Ever Present Though Always Denied* (Ann Arbor: University of Michigan Centre for European Studies, 2003).

David Marquand, *The Unprincipled Society* (London: Jonathan Cape, 1988).

Luke Martell, *Globalizations* (Cambridge: Polity, forthcoming).

Mark Mazower, *Dark Continent: Europe's Twentieth Century* (London: Allen Lane, 1998).

Walter Russell Mead, *God and Gold: Britain, America and the Making of the Modern World* (London: Atlantic, 2007).

John Micklethwait, 'The Bush Re-Election and Foreign Policy after Bush', *International Politics* (2005), vol. 42, pp. 499–510.

John Micklethwait and Adrian Wooldridge, *The Right Nation: Why America Is Different* (London: Penguin, 2004).

Alan Milward, 'Approaching Reality: Euro-Money and the Left', *New Left Review* (1996), vol. I/216, pp. 55–65.

Alan S. Milward, *The Rise and Fall of a National Strategy 1945–63* (London: Whitehall History Publishing, 2002).

Jean Monnet, *Memoirs*, tr. Richard Mayne (London: Collins, 1978).

Geoff Mulgan, *Connexity: How to Live in a Connected World* (London: Chatto & Windus, 1997).

Robin Niblett, 'Europe Inside Out', *Washington Quarterly*, Winter 2005–06.

Pippa Norris and Joni Lovenduski, 'Why Parties Fail to Learn: Electoral Defeat, Selective Perception, and British Party Politics', *Party Politics* (2004), vol. 10, pp. 83–102.

Richard Norton-Taylor and Tania Branigan, 'Army chief: British troops must pull out of Iraq soon', *Guardian*, 13 October 2006.

Joseph S. Nye Jr, 'U.S. Power and Strategy after Iraq', *Foreign Affairs*, July–August 2003.

Clara Marina O'Donnell and Richard G. Whitman, 'European Policy under Gordon Brown: Perspectives on a Future Prime Minister', *International Affairs* (2007), vol. 83, pp. 253–72.

George Orwell, *The Road to Wigan Pier* (London: Victor Gollancz, 1937).

Constantine A. Pagedas, *Anglo-American Strategic Relations and the French Problem 1960–1963: A Troubled Partnership* (London: Frank Cass, 2000).

Mića Panić, 'Does Europe Need Neoliberal Reforms?', *Cambridge Journal of Economics* (2007), vol. 31, pp. 145–69.

Chris Patten, *Not Quite the Diplomat: Home Truths about World Affairs* (London: Allen Lane, 2005).

Nick Pearce and Julia Margo (eds), *Politics for a New Generation: The Progressive Moment* (Basingstoke: Palgrave Macmillan, 2007).

Ed Pilkington, '300 million and counting. . .: US reaches population milestone', *Guardian*, 13 October 2006.

Ben Pimlott, *Harold Wilson* (London: HarperCollins, 1992).

Robert Putnam, *Bowling Alone: The Collapse and Revival of American Community* (New York: Simon & Schuster, 2000).

Jason Ralph, *Tony Blair's 'New Doctrine of International Community' and the UK Decision to Invade Iraq* (Leeds: University of Leeds School of Politics and International Studies, 2005).

Andrew Rawnsley, 'It wasn't the "Yo" that was humiliating, it was the "No"', *Observer*, 23 July 2006.

John Rentoul, 'His policy on Europe is a failure. But can you really blame the man?', *Independent on Sunday*, 20 June 2004.

David Reynolds, *From World War to Cold War: Churchill, Roosevelt and the International History of the 1940s* (Oxford: Oxford University Press, 2007).

Condoleezza Rice, 'Campaign 2000: Promoting the National Interest', *Foreign Affairs*, January–February 2000.

Peter Riddell, *The Unfulfilled Prime Minister: Tony Blair's Quest for a Legacy* (London: Politico's, 2005).

Jeremy Rifkin, *The European Dream: How Europe's Vision of the Future Is Quietly Eclipsing the American Dream* (Cambridge: Polity, 2004).

Andrew Roberts, *A History of the English-Speaking Peoples since 1900* (London: Weidenfeld & Nicolson, 2006).

Paul Rogers, 'Gordon Brown's white elephants', OpenDemocracy website, 26 July 2007.

Arthur M. Schlesinger, *War and the American Presidency* (New York: W. W. Norton, 2004).

Tom Sefton, *A Fair Share of Welfare: Public Spending on Children in England* (London: Centre for Analysis of Social Exclusion, 2004).

P. Sharp, 'British Foreign Policy under Margaret Thatcher', in T. G. Otte (ed.), *The Makers of British Foreign Policy* (Basingstoke: Palgrave Macmillan, 2001).

Andrew Shonfield, *Modern Capitalism: The Changing Balance of Public and Private Power*, 2nd ed. (Oxford: Oxford University Press, 1969).

Larry Siedentop, *Democracy in Europe* (London: Allen Lane, 2000).

'The sound of dissent', *Daily Telegraph*, 29 January 2006.

Gene Sperling, *The Pro-Growth Progressive: An Economic Strategy for Shared Prosperity* (New York: Simon & Schuster, 2005).

Michael Spicer, *A Treaty Too Far: A New Policy for Europe* (London: Fourth Estate, 1992).

Irwin Stelzer (ed.), *Neo-Conservatism* (London: Atlantic, 2004).

Philip Stephens, 'Capital E', *E!Sharp*, September–October 2006.

Philip Stephens, 'The debate about Europe is haunted by shared delusions', *Financial Times*, 22 June 2007.

Philip Stephens, 'Europe cannot afford to retreat from the world', *Financial Times*, 12 July 2005.

Philip Stephens, 'A political awakening that recasts the global landscape', *Financial Times*, 13 July 2007.

Philip Stephens, 'Time for Britain to look at the world afresh', *Financial Times*, 21 February 2006.

Philip Stephens, *Tony Blair: The Making of a World Leader* (New York: Viking, 2004).

A. J. P. Taylor, *English History* (London: Penguin, 1957).

Polly Toynbee, 'In Europe, not America', *Guardian*, 17 June 2005.

Loukas Tsoukalis, *What Kind of Europe?* (Oxford: Oxford University Press, 2003).

Peter Unwin, *Hearts, Minds and Interests: Britain's Place in the World* (London: Profile, 1998).

Rhiannon Vickers, 'Harold Wilson, the Labour Party and the War in Vietnam', paper presented to the British International Studies Association annual conference, Cork, 18–20 December 2006.

Rhiannon Vickers, *The Labour Party and the World, vol. 1: The Evolution of Labour's Foreign Policy 1900–51* (Manchester: Manchester University Press, 2004).

Kurt Volker, 'The United States and the European Union: A Renewed Partnership Delivering Results', remarks at the New Instruments of International Governance: Transatlantic and Global Perspectives conference, Good Governance Consortium, Vienna, 11 May 2006.

Conrad P. Waligorski, *John Kenneth Galbraith: The Economist as Political Theorist* (Lanham, MD: Rowman & Littlefield, 2006).

Stephen Wall, 'In hock to George Bush', *Guardian*, 28 July 2006.

William Wallace, 'Europe should fill the global leadership gap', *Financial Times*, 27 September 2006.

Anthony Wells, 'What Britain thinks of the USA', UK Polling Report website, 4 July 2006.

Paul D. Williams, *British Foreign Policy under New Labour 1997–2005* (Basingstoke: Palgrave Macmillan, 2005).

Hugh Williamson, 'Germany's military to take on global role', *Financial Times*, 25 October 2006.

James K. Wither, 'British Bulldog or Bush's Poodle?: Anglo-American Relations and the Iraq War', *Parameters*, Winter 2003–4.

Daniel Yankelovich, 'Poll Positions: What Americans Really Think about US Foreign Policy', *Foreign Affairs*, September–October 2005.

Hugo Young, *This Blessed Plot: Britain and Europe from Churchill to Blair* (London: Macmillan, 1998).

Philip Ziegler, *Wilson: The Authorized Life of Lord Wilson of Rievaulx* (London: Weidenfeld & Nicolson, 1993).

Index

9/11 *see* September 11 2001 attacks

Acheson, Dean 4, 22, 30, 167
Addison, Paul 3
Aden 102
Adenauer, Konrad 138
Afghanistan xxiii, 44, 61, 65, 103, 118–20, 165
   insurgency by Jihad militant 119
   missile attacks by USA (1998) 63
   polls suggest UK is a greater terrorist target following war 76
   proportionate action by USA xxv
Africa 118, 121
   shrinking of British Empire 2, 125
   see also east Africa; north Africa; west Africa
AIDS 157
Al Qaeda xxv, 66–7, 90–91, 125
Algeria 15
American Civil War *see* United States of America
Anderson, Benedict xvii
Argentina 29
Arizona 99
ASEAN 158

Ashdown of Norton-sub-Hamdon, Lord 56–7
Asia xxvii, 50, 82, 94, 125, 161
Association of South East Asian Nations *see* ASEAN
Atatürk, Kemal 65
Atta, Mohammed 66
Attlee, Clement xvii, 70, 87, 132
   believes UK's empire days over 1
   convertibility crisis (1947) 21
   refuses to join Schuman plan 4, 22, 138–9
   role in persuading USA to assume global responsibilities after WWII 69
   sees need for greater European unity 16
Australia 6
avian flu 157

Baghdad 31, 64
Baker, James 60
Balkans 87, 107, 118
   Blair and Clinton clash over use of ground forces to secure victory 54, 56, 62
   coherence and full responsibility of Europe towards 120

military and political weakness
  of Europeans 42, 115
  see also Kosovo
Balls, Ed 143
Bank of England 143, 147
  Monetary Policy Committee
    144
Battle of Britain 132
beef wars 138
Berger, Sandy 43
Berlin 10, 32
  crisis (1961) 3
  Wall 78, 96, 163
Berlin, Isaiah 101
Bevin, Ernest 16, 38, 129
bin Laden, Osama 91
biological weapons 58, 90, 157
Black Sea 107, 161
Blair, Tony ix, 11, 106, 166–7
  2001 Labour conference
    speech 67
  announces 'doctrine of
    international community'
    35–6, 59, 86
  at St Malo summit (1998)
    42–3, 53, 110–11, 161
  attacked by Cameron over
    relationship with USA
    74–5
  attempts to bridge divide
    between USA and Europe
    4, 34, 43–4, 72
  believes rogue states should be
    confronted by international
    community 45
  Bush, George W.
    Blair described as 'Bush's
      poodle' xi, 67
    differences xxiv, 36, 44,
      59–60, 66, 74, 85, 119

  similarities xxiv, 36
  compared to Gladstone 36, 71
  confidence that UK would
    emerge as a pivotal power
    37–8
  constitutional reforms 39, 48,
    133
  cultivates relationships with
    foreign policy intellectuals
    35
  described as 'foreign minister
    for the United States' by
    Mandela 5
  development of global strategy
    for UK 34–46, 67
  difficulty sustaining
    USA–Europe balancing act
    xi, xv, xxviii, xxxi, 94,
    151, 160, 162
  'dodgy dossier' (September
    2002) 57–8, 73
  economic policy 48
  elected Prime Minister in 1997
    34
  fails to end UK distance and
    hesitation towards Europe
    xxviii–xxix, 152
  as foreign policy traditionalist
    41, 46
  as instinctive multiculturalist
    and multilateralist 36, 71
  Iraq War
    damage inflicted 45, 52,
      54–85
    endorses US unilateral
      military action 11, 45, 55,
      69, 72–3
    realises need for full UN
      backing for invasion 57,
      68, 119

reasons for going to war 54–85
links globalisation with foreign and security policy 86–95
maintains intimate ties with Washington xvi, 32, 35, 42–3, 45, 58, 72, 94, 119
opinion polls suggest UK tied too closely to USA 76
persuades Labour to change foreign policy values 38
as pro-European 37, 138, 141, 151
  problems over euro 41, 140, 144
  seeks to strengthen ties with Europe 40–42
relationship with Clinton 6, 10, 39, 43–4, 141, 156
  clashes over use of ground forces in Balkans 54, 56, 62
  clashes over Northern Ireland 54
seeks to fundamentally change politics of decline xvi
seen as punching above UK's weight 42, 52, 164
special relationship
  accepts primacy of x, 2, 12, 72
  defines 34, 47
  origins 13
  preference towards USA over Europe 12, 39–40, 45
speech at Bush Presidential Library (2002) 36
stresses risks of allowing Saddam to possess WMD 55

Sun newspaper article 138
takes stance against dictatorships 56
Third Way philosophy 59, 74, 121, 141, 164
unwavering support for USA post-9/11 xxiii, 44, 56, 58, 90, 106, 125
Boer War 70
Bogdanor, Vernon 133
Bosnia-Herzegovina 118
Bowling Alone 83
Boyce, Sir Michael 90, 92–3
Braithwaite, Sir Rodric 79
Brazil 3, 147, 158, 164
British Empire, shrinking after WWII 2, 125
Brown, Gordon xiv, 12, 69, 142–3
Brussels 45, 103
Bulgaria 36, 102
Burke, Edmund 105, 137
Bush, George Sr 36, 60, 77
  attempts to strengthen links with Germany 42, 141
Bush, George W. 56, 86
  Blair, Tony
    described as 'poodle' xi, 67
    differences xxiv, 36, 44, 59–60, 66, 74, 85, 119
    similarities xxiv, 36
    unwavering support post-9/11 xxiii, 44, 58, 125
  Iraq War
    damage of 45, 52, 54–85
    fails to win German and French support for invasion xii, 10, 52, 73–4, 102, 117
    persuaded by Blair to seek UN backing 57, 68, 119

reasons for going to war 54–85
unilateral military action endorsed by Blair 11, 45, 55, 69, 72–3
proportionate action by USA in Afghanistan xxv
relationship with UK xxii, 54, 164
personal unpopularity xxv, 76, 78, 85
relationship with Europe 110, 155, 160
personal unpopularity xxv, 77–8, 96, 104
talks about 'axis of evil' 45, 57, 65, 92, 94
talks about 'war on terror' x, xvii, xix, xxiii, 46, 61, 64–5, 73–4, 76, 85, 91, 93, 156
UK's false assumptions regarding foreign policy 60
unilateralist foreign policy xiii, xviii, 11, 44–5, 53, 60–62, 66–8, 73, 76, 85, 92, 110, 114, 119, 154, 160, 166

California 99
Callaghan, James 26, 38
Cambridge Journal of Economics 146
Cameron, David 74, 82
criticises Blair over alliance with USA 74–5
Camp David 28
Canada 6
Caribbean, shrinking of British Empire 2
Carter, Jimmy 26, 28

Cato Institute 100
Caucasus 87, 114, 161
Central Intelligence Agency (CIA) 15, 32
Chamberlain, Joseph 1, 138
chemical weapons 57–8, 90, 103, 157
Cheney, Dick 63–6
Chesterton, G. K. 100
Chicago Press Club 35–6, 59, 86
China xvii, 86, 109, 120–21, 147, 158, 164
pre-communist 3
Chirac, Jacques 74, 102, 110, 151
Churchill, Winston xxi, xxix, 1–2, 6, 9, 12, 48, 137, 148, 150
speech at Fulton, Missouri (1946) 7–8
CIA *see* Central Intelligence Agency
Clarke, Peter xii
climate change 164
Clinton, Bill 42, 60, 63–5, 70, 74, 97, 121, 164
relationship with Blair 6, 10, 38–9, 43–4, 141, 156
clashes over Northern Ireland 54
clashes over use of ground forces to secure victory in Balkans 54, 56, 62
Coates, David 68, 70, 74, 94, 122
Coker, Christopher 13
Cold War xv, xvii, xxii, xxiv, xxvi, 8, 11, 15, 17–19, 24, 26–8, 30–32, 44, 50–52, 58, 62–3, 80, 85–6, 88–9,

97–8, 114, 116, 125, 141, 150–51, 157, 160, 165–6
Common Agricultural Policy 74, 125
Common Foreign and Security Policy 115
communism xxix, 17, 19, 28, 88, 119
  collapse 116
Conservative Party 16–18, 27, 69, 74, 76, 80, 82, 138–9
  general elections
    1983 31–2, 128
    1987 31–2
    1997 40, 128
  maintaining post-war consensus 18
  as party of Europe 24–5, 31
  reflects on implications of 'special relationship' xxvi
  split over global strategy after WWII 5
  supports USA under Thatcher 31
Cook, Robin 54, 68, 75
  resigns over Iraq War 71
Cooper, Robert 35, 68, 87–8, 117, 154
Council of Foreign Ministers 123
Cronin, James 27
Crosland, Anthony 140
Cuban missile crisis 3–4
Cyprus 102
Czech Republic 66, 102–3

Daalder, Ivo x
d'Ancona, Matthew 73
Dannatt, Sir Richard 91
Darfur, genocide x

Democratic Party 18, 38, 40, 60, 63–4, 119
Dimbleby, David 25
Disraeli, Benjamin 138
drug-trafficking 107, 112
Dulles, John Foster 15

east Africa 63
East Timor 112
Eden, Sir Anthony 2
EEC *see* European Economic Community
Egypt 158
Eisenhower, Dwight 13, 15, 23
  not influenced by Macmillan in dealings with Khrushchev 21
elected mayors in UK 40
Elizabeth II, Queen 29
ERM *see* Exchange Rate Mechanism
ESDI *see* European Security and Defence Initiative
ESS *see* European Security Strategy
Estonia 102
Etzioni, Amitai xiii, 166
EU *see* European Union
euro ix, 41, 140, 144
European Coal and Steel Community 135
European Commission 134, 146, 148, 158
European Commissioner for External Relations 115
European Commissioner for Foreign Affairs 123
European Court of Justice 134
European Economic Community (EEC) 3–4, 107–8

de Gaulle vetoes UK's entry
(1963) 5, 22, 53, 117
Thatcher favours USA 31
treaty of Rome 3
UK joins (1973) 25, 134
UK refuses to join Schuman
plan (1950) 4, 22, 138–9
UK's early abstention 41–2,
128, 53, 110, 128, 135,
137–8
see also European Union
European External Action Service
115
European Growth and Jobs Monitor
145
European Monetary Union 147
European reform treaty xxvii
European Security and Defence
Initiative (ESDI) 41
European Security Strategy (ESS)
111, 114
European Social Chapter 141
European Union (EU) ix,
xvii–xviii, xxii, xxvi–xxxi,
7, 10, 17, 25, 31, 40, 71,
92, 94, 95–6, 102–7, 109,
117–18, 121, 124, 128,
135, 140–42, 145, 147,
149–50, 154–5, 158, 160,
162–6
  constitution 78
  Council of Ministers 111, 134,
148
  Secretariat 115
  discovery of active terrorist
cells within Europe 92
  opposition to Turkish
membership 108
  reasons for establishment 114
  and United Kingdom

  beef wars during 1990s 138
  Blair, Tony
  doubts about European
support post-9/11 72
  fails to bridge USA–Europe
divide xi, xv–xvi, xxviii,
xxxi, 4, 34, 43–4, 72, 94,
151, 160, 162
  fails to end decades of
hesitation and distance
xxviii–xxix, 152
  as a pro-European 37, 138,
141, 151
  coherence and full
responsibility towards
Balkans of Europe and UK
120
  failure to win German or
French support for Iraq
War xii, 10, 52, 73–4,
102, 117
  France and Germany fail to
prove themselves as reliable
strategic partners to UK
xxiv
  future closer integration
between Europe and UK
xxi, 150
  problems over euro ix, 41,
140, 144
  protests over EU budget
138
  refusal to sign Maastricht treaty
107, 135
  St Malo summit 42–3, 53,
110–11, 161
  suspicion towards Europe xiii,
xxi, 16–17, 40, 42, 110,
139–41, 148
  UK believes Europe militarily

and politically weak in
  Balkans 42, 115
and USA
  anger over St Malo summit
    42–3, 110–11
  failure to win German or
    French support for Iraq
    War xii, 10, 52, 73–4,
    102, 117
  personal unpopularity of
    George W. Bush within
    EU xxv, 77–8, 96, 104
  USA believes Europe is
    militarily and politically
    weak in Balkans 42, 115
  see also European Economic
    Community
Euroscepticism xiii, xxi, 40, 42,
  110, 148
Exchange Rate Mechanism
  (ERM) 135, 141

F-35 strike aircraft 89
Falkland Islands, conflict 29,
  49
Federal Republic of Germany see
  Germany
Ferguson, Niall 102, 163
Financial Services Authority 40
Finland 111
First Gulf War 30–31, 49, 63,
  68, 72
  see also Iraq
First World War 7, 62, 70
Florida 60, 99
Ford, Gerald 26
Ford, Henry 17
France xxi, 14–15, 111, 114–17,
  127, 136, 143, 161–6
  beef wars with UK 138

discovery of active terrorist
  cells 92
economy 139, 147
failure to prove itself a reliable
  strategic partner to UK
  xxiv
future closer integration with
  UK xxi, 150
and Germany 3, 10, 40, 88,
  128
opposes Turkey's EU
  membership 108
opposes war in Iraq xii, 52,
  73–4, 102, 117
and UK
  relationship post-Suez 4, 41,
    117, 166
  St Malo summit 42–3, 53,
    110–11, 161
  vetoes entry into EEC 5, 22,
    53, 117
and USA 23
  de Gaulle refuses to
    subordinate to US foreign
    policy 3, 41, 48
  restores ties after Iraq War
    ends 85
Freedman, Lawrence 35
Friedman, Thomas L. 63, 163
Frum, David 60, 65
Fulton, Missouri, Churchill
  delivers speech 7–8

Gaitskell, Hugh 38, 134, 138
Galbraith, J. K. 97
Gamble, Andrew ix, xii, xiv, 6,
  45, 80, 127, 139–40, 160
Garton-Ash, Timothy 35
GATT see General Agreement on
  Tariffs and Trade

Gaulle, Charles de
  refuses to subordinate to US foreign policy 3, 41, 48
  vetoes UK's entry into EEC 5, 22, 53, 117
Gaza strip 115
GCHQ (Government Communications Headquarters) 15
General Agreement on Tariffs and Trade (GATT) 18, 69
  see also World Trade Organization
Georgetown University 89
Georgia 161
German Marshall Fund of the United States 17
Germany 21, 23, 26, 77, 132, 136, 139, 141, 162, 166
  defeated in WWII 1, 9, 33, 62, 88, 136
  discovery of active terrorist cells 92
  economy 139
    adopts single currency 144
    stagnation during mid-1990s 143–4
  fails to prove itself a reliable strategic partner to UK xxiv
  opposes Turkey's EU membership 108
  opposes war in Iraq xii, 52, 73–4, 102, 117
  and USA
    asks USA to locate cruise missiles in Europe 26
    restores ties after Iraq War ends 85
    USA attempts to strengthen links following reunification 42, 141
    USA supports reunification 28
  post-war relationship with France 3, 10, 40, 88, 128
  restructuring of military 113
Gladstone, William, Blair compared to 36, 71
globalisation xiv, 11, 34–6, 89–90, 106–7, 148, 163–4
'Glorious Revolution' 133–4
Gore, Al 60
Government Communications Headquarters *see* GCHQ
Great Britain *see* United Kingdom
Grenada, US invasion of 29
Guantánamo Bay xxiv
Guthrie, Charles 35

Haass, Richard 166
Habermas, Jürgen xxx, 109, 166
Harvard University 42
Healey, Denis 29
Heath, Edward x, 24–5, 29, 138, 143
Held, David xxx
Helms, Jesse 113
Helsinki 116
Hennessy, Peter 128
Heritage Foundation 100
Hitler, Adolf 9, 13, 33
Hobbes, Thomas 137, 155
Hong Kong 15, 81
Hopkins, Harry 6
House of Commons 134
House of Lords, reform 48–9
A Human Security Doctrine for Europe 111

Human Security Response Force
   111
human trafficking 107, 112
Hungary 102–3
Hurd, Douglas 75
Hussein, Saddam *see* Saddam
   Hussein

ICC *see* International Criminal
   Court
immigration xviii, 52, 97–9,
   106–7
Independent Labour Party 70
   see also Labour Party
India xvii, 18, 86, 102, 109, 121,
   147, 158
Indonesia 20, 158
The Innocent 32
International Criminal Court
   (ICC) 103, 154
International Monetary Fund 18,
   164
Iran 45, 62, 65, 87, 115, 120–21,
   155–6, 162
   hostage crisis 28
Iraq ix–xiv, xvii, xix, xxii, xxix,
   5, 10–11, 31–2, 37, 43–5,
   53–7, 59, 61, 63–74, 76,
   78–9, 84–5, 87, 90–91, 94,
   102–4, 106, 114–15,
   117–18, 120, 125, 149,
   154, 156, 160, 166
   alleged WMD capabilities
      54–7, 59, 65–6, 73–4,
      90–91, 159
   UN role post-war xxiv
   see also First Gulf War
Iraq War
   Blair endorses unilateral
      military action by USA 11,
      45, 55, 69, 72–3
   Blair realises need for full UN
      backing over invasion 57,
      68, 119
   compared to Suez xiii, 55, 79
   compared to Vietnam 76
   France and Germany restore
      ties with USA after war
      ends 85
   French and German opposition
      xii, 52, 73–4, 102, 117
   impact on UK's European
      relations 52–3, 73–4, 102,
      117
   UK reasons for going to war
      54–85
   US reasons for going to war
      54–85
Islam 61
   relationship with West
      xvii–xviii, 11, 65, 84, 88,
      98, 118–20
Islamic fundamentalism xxvi, 86,
   88, 108, 150
isolationism xiii, xxix, 36, 40,
   42, 53, 62, 133, 157
Israel 3, 68, 115–16
   peace process with Palestine
      xxiv, xxvii, 68–9, 120, 161
   see also Middle East
Italy 77, 92, 143–4

Japan 21, 91, 139
Johnson, Lyndon 24, 97
Joint Intelligence Committee 79
Judt, Tony 14, 78, 116

Kagan, Robert 154–5
Kampfner, John 58
Kant, Immanuel 155

Kearns, Iain 89
Kelly, David 73
Kennedy, John F. 4, 17, 23, 74
   assassination 22
   threatens to abandon Skybolt 5
Kennedy, Paul 158
Kenya 20, 102
Keynes, John Maynard 7, 21, 27
Khrushchev, Nikita 21
Kinnock, Neil 67–8
Kissinger, Henry 3, 14, 28, 92, 115
Kohl, Helmut 138
Korea 91, 122
   see also North Korea
Korean War 30, 49
Kosovo 35–6, 44, 58, 63, 72, 112–13, 164
   Blair and Clinton clash over use of ground forces to secure victory 54, 56, 62
   see also Balkans
Krieger, Joel 68, 70, 74, 94, 122
Kupchan, Charles 89
Kuwait 56
Kyoto protocol 78, 154

Labour Party xiv, xxvi, 21, 24, 34, 60, 74, 76, 80, 106–7, 134, 139–43, 145
   accepts days of empire are over 1–2
   anti-Americanism 76
   believes Saddam to be a menace from early 1990s 67
   bipartisan agreement on security following WWII 16
   creates Atlantic alliance following WWII 17, 70
   downgrades UK's global commitments 21
   foreign policy under New Labour 34, 37, 40–41, 43–4, 55, 57, 69–73, 86–95, 106
   future strategy xxvi, 107
   general elections
      1983 31–2, 128
      1987 31–2, 128
      1997 34, 37, 40–41, 55, 57, 71, 81, 128
   policy of unilateral nuclear disarmament during 1980s 38, 69
   reframes economic policy at start of 1990s 40
   refuses to support USA in Vietnam War xiv, 22–4
   suspicious of European project 16–17, 139–41
   overcomes suspicion during 1980s 140
   Third Way philosophy 59, 74, 121, 141, 164
   see also Independent Labour Party
Latin America 50, 99
Latvia 102
Lebanon 28, 116, 165
Liberal Democrats 57, 76
Libya 29
Lindsay, James x
Lipset, Seymour Martin 100
Lisbon 145
Lithuania 102
London
   City of xxx, 18, 136, 143, 164

relationship with Washington xxiii, 26, 42–3, 59–60, 66–7, 80, 121, 152
terrorist bombings 92, 118
London School of Economics and Political Science xxx, 146

Maastricht treaty 107, 135
MacDonald, Ramsay 70
McEwan, Ian 32
Machiavelli, Niccolò ix
McMahon Act 15
Macmillan, Harold xvii, 2, 4–5, 9, 15, 22, 24, 32, 41, 84, 87, 98, 143, 159
restores close ties with Washington following Suez crisis 2–3
unable to influence Eisenhower in dealings with Khrushchev 21
Madrid, terrorist bombings 92, 118
Major, John 40, 68
beef wars with France 138
Malaya 20
Mandela, Nelson, refers to Blair as 'foreign minister of the USA' 5
Manning, Sir David 57, 84
Mazower, Mark 116
Mead, Walter Russell 151
Mediterranean Sea 108
Menwith Hill 15, 89
Mercosur 158
Merkel, Angela 113, 151
Messina 135
metric martyrs 135
Meyer, Sir Christopher 43
MI6 32

Micklethwait, John 100
Middle East xxvii, 15, 20, 26, 54, 59, 63–9, 76, 87, 91–2, 94, 99, 114–15, 155, 165
threat to region from US war on terror 58, 61, 64, 66, 76, 120–22, 124–5, 160–61
UK urges USA to push for resolution in peace process xxiv, xxvii, 68–9, 120, 161
Milošević, Slobodan 56, 164
Milward, Alan xv
Mitterrand, François 138
Monnet, Jean 114, 123, 134
Monroe doctrine 29
Morgan, J. P. 8
Moscow 79, 87
Murdoch, Rupert 69, 138

NAFTA 158
Nairn, Tom 12
National Health Service 82
National Review 100
National Security Agency (NSA) 15
NATO *see* North Atlantic Treaty Organisation
Nazism xxix, 1, 9, 62, 88
Netherlands 10, 92, 145, 163
Nevada 99
New Deal (UK) 40
New Deal (USA) 97
New Labour *see* Labour Party
New Zealand 6
Niblett, Robin 107
Nigeria 158
Nixon, Richard 24–5, 29
north Africa 107–8, 114
North American Free Trade Agreement *see* NAFTA

North Atlantic Treaty
    Organisation (NATO) 13,
    15–16, 18–19, 29, 35, 38,
    41–3, 51, 62, 69, 71, 103,
    105, 110–11, 117–18, 122,
    141, 150, 159
  security and intelligence
    relationship with USA
    xviii–xix
North Korea 45, 65, 92, 156,
    162
Northern Ireland 39
  Blair and Clinton clash 54
NSA *see* National Security
    Agency
nuclear weapons 15–16, 21, 23,
    27–8, 32, 38, 51, 54, 58,
    65, 85, 87–8, 90, 92, 105,
    115, 118, 121, 130, 157,
    162
Nye, Joseph 42–3

oil crisis (1973–4) 116
Operation Desert Fox 31, 43,
    53, 55, 68
Organisation for Economic Co-
    operation and
    Development 81
Orwell, George 132

Pakistan 18
Palestine 54, 68, 121
  Palestinian Authority 115
  peace process with Israel xxiv,
    xxvii, 68–9, 120, 161
Palmerston, Lord 12
Panić, Mića 146
Paris 10
Patten, Chris 88
Pearl Harbor 90

Peel, Robert 127
Pentagon 43, 60
Perle, Richard 61, 64–5
Persian Gulf 20, 43
Pew Global Attitudes 76–7,
    104
Poland 102–4, 116
Polaris submarine-based system
    5, 15
Portugal 10, 77
Postwar 116
Potsdam peace conference 2
poverty relief 164
Powell, Colin 60–61, 63, 66
Powell, Jonathan 35
Prague 66
Putnam, Robert 83

Rafah crossing point 115
Reagan, Ronald
  conservative foreign policy
    unpopular with UK left-
    wingers 77, 97
  and Thatcher xv, 9, 26–30,
    38, 156
Republican Party 18, 63–4, 74
Reynolds, David 13, 25
Rhodesia 102
Rice, Condoleezza 65, 110
Riddell, Peter xi
Rifkin, Jeremy xxx, 157
Roberts, Andrew 9
Rogers, Paul 89
Romania 102
Roosevelt, Franklin 6, 9, 62, 74
Roosevelt, Theodore 56
Rove, Karl 63–4
Royal Navy 5
Rumsfeld, Donald 61, 63–6,
    102, 115–16

Russia 109, 161
  growing dependency on gas from 160
  see also Soviet Union
Rwanda 121

Saddam Hussein xxv, 31, 43, 54, 56, 59, 61, 65, 67–8, 73, 77
  offers rewards to families of suicide bombers 66
St Malo summit 42–3, 53, 110–11, 161
Sarkozy, Nicolas 151
Saudi Arabia 62–3, 158
Schlesinger, Arthur M. 62
Schmidt, Helmut 26
Schroeder, Gerhard 10, 74, 151
Schuman plan 4, 22, 138–9
Scotland 39
  Scottish Parliament 48
Second World War xxix, 6, 32, 98, 116, 119, 131–4, 137, 150–52, 156, 165
  afterwards
    EU established to prevent further attacks on European soil 114
    UK develops model welfare state 82
    USA becomes pillar of collective security x, xiv–xv, 1, 10, 12–13, 20, 45, 49, 52, 69, 80, 94, 111, 131–4, 137
September 11 2001 attacks x, xvii, 44, 50, 66, 77, 87, 114, 118, 120, 150, 155, 163
  Blair, Tony
    delivers 2001 Labour conference speech just after attacks 67
    fears over lack of European support 72
    unwavering support for USA in aftermath xxiii, 44, 56, 58, 90, 106, 125
  Bush, George W.
    allows State Department and Pentagon to pursue rival agendas afterwards 60
    believes attacks would banish partisan politics 64
    believes USA subsequently engaged in 'war with Islam' 119
    compared to falling of Berlin Wall xxiii
    compared to Pearl Harbor 90
    Europeans support subsequent military action against Al Qaeda xxv
    opinion polls highlight Americans' belief in Iraqi complicity 66
    political climate in USA afterwards 64
    proportionate action by USA in Afghanistan afterwards xxv
    role of UN subsequently 90, 125
    UK public opinion subsequently 73
Shakespeare, William xxix
Shonfield, Andrew 131
Short, Clare, resigns over Iraq War 71
Sierra Leone 44, 58, 72, 112

Sinai 28
Skybolt stand-off missile system 5, 21, 53
Slovakia 102
Slovenia 102
Solana, Javier 115
South Africa 5, 158
Soviet Union xxix, 1, 8, 13–14, 17, 19, 21, 23, 25, 27–8, 62, 80, 88, 108, 119, 161–2
  collapse xxii, 136
  pipeline dispute (1981) 29
  see also Russia
Spain 77, 144
  Spanish Civil War 139
Stalin, Iosif 1
Stevens, Philip xii, 32, 41, 87
Stewart, Michael 23
Straw, Jack 68
Suez crisis 1, 21, 25, 52, 102, 128, 130
  Anglo-French relations suffer as a result 4, 41, 117, 166
  compared to Iraq War in terms of failure xiii, 55, 79
  demonstrates one-sidedness of special relationship 2
  Macmillan restores close ties with Washington afterwards 2–3
  relationship with USA subsequently becomes pivotal for UK xv, xix, xxii, 2, 9, 14, 41, 48, 87
Sun 138
Sutton, John 146
Sweden 139, 144
Syria 87, 116, 155–6

Taiwan 91, 109
Talbott, Strobe 43
Taliban 67
Taylor, A. J. P. 132
Tehran peace conference 2
terrorism xi, 107, 157, 160
Texas 44, 99
Thatcher, Margaret xiv, 32, 80, 127, 139–41
  economy under 31, 39–40, 48, 81, 140, 142
  neo-liberal policies xiv
  protests over EU budget 138
  and Reagan xv, 9, 26–30, 38, 156
Third Way 59, 74, 121, 141, 164
treaty of Rome 3
Trevelyan, G. M. 137
Trident weapons systems xiv, 15, 106
Truman, Harry 62
  complains at UK reticence towards EEC participation 110
Turkey 74, 161
  France and Germany oppose EU membership 108

Ukraine 161
United Kingdom
  British identity xi, xiii–xiv, xxix, 1, 8–9, 39, 80, 127, 134, 137, 139, 153, 157, 162
  constitutional reforms 39–40, 48–9, 133
  damage of Iraq War to 45, 52, 54–85
  develops model welfare state after WWII 82

'dodgy dossier' on Iraq's
  WMD capabilities 57–8,
  73
and Europe
  beef wars with France 138
  believes Europe militarily and
    politically weak in Balkans
    42, 115
  Blair, Tony
    doubts about European
      support post-9/11 72
    fails to bridge USA–Europe
      divide xi, xv–xvi, xxviii,
      xxxi, 4, 34, 43–4, 72, 94,
      151, 160, 162
    fails to end decades of UK
      hesitation and distance
      xxviii–xxix, 152
    failure to win German or
      French support for Iraq
      War xii, 10, 52, 73–4,
      102, 117
    finds it difficult to sustain
      balancing act between USA
      and Europe xi, xv, xxviii,
      xxxi, 94, 151, 160, 162
    as a pro-European 37, 138,
      141, 151
  France and Germany fail to
    prove themselves reliable
    strategic partners xxiv
  France vetoes UK entry into
    EEC 5, 22, 53, 117
  future closer integration xxi,
    150
  problems regarding euro ix,
    41, 140, 144
  protests over EU budget 138
  refuses to join Schuman plan
    (1950) 4, 22, 138–9
  refuses to sign Maastricht
    treaty 107, 135
  St Malo summit 42–3, 53,
    110–11, 161
  suspicion towards Europe
    xiii, xxi, 16–17, 40, 42,
    110, 139–41, 148
Falklands conflict 29, 49
polls suggest UK is a greater
  terrorist target following
  war in Afghanistan 76
seen as punching above its
  weight on international
  stage 42, 52, 164
and USA
  accepts primacy of USA in
    special relationship x, 2,
    12, 72
  accused of reticence over
    EEC participation 110
  believes rogue states should
    be confronted by
    international community
    45
  Blair described as 'Bush's
    poodle' xi, 67
  Blair fails to bridge
    USA–Europe divide xi,
    xv–xvi, xxviii, xxxi, 4, 34,
    43–4, 72, 94, 151, 160, 162
  clash over use of ground
    troops in Balkans 54, 56,
    62
  convertibility crisis (1947) 21
  convinces USA that it is not
    in a 'war with Islam' post-
    9/11 119
  differing prime ministerial
    definitions of special
    relationship

Blair 34, 47
Heath 29–30
Macmillan 2, 4, 9, 15, 21, 84, 98
Thatcher 26–30
Wilson 23–4
disagree over detaining prisoners at Guantanamo Bay xxiv
endorses unilateral military action in Iraq 11, 45, 55, 69, 72–3
fails to influence USA in dealings with Khrushchev 21
as favoured allies over Europe 12, 40, 45
intimate ties between London and Washington xvi, 32, 35, 42–3, 45, 58, 72, 94, 119
lack of support towards USA among British xvi, xxv, 77–8, 96, 104
makes false assumptions regarding US foreign policy under George W. Bush 60
opinion polls suggest UK tied too closely to USA under Blair 76
personal relationship between Prime Ministers and Presidents
  Blair and Bush xxiv, 36, 44, 59–60, 66, 74, 85, 119
  Blair and Clinton 6, 10, 38–9, 43–4, 141, 156
  Churchill and Roosevelt 9
  Heath and Nixon 29–30
  Macmillan and Eisenhower 2–3, 15, 21
  Macmillan and Kennedy 21–2
  Thatcher and Reagan xv, 9, 26–30, 38, 156
  Wilson and Johnson 24
persuades USA to seek UN backing for invasion of Iraq 57, 68, 119
post-war friction 4–5, 7, 20–25
public opinion following 9/11 73
realises that good relations with USA pivotal after Suez xv, xix, xxii, 2, 9, 14, 41, 48, 87
refuses to allow USA to use its bases during Yom Kippur War 30
refuses to support USA in Vietnam xiv, 22–4
unwavering support of USA post-9/11 xxiii, 44, 56, 58, 90, 106, 125
urges USA to push for resolution in Middle East peace process xxiv, xxvii, 68–9, 120, 161
US anger towards UK over St Malo summit 42–3, 110–11
USA agrees to sell Polaris submarine-based system to UK 5, 15
United Nations 18, 43, 55, 62, 68, 71–3, 119
  Charter 112
  role in post-war Iraq xxiv

role following 9/11 attacks 90, 125
Security Council 35, 44, 66, 90, 130, 163–4
  resolution authorising military intervention in Iraq 57
United States of America
  American Civil War 97
  American Revolution 6
  becomes essential pillar of collective security after WWII x, xiv–xv, 1, 10, 12–13, 20, 45, 49, 52, 69, 80, 94, 111, 131–4, 137
  defence spending 122
  domestic political climate after 9/11 64
  and Europe
    anger over St Malo summit 42–3, 110–11
    believes Europe militarily and politically weak in Balkans 42, 115
    discovery of active terrorist cells within Europe 92
    Europeans support military action in Afghanistan following 9/11 xxv
    fails to win German or French support for Iraq War xii, 10, 52, 73–4, 102, 117
    personal unpopularity of George W. Bush xxv, 77–8, 96, 104
  Germany
    requests that USA locates cruise missiles in Europe 26
    USA attempts to strengthen links following
    reunification 42, 141
    launches missile attacks against Afghanistan (1998) 63
    and NATO, close security and intelligence relationship xviii–xix
    opinion polls highlight Americans' belief in Iraqi complicity in 9/11 attacks 66
    significance of 9/11 attacks compared to falling of Berlin Wall xxiii
    significance of 9/11 attacks compared to Pearl Harbor 90
  and UK
    accuses UK of reticence over EEC participation 110
    agrees to sell Polaris submarine-based system 5, 15
    anger towards UK over St Malo summit 42–3, 110–11
    Blair described as 'Bush's poodle' xi, 67
    Blair fails to bridge USA–Europe divide xi, xv–xvi, xxviii, xxxi, 4, 34, 43–4, 72, 94, 151, 160, 162
    clash over use of ground troops in Balkans 54, 56, 62
    convertibility crisis (1947) 21
    differing prime ministerial definitions of special relationship
    Blair 34, 47

214　SHIFTING ALLIANCES

Heath 29–30
Macmillan 2, 4, 9, 15, 21, 84, 98
Thatcher 26–30
Wilson 23–4
disagree over detaining prisoners at Guantanamo Bay xxiv
as favoured allies over Europe 12, 40, 45
intimate ties between London and Washington xvi, 32, 35, 42–3, 45, 58, 72, 94, 119
lack of support among British xvi, xxv, 77–8, 96, 104
not influenced by UK over dealings with Khrushchev 21
opinion polls suggest UK tied too closely to USA under Blair 76
personal relationship between Presidents and Prime Ministers
 Bush and Blair xxiv, 36, 44, 59–60, 66, 74, 85, 119
 Clinton and Blair 6, 10, 38–9, 43–4, 141, 156
 Eisenhower and Macmillan 2–3, 15, 21
 Johnson and Wilson 24
 Kennedy and Macmillan 21–2
 Nixon and Heath 29–30
 Reagan and Thatcher xv, 9, 26–30, 38, 156
 Roosevelt and Churchill 9
post-war friction 4–5, 7, 20–25

UK accepts US primacy in special relationship x, 2, 12, 72
UK believes rogue states should be confronted by international community 45
UK convinces USA that it is not in a 'war with Islam' post-9/11 119
UK endorses unilateral military action in Iraq 11, 45, 55, 69, 72–3
UK makes false assumptions regarding US foreign policy under George W. Bush 60
UK persuades USA to seek UN backing for invasion of Iraq 57, 68, 119
UK public opinion following 9/11 73
UK realises that good relations with USA pivotal after Suez xv, xix, xxii, 2, 9, 14, 41, 48, 87
UK refuses to allow USA to use its bases during Yom Kippur War 30
UK refuses to support USA in Vietnam xiv, 22–4
UK urges USA to push for resolution in Middle East peace process xxiv, xxvii, 68–9, 120, 161
unwavering support of UK post-9/11 xxiii, 44, 56, 58, 90, 106, 125
unilateralist foreign policy xiii, xviii, 11, 44–5, 53, 60–62,

66–8, 73, 76, 85, 92, 110, 114, 119, 154, 160, 166
Vietnam War xiv, 22–4, 26, 28, 62, 76
war on terror x, xvii, xix, xxiii, 46, 61, 64–5, 73–4, 76, 85, 91, 93, 156
University of Bradford 89
University of Oxford 133
USA *see* United States of America
USSR *see* Soviet Union

Vickers, Rhiannon 17
Vietnam War 26, 28, 62, 76
   UK refuses to support USA xiv, 22–4
Vīķe-Freiberga, Vaira 102
Volker, Kurt 155

Wales 39
   Welsh Assembly 48
Wall, Sir Stephen 94, 159
Wall Street 8
war on terror x, xvii, xix, xxiii, 46, 61, 64–5, 73–4, 76, 85, 91, 93, 156
Warsaw 104
Washington xxi–xxii, 10, 18, 103
   relationship with London xxiii, 26, 42–3, 59–60, 66–7, 80, 121, 152
Watergate scandal 26
weapons of mass destruction (WMD) 54–9, 65–6, 73–4, 90–91, 159
west Africa 122
Whitehall 136
Wilson, Harold 20–21, 23, 26, 138
   defines relationship with USA 24
WMD *see* weapons of mass destruction
Wolfowitz, Paul 60, 64–5
Wooldridge, Adrian 100
Woolsey, James 15
World Bank 18, 69, 164
World Trade Organization 18, 146
   see also General Agreement on Tariffs and Trade

Yale University 65
Yalta peace conference 2
Yankelovich, Daniel 98
Yemen 63
Yom Kippur War 30
Young, Hugo xxvii, 57, 135
Yugoslavia 35, 115